Service Support

London: The Stationery Office

First published 2000
Third impression 2001

ISBN 0 11 330015 8

ITIL® is a registered trademark of OGC

Titles within the ITIL series include:

Service Support (Published 2000)
Service Desk and the Process of Incident
Management, Problem Management, Configuration
Management, Change Management and
Release Management .... ISBN 0 11 330015 8

Service Delivery (Published 2001)
Capacity Management, Availability Management,
Service Level Management, IT Service Continuity,
Financial Management for IT Services and
Customer Relationship Management .... ISBN 0 11 330017 4

Customer Liaison	ISBN 0 11 330546 X
Managing Supplier Relationships	ISBN 0 11 330562 1
Managing Facilities Management	ISBN 0 11 330526 5
IT Service Management Case Studies	ISBN 0 11 330676 8
Network Services Management	ISBN 0 11 330558 3
A Guide to Business Continuity Management	ISBN 0 11 330675 X
Business and Management Skills	ISBN 0 11 330686 5
In Times of Radical Change	ISBN 0 11 330687 3
Understanding and Improving	ISBN 0 11 330679 2
Surviving IT Infrastructure Transitions	ISBN 0 11 330678 4
Security Management	ISBN 0 11 330014 X
Service Delivery Tools	ISBN 0 11 330633 4
Quality Management for IT Services	ISBN 0 11 330555 9

Published by The Stationery Office and available from:

The Stationery Office
(mail, telephone and fax orders only)
PO Box 29, Norwich NR3 1GN
Telephone orders/General Enquiries 0870 600 5522
Fax orders 0870 600 5533

www.thestationeryoffice.com

The Stationery Office Bookshops
123 Kingsway, London WC2B 6PQ
020 7242 6393 Fax 020 7242 6394
68-69 Bull Street, Birmingham B4 6AD
0121 236 9696 Fax 0121 236 9699
33 Wine Street, Bristol BS1 2BQ
0117 926 4306 Fax 0117 929 4515
9-21 Princess Street, Manchester M60 8AS
0161 834 7201 Fax 0161 833 0634
16 Arthur Street, Belfast BT1 4GD
028 9023 8451 Fax 028 9023 5401
The Stationery Office Oriel Bookshop
18-19 High Street, Cardiff CF1 2BZ
029 2039 5548 Fax 029 2038 4347
71 Lothian Road, Edinburgh EH3 9AZ
0870 606 5566 Fax 0870 606 5588

The Stationery Office's Accredited Agents
(see Yellow Pages)

and through good booksellers

For further information on OGC products,
contact:

OGC Help Desk
Rosebery Court
St Andrews Business Park
Norwich NR7 0HS
Telephone 01603 704567 GTN 3040 4567

This document has been produced using
procedures conforming to
BS 5750 Part 1: 1987; ISO 9001: 1987

Contents

Foreword by Bob Assirati   xiii

Preface   xv

Chapter 1: Introduction   1
1.1   The IT Infrastructure Library   1
               1.1.1   Public domain framework   1
               1.1.2   Best practice framework   1
               1.1.3   *De facto* standard   2
               1.1.4   Quality approach   2
               1.1.5   itSMF   3
1.2   Restructuring the IT Infrastructure Library   3
1.3   Target audience   4
1.4   Navigating the IT Infrastructure Library   4
1.5   Why choose a jigsaw concept?   6
1.6   The Service Support book   6
1.7   Service Management   7
1.8   Customers and Users   7
1.9   A Code of Practice for IT Service Management – PD0005   8
1.10   Service Management: a process approach   8
1.11   Recommended reading   9

Chapter 2: Relationship between processes   11
2.1   Configuration Management   11
2.2   Change Management   12
2.3   Release Management   12
2.4   Incident Management   13
2.5   Problem Management   13
2.6   Service Desk   13
2.7   Service Level Management   13
2.8   Capacity Management   14
2.9   Financial Management for IT Services   14
2.10   Availability Management   14
2.11   IT Service Continuity Management   15
2.12   Customer Relationship Management   15
2.13   ICT Infrastructure Management   15
2.14   Application Management   15
2.15   Security Management   15
2.16   Environmental infrastructure processes   16
2.17   Project Management   16

Chapter 3: Getting started   17

3.1   Service Management benefits   17

3.2   A process led approach   18

3.3   Management commitment   19

    3.3.1   Aspects of management commitment   20

    3.3.2   Management commitment in the planning stage   20

3.4   Cultural aspects   20

    3.4.1   What is culture?   21

    3.4.2   Responsibilities   22

    3.4.3   What is meant by 'service culture'?   22

    3.4.4.   How is this relevant to IT service provision   22

    3.4.5   What do Customers want?   22

    3.4.6   Common excuses for conducting 'business as usual'   24

    3.4.7   How much will all this cost?   24

    3.4.8   What are the potential benefits of Customer care?   25

    3.4.9   Service Management training   25

Chapter 4: The Service Desk   27

4.1   Overview   27

    4.1.1   Why do we need a Service Desk?   27

    4.1.2   The support problem   28

    4.1.3   Call Centre   29

    4.1.4   Help Desk   29

    4.1.5   Service Desk   29

    4.1.6   How can a Service Desk help my organisation?   29

    4.1.7   Charging for support services   30

    4.1.8   Business and operational benefits   31

    4.1.9   The role and direction of the Service Desk   31

    4.1.10   Customer interaction   31

    4.1.11   Keeping the Customer and User informed   32

    4.1.12   Physical attendance   33

    4.1.13   Monitored infrastructure events   34

    4.1.14   Actioned infrastructure Incidents   34

    4.1.15   Infrastructure Incident model   34

    4.1.16   Benefits   35

    4.1.17   Use of Internet technology   35

4.2   Implementing the Service Desk infrastructure   36

    4.2.1   Staff resourcing   36

    4.2.2   Target effectiveness metrics   36

    4.2.3   Key considerations   37

    4.2.4   Selecting the right Service Desk structure   37

    4.2.5   Types of Service Desk structure   37

    4.2.6   Local Service Desk considerations   38

    4.2.7   Central Service Desk considerations   38

	4.2.8	Virtual Service Desk considerations	39
	4.2.9	Service Desk Configuration considerations	41
	4.2.10	Global 'follow the sun' support	41
	4.2.11	Incident classification	42
	4.2.12	Classification Process Review	42
4.3		Service Desk technologies	43
	4.3.1	The computerised Service Desk	43
	4.3.2	Computerised Service Desk benefits	44
	4.3.3	Build or buy?	44
	4.3.4	Running in a multiplatform environment	44
	4.3.5	Running in a Wide-Area Network (WAN) infrastructure	45
	4.3.6	Intelligent phone systems, voicemail and email usage	45
	4.3.7	Deploying a self-service strategy	45
	4.3.8	Critical success factors	46
	4.3.9	Implementation considerations	46
	4.3.10	Outsourcing a Service Desk	47
4.4		Service Desk responsibilities, functions, staffing levels etc	48
	4.4.1	Service Desk functions	48
	4.4.2	Which Requests should be registered	49
	4.4.3	Service Desk empowerment	49
	4.4.4	Escalation management	50
	4.4.5	Service Desk staffing levels	51
	4.4.6	Staff turnover considerations	52
	4.4.7	Workload monitoring	52
	4.4.8	Customer satisfaction analysis and surveys	53
	4.4.9	Service Desk resourcing for smaller support units	53
	4.4.10	Second-line staff awareness	53
	4.4.11	Identifying training needs	54
	4.4.12	Call rate reduction	54
	4.4.13	Workload definitions requests types	54
4.5		Service Desk staffing skill set	55
	4.5.1	Major customer requirements	55
	4.5.2	Fix rates	55
4.6		Setting up a Service Desk environment	56
	4.6.1	Service Desk environment considerations	56
	4.6.2	Defining your services	56
	4.6.3	Service Desk pre-Release requirements	57
	4.6.4	Advertising and selling the Service Desk	58
	4.6.5	Quick wins	59
4.7		Service Desk education and training	59
	4.7.1	Soft skills	59
	4.7.2	Managerial focus	60
	4.7.3	Service Desk staff profile	60
	4.7.4	Service staff responsibilities and mindset	61

	4.7.5	Working with Customers	61
	4.7.6	Active listening	62
	4.7.7	Service Desk staff training	63
4.8		Service Desk processes and procedures	63
	4.8.1	Considerations	63
	4.8.2	Common structured interrogation technique	63
	4.8.3	Customers details and identification	64
	4.8.4	Maintaining the Customer database	64
	4.8.5	Marketing the Service Desk amongst Customers	65
4.9		Incident reporting and review	65
	4.9.1	Effective workload analyses	66
	4.9.2	Frequency of reporting and review	66
	4.9.3	Archiving Service Desk records	67
4.10		Conclusions	68
	4.10.1	Critical success factors	68
	4.10.2	Service Desk implementation guidance	68
	Annex 4A	Sample Release Document	69

Chapter 5: Incident Management 71

5.1		Goal of Incident Management	71
5.2		Scope of Incident Management	71
5.3		Basic concepts	73
	5.3.1	Incident Handling	73
	5.3.2	First, second- and third-line support	74
	5.3.3	Functional versus hierarchical escalation	75
	5.3.4	Priority	76
	5.3.5	Relationship between Incidents, Problems, Known Errors and RFCs	76
5.4		Benefits of Incident Management	78
5.5		Planning and implementation	78
	5.5.1	Timing and planning	78
	5.5.2	Critical success factors	79
	5.5.3	Possible problem areas	80
5.6		Incident Management activities	80
	5.6.1	Incident detection and recording	80
	5.6.2	Classification and initial support	81
	5.6.3	Investigation and diagnosis	83
	5.6.4	Resolution and recovery	84
	5.6.5	Incident closure	85
	5.6.6	Ownership, monitoring, tracking and communication	86
5.7		Handling of major incidents	87
5.8		Roles of the Incident Management process	87
	5.8.1	Incident Manager	87
	5.8.2	Incident-handling support staff	87

5.9	Key Performance Indicators	88
5.10	Tools	88
	Annex 5A	Example coding system for Incident/request classification	90
	Annex 5B	Example of a priority coding system	91
	Annex 5C	Data requirements for service Incident records	92
	Annex 5D	The process of Incident investigation	93
	Annex 5E	Incident handling on the Service Desk (flow)	94

Chapter 6: Problem Management 95

6.1	Goal of Problem Management	95
6.2	Scope of Problem Management	95
6.3	Basic concepts	96
	6.3.1	What is the difference between Incident Management and Problem Management?	97
	6.3.2	Problem control	97
	6.3.3	Error control	97
	6.3.4	Proactive Problem Management	98
	6.3.5	Completion of major Problem reviews	98
6.4	Benefits of Problem Management	98
6.5	Planning and implementation	99
	6.5.1	Timing and planning	99
	6.5.2	Key success factors	99
	6.5.3	Risks	100
6.6	Problem control activities	100
	6.6.1	Problem identification and recording	101
	6.6.2	Problem classification	102
	6.6.3	Problem investigation and diagnosis	104
	6.6.4	Tips on Problem control	105
6.7	Error control activities	105
	6.7.1	Error identification and recording	106
	6.7.2	Error assessment	107
	6.7.3	Error resolution recording	108
	6.7.4	Error closure	108
	6.7.5	Problem/error resolution monitoring	108
	6.7.6	Tips on error control	109
6.8	Proactive Problem Management	109
	6.8.1	Trend Analysis	110
	6.8.2	Targeting preventive action	110
	6.8.3	Tips on proactive Problem Management	111
	6.8.4	Major Problem reviews	111
6.9	Providing information to the support organisation	111
	6.9.1	Providing management information	112
	6.9.2	Cascading information	112

6.10		Metrics	112
	6.10.1	Problem/error control reporting	112
	6.10.2	Periodic audits	113
	6.10.3	Tips on metrics	113
6.11		Roles within Problem Management	114
	6.11.1	Problem Manager	114
	6.11.2	Problem support	115
	Annex 6A	An example of a coding structure for Problem/error categorisation	116
	Annex 6B	Kepner and Tregoe analysis	118
	Annex 6C	Ishikawa diagrams	120

Chapter 7: Configuration Management — 121

7.1		Goal of Configuration Management	121
7.2		Scope of Configuration Management	121
7.3		Basic concepts	122
	7.3.1	Configuration Management planning	122
	7.3.2	Configuration identification and CIs	122
	7.3.3	Configuration control	123
	7.3.4	Configuration status accounting	123
	7.3.5	Configuration verification and audit	123
	7.3.6	Configuration baseline	123
	7.3.7	Configuration Management Database	124
	7.3.8	Software and document libraries	125
	7.3.9	Definitive Software Library	125
	7.3.10	Licence management	125
7.4		Benefits and possible problems	125
	7.4.1	Benefits	125
	7.4.2	Possible problems	126
7.5		Planning and implementation	127
	7.5.1	Initial planning	128
	7.5.2	Agreement on purpose, objectives, scope, priorities and implementation approach aligned with business objectives	128
	7.5.3	Appointment of a Configuration Manager and planning a Configuration Management team	129
	7.5.4	Analysis of existing systems	130
	7.5.5	Developing Configuration Management plans and system design	130
	7.5.6	Detailed planning for implementation	131
	7.5.7	Populating the CMDB and DSL	133
	7.5.8	Cutover to new processes	134
	7.5.9	Other implementation considerations	134
	7.5.10	Costs	135
7.6		Activities	136
	7.6.1	Configuration Management planning	136
	7.6.2	Configuration identification	137

	7.6.3	Control of CIs	144
	7.6.4	Configuration status accounting	147
	7.6.5	Configuration verification and audit	148
	7.6.6	CMDB back-ups, archives and housekeeping	149
	7.6.7	Providing a Configuration Management service	149
7.7	Process control		149
	7.7.1	Management reporting	150
	7.7.2	Key performance indicators	150
7.8	Relations to other processes		151
7.9	Tools specific to the Configuration Management process		153
	7.9.1	Configuration Management system	153
	7.9.2	Software Configuration Management	154
	7.9.3	Change Management and Release Management support	154
	7.9.4	Configuration auditing	154
	7.9.5	Enterprise system and tools	155
	7.9.6	Other tools	155
7.10	Impact of new technology		156
7.11	Guidance on Configuration Management		156
	7.11.1	Level of control	156
	7.11.2	Versions or variants?	157
	7.11.3	Selection of Configuration Management tools	157
	Annex 7A	The central function for Change, Configuration and Release Management	158
	Annex 7B	Specific responsibilities of the Configuration Management team	162
	Annex 7C	Suggested CI attributes	164
Chapter 8: Change Management			165
8.1	Goal of Change Management		165
	8.1.1	Purpose	165
	8.1.2	Best practice	165
	8.1.3	Program/project management and Change Management	165
8.2	Scope of Change Management		166
	8.2.1	Why Change is important	168
	8.2.2	Boundaries between Incident resolution and Change Management	169
	8.2.3	Application development and Change Management	169
	8.2.4	Business change and Change Management	170
8.3	Basic concepts		170
	8.3.1	Requests for Change	173
	8.3.2	Change Advisory Board	175
	8.3.3	Change metrics	176
	8.3.4	The Forward Schedule of Change, and Change models	176
	8.3.5	Outsourcing and Change Management	178
	8.3.6	Critical outage plan	179

8.4		Benefits, costs and possible problems	179
	8.4.1	Benefits	179
	8.4.2	Costs	180
	8.4.3	Possible problems	180
8.5		Activities	181
	8.5.1	Planning the implementation of operational processes	182
	8.5.2	Change logging and filtering	182
	8.5.3	Allocation of priorities	183
	8.5.4	Change categorisation	183
	8.5.5	CAB meetings	184
	8.5.6	Impact and resource assessment	185
	8.5.7	Change approval	186
	8.5.8	Change scheduling	186
	8.5.9	Change building, testing and implementation	187
	8.5.10	Urgent Changes	188
	8.5.11	Urgent Change building, testing and implementation	190
	8.5.12	Change review	191
	8.5.13	Reviewing the Change Management, process for efficiency and effectiveness	191
	8.5.14	Roles and responsibilities	192
8.6		Planning and implementation	194
	8.6.1	Designating the Change Manager role	194
	8.6.2	Deciding on a Change Management system	194
	8.6.3	Planning system reviews	195
	8.6.4	Implementation planning	195
	8.6.5	Guidance	195
8.7		Metrics and management reporting	197
	8.7.1	Auditing for compliance	198
8.8		Software tools	199
8.9		Impact of new technology	200
	8.9.1	The business domain	200
	8.9.2	Technology	201
Chapter 9: Release Management			**203**
9.1		Goal of Release Management	203
9.2		Scope of Release Management	203
9.3		Basic concepts	205
	9.3.1	Release	205
	9.3.2	Release policy and planning	206
	9.3.3	Release unit	206
	9.3.4	Release identification	207
	9.3.5	Types of Release	207
	9.3.6	Definitive Software Library	208
	9.3.7	Definitive Hardware Store (DHS)	210

	9.3.8	Configuration Management Database (CMDB)	210
	9.3.9	Build management	210
	9.3.10	Testing	210
	9.3.11	Back-Out plans	211
9.4		Benefits and possible problems	212
	9.4.1	Benefits	212
	9.4.2	Possible problems	213
9.5		Planning and implementation	214
	9.5.1	Planning	214
	9.5.2	Implementation	221
	9.5.3	Costs	222
9.6		Activities	223
	9.6.1	Release planning	223
	9.6.2	Designing, building and configuring a Release	223
	9.6.3	Release acceptance	224
	9.6.4	Rollout planning	225
	9.6.5	Communication, preparation and training	228
	9.6.6	Distribution and installation	228
9.7		Process control	229
	9.7.1	Key performance indicators	229
	9.7.2	Management reporting	230
9.8		Relations to other processes	231
	9.8.1	Configuration Management	231
	9.8.2	Change Management	231
	9.8.3	Software from Developers and suppliers	231
	9.8.4	Problem Management and the Service Desk	231
	9.8.5	Project Management and PRINCE2	232
9.9		Tools specific to the Release Management process	232
	9.9.1	Change Management tools	232
	9.9.2	Configuration Management tools	232
	9.9.3	Software Configuration Management (SCM) tools	232
	9.9.4	Build management tools	232
	9.9.5	Electronic software distribution	234
	9.9.6	Software and hardware auditing tools	235
	9.9.7	Desktop management tools	235
	9.9.8	Server management tools	236
9.10		Impact of New Technology	236
	9.10.1	The future of support tools	236
	9.10.2	'Thin client'	236
	9.10.3	Multi-tier systems	236
	9.10.4	Internet applications	237
	9.10.5	Software updates via the Internet	238
9.11		Guidance for successful Release Management	239

		9.11.1	Configuration Management	239
		9.11.2	Change Management	239
		9.11.3	Release Management	239
		9.11.4	Application design issues	240
		9.11.5	The positioning of software: what to put where	240
		Annex 9A	Checklist to use when reviewing rollout plans	242
		Annex 9B	Sample Release Management objectives for distributed systems	243

Chapter 10: Service Management software tools 245

10.1	Types of tools	245
10.2	Summary of tool-evaluation criteria	246
	10.2.1	Service Management tools	246
10.3	Product training	247

Chapter 11: Planning for the implementation of Service Management 249

11.1	A Service Management project	249
11.2	Feasibility study	249
11.3	Assessing the current situation	250
	11.3.1	Introduction	250
	11.3.2	A 'health check'	250
11.4	General guidelines on project planning	251
	11.4.1	Project characteristics	251
	11.4.2	Business case for the project	252
	11.4.3	Critical success factors and possible problems	252
	11.4.4	Project costs	253
	11.4.5	Organisation	253
	11.4.6	Products	254
	11.4.7	Planning	254
	11.4.8	Communication plan	254
11.5	Project review and management reporting	255
	11.5.1	Progress reporting	255
	11.5.2	Evaluation of the project	256
	11.5.3	Post-project review	256
	11.5.4	Auditing for compliance using quality parameters	256
	11.5.5	Auditing for improvement using key performance indicators	257
	11.5.6	Management reporting	258

Chapter 12: Bibliography 259

| 12.1 | References | 259 |
| 12.2 | Other sources | 262 |

Appendix A: Terminology 263

| A.1 | List of acronyms | 263 |
| A.2 | Glossary of terms | 265 |

Appendix B:	**Process theory and practice**		271
B.1	Process theory		271
	B.1.1	The product-oriented organisation	271
	B.1.2	Moving towards a process-oriented organisation	271
	B.1.3	The process approach	272
B.2	Process modelling case study: Service Support example		273
	B.2.1	Introduction	273
	B.2.2	The approach	274
	B.2.3	Process analysis	274
	B.2.4	Conclusion	277
Appendix C:	**Implementing Service Management processes – issues to consider**		279
C.1	Process implementation		279
C.2	Applicability / scalability		279
	C.2.1	Large and small IT units	280
C.3	Process implementation projects: a checklist		280
	C.3.1	Procedures	280
	C.3.2	Dependencies	281
	C.3.3	People	281
	C.3.4	Timing	281
C.4	Impact on an organisation		281
	C.4.1	Hierarchical structure	281
	C.4.2	Matrix organisation	282
	C.4.3	Self-learning teams (coaching management)	282
C.5	Benchmarking		282
C.6	A sample implementation strategy		283
	C.6.1	Phase 1	283
	C.6.2	Phase 2	283
	C.6.3	Phase 3	283
	C.6.4	Phase 4	284
	C.6.5	Phase 5	284
	C.6.6	Phase 6	284
C.7	Process improvement		284
Appendix D:	**Quality**		287
D.1	Quality Management		287
	D.1.1	Ongoing quality improvement: The Deming Cycle	287
	D.1.2	Quality standards	287
	D.1.3	Total Quality Systems: EFQM	289
Appendix E:	**Example of cost-benefit analysis for Service Management processes**		293
Appendix F:	**The Service Support Process Model**		296
Index			297

FOREWORD

Organisations are increasingly dependent on electronic delivery of services to meet customer needs. This means a requirement for high-quality IT services, matched to business needs and user requirements as they evolve.

OGC's IT Infrastructure Library (ITIL) is the most widely accepted approach to IT Service Management in the world. ITIL provides a cohesive set of best practice, drawn from the public and private sectors internationally, supported by a comprehensive qualification scheme, accredited training organisations, implementation and assessment tools.

Bob Assirati

Director IT Directorate
Office of Government Commerce

May 2000

PREFACE

The ethos behind the development of the IT Infrastructure Library (ITIL) is the recognition that organisations are increasingly dependent upon IT to satisfy their corporate aims and meet their business needs. This growing dependency leads to growing needs for quality IT services – quality that is matched to business needs and user requirements as they emerge.

This is true no matter what type or size of organisation, be it national government, a multinational conglomerate, a decentralised office with either a local or centralised IT provision, an outsourced service provider, or a single office environment with one person providing IT support. In each case there is the requirement to provide an economical service that is reliable, consistent and of the highest quality.

IT Service Management is concerned with delivering and supporting IT services that are appropriate to the business requirements of the organisation. ITIL provides a comprehensive, consistent and coherent set of best practices for IT Service Management processes, promoting a quality approach to achieving business effectiveness and efficiency in the use of information systems. ITIL processes are intended to be implemented so that they underpin but do not dictate the business processes of an organisation. IT service providers will be striving to improve the quality of the service, but at the same time they will be trying to reduce the costs or, at a minimum, maintain costs at the current level.

For each of the processes described in this book, one or more roles are identified for carrying out the functions and activities required. It should be noted that organisations may allocate more than one role to an individual within the organisation (although this book indicates where specific roles should *not* be merged), or may allocate more than one individual to a role. The purpose of the role is to locate responsibility rather than to create an organisational structure.

The best-practice processes described in this book both support and are supported by the British Standards Institution's Code of Practice for IT Service Management (PD0005), and in turn underpin the ISO quality standard ISO9000.

The authors

The guidance in this book was distilled from the experience of a range of authors working in the private sector in IT service management. The material was written by:

Michiel Berkhout	Pink Elephant
Roy Harrow	Friends Provident, and Secretary of the BCS Configuration Management Specialist Group
Brian Johnson	Pink Elephant
Shirley Lacy	Change IT Ltd
Vernon Lloyd	Ultracomp
Don Page	Marval Software
Marc van Goethem	Pink Elephant
Hans van den Bent	Pink Elephant
Guus Welter	Pink Elephant

Significant contributions about process modelling were received from:

Gail Fosbrook	EDS
David Hinley	DS Hinley Assoc.

The project was managed and co-ordinated by Brian Johnson of Pink Elephant.

A wide-ranging national and international quality assurance (QA) exercise was carried out by people proposed by OGC and itSMF. OGC and Pink Elephant wish to express their particular appreciation to the following people, who spent considerable time and effort (far beyond the call of duty!) on QA of the material:

Dave Bingham	DMR Consulting Group
Tony Brough	Exel Logistics
Martin Carr	OGC
Kevin E. Ellis, BA.	Regional Information Technology Analyst/ Union Gas Ltd., Sudbury, Ontario, Canada
Karen M Ferris	ProActive Services Pty Ltd
Mary Fishleigh	F.I.Group and itSMF
Neville Greenhalgh	Documentation Services
John Groom	OGC
Lex Hendriks	EXIN
Marc Hodes	Fidus
Hilary Holman	F.I.Group
Steve Ingall	Ultracomp
Moira Ingham	F.I.Group
Tom Ivison	Siemens Business Services
David Johnston	Fox IT
Chris Keeling	Insight Consulting
Vladimir Kufner	Logica
Chris Littlewood	F.I.Group
Ivor Macfarlane	Axios Systems Ltd
Bernard Melson	ImagoQA
Phil Montanaro	EDS
John Palmer	Merant
Louk Peters	Pink Elephant
René Posthumus	Mainland Sequoia
David Pultorak	Visalign, USA
Marcel Rispens	Rabobank Nederland Securities Services
Colin Rudd	IT Enterprise Management Ltd. (itEMS)
Frances Scarff	OGC
Manfred Talle	IT Service Manager, Kivision bv
Bridget Veitch	F.I.Group
David Wheeldon	Ultracomp

Contact information

Full details of the range of material published under the ITIL banner can be found at www.itil.co.uk

For further information on this and other OGC products, please visit the OGC website at www.ogc.gov.uk/. Alternatively, please contact:

OGC Service Desk
Rosebery Court
St Andrews Business Park
Norwich
NR7 0HS
United Kingdom
Tel: +44 1603 704567
Email: ServiceDesk@ogc.gsi.gov.uk

1 INTRODUCTION

This book is one of a series issued as part of the updated IT Infrastructure Library that documents industry best practice for the support and delivery of IT services. Although this book can be read in isolation, it is recommended that it be used in conjunction with the other IT Infrastructure Library books. Service Management is a generic concept and the guidance in the new IT Infrastructure Library books is applicable generically. The guidance is also scaleable – applicable to both small and large organisations. It applies to distributed and centralised systems, whether in-house or supplied by third parties. It is neither bureaucratic nor unwieldy if implemented sensibly and in full recognition of the business needs of your organisation.

1.1 The IT Infrastructure Library

Developed in the late 1980's, the IT Infrastructure Library (ITIL) has become the world-wide *de facto* standard in Service Management. Starting as a guide for UK government, the framework has proved to be useful to organisations in all sectors through its adoption by many Service Management companies as the basis for consultancy, education and software tools support. Today, ITIL is known and used worldwide.

The reasons for its success are explained in the remainder of this section:

1.1.1 Public domain framework

From the beginning, ITIL has been publicly available. This means that any organisation can use the framework described by the CCTA in its numerous books. Because of this, the IT Infrastructure Library guidance has been used by such a disparate range of organisations, local and central government, energy, public utilities, retail, finance, and manufacturing. Very large organisations, very small organisations and everything in between have implemented ITIL processes.

1.1.2 Best practice framework

The IT Infrastructure Library documents industry best practice guidance. It has proved its value from the very beginning. Initially, CCTA collected information on how various organisations addressed Service Management, analysed this and filtered those issues that would prove useful to CCTA and to its Customers in UK central government. Other organisations found that the guidance was generally applicable and markets outside of government were very soon created by the service industry.

Being a framework, ITIL describes the contours of organising Service Management. The models show the goals, general activities, inputs and outputs of the various processes, which can be incorporated within IT organisations. ITIL does not cast in stone every action you should do on a day-to-day basis because that is something which will differ from organisation to organisation. Instead it focuses on best practice that can be utilised in different ways according to need.

Thanks to this framework of proven best practices, the IT Infrastructure Library can be used within organisations with existing methods and activities in Service Management. Using ITIL doesn't imply a completely new way of thinking and acting. It provides a framework in which to place existing methods and activities in a structured context. By emphasising the relationships between the processes, any lack of communication and co-operation between various IT functions can be eliminated or minimised.

ITIL provides a proven method for planning common processes, roles and activities with appropriate reference to each other and how the communication lines should exist between them.

1.1.3 *De facto* standard

By the mid-1990s, ITIL was recognised as the world *de facto* standard for Service Management. A major advantage of a generally recognised method is a common language. The books describe a large number of terms that, when used correctly, can help people to understand each other within IT organisations.

An important part of IT Infrastructure Library projects is getting people to speak that common language. That is why education is the essential basis of an implementation or improvement program. Only when the people involved use a common language can a project be successful.

1.1.4 Quality approach

In the past, many IT organisations were internally focused and concentrated on technical issues. These days, businesses have high expectations towards the quality of services and these expectations change with time. This means that for IT organisations to live up to these expectations, they need to concentrate on service quality and a more Customer oriented approach. Cost issues are now high on the agenda as is the development of a more businesslike attitude to provision of service.

ITIL focuses on providing high quality services with a particular focus on Customer relationships. This means that the IT organisation should provide whatever is agreed with Customers, which implies a strong relationship between the IT organisation and their Customers and partners.

Tactical processes are centred on the relationships between the IT organisation and their Customers. Service Delivery is partially concerned with setting up agreements and monitoring the targets within these agreements. Meanwhile, on the operational level, the Service Support processes can be viewed as delivering service as laid down in these agreements. On both levels you will find a strong relationship with quality systems such as ISO9000 and a total quality framework such as European Foundation for Quality Management (EFQM). ITIL will support these quality systems by providing defined processes and best practice for the management of IT Services, enabling a fast track towards ISO certification.

Appendix D provides more information on quality management. Generic benefits include:

- improved quality service provision
- cost justifiable service quality
- services that meet business, Customer and User demands
- integrated centralised processes
- everyone knows their role and knows their responsibilities in service provision
- learning from previous experience
- demonstrable performance indicators.

Business case for using the ISO9000 quality standards

Many companies require their suppliers to become registered to ISO9001 and because of this, registered companies find that their market opportunities have increased. In addition, a company's compliance with ISO9001 ensures that it has a sound Quality Assurance system.

Registered companies have had dramatic reductions in Customer complaints, significant reductions in operating costs and increased demand for their products and services.

ISO9000 registration is rapidly becoming a should for any company that does business in Europe. Many industrial companies require registration by their own suppliers. There is a growing trend toward universal acceptance of ISO9000 as an international standard.

Of course this applies to other standards, for example the British Standards, and in fact most European and many other standards world-wide have been consolidated in the new ISO9000-2000 standards.

1.1.5   itSMF

The itSMF (IT Service Management Forum) was set up to support and influence the IT Service Management industry. It has through its very large membership been influential in promoting industry best practice and driving updates to ITIL.

1.2   Restructuring the IT Infrastructure Library

The concept of managing IT services for the improvement of business functions is not new; it predates ITIL. The idea to bring all of the Service Management best practice together under one roof however was both radical and new. The first series of ITIL amalgamated Service Management from an IT standpoint but could have done more to capture the interest of the business. The business perspective series was published to bridge the gap between business and management and although a success, the series was published at a time when the original ITIL guidance was becoming outdated in some areas. The impact of the new series was therefore limited in the market, but a catalyst in the Service Management industry.

ITIL was originally produced in the late 1980s and consisted of ten core books covering the two main areas of Service Support and Service Delivery. These core books were further supported by 30 complementary books covering a range of issues from Cabling to Business Continuity Management. In this revision, ITIL has been restructured to make it simpler to access the information needed to manage your services. The core books have now been pulled together into two books, covering the areas of Service Support and Service Delivery, in order to eliminate duplication and enhance navigation. The material has also been updated and revised for consistency and sharpness of focus. Lastly, the material has been re-engineered to focus on the business issues of infrastructure management as well as to ensure a closer synergy with the new IS guides published by CCTA.

1.3   Target audience

This book is relevant to anyone involved in the delivery or support of services. It is applicable to anyone involved in the management or day-to-day practice of Service Management, in-house or outsourced, as well as anyone defining new processes or refining existing processes. Business managers will find the book helpful in understanding and establishing best practice IT services and support. Managers from supplier organisations will also find this book relevant when setting up agreements for the delivery and support of services.

1.4   Navigating the IT Infrastructure Library

Following consultation with Service Management organisations and User groups, CCTA designed the diagram shown in Figure 1.1. This illustrates that the new library series will comprise five principal elements, each of which will have interfaces and overlaps with each of the other four. The elements are:

- the Business Perspective
- managing Applications
- deliver IT Services
- support IT Services
- manage the Infrastructure.

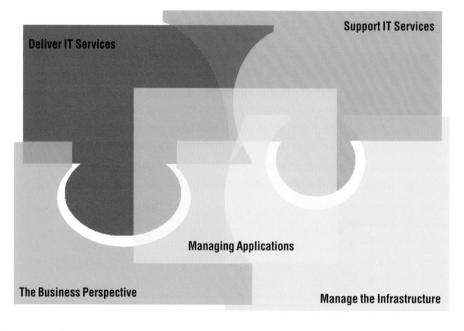

Figure 1.1 - Jigsaw Diagram

The Business Perspective book will cover a range of issues concerned with understanding and improving IT service provision, as an integral part of an overall business requirement for high quality IS management. These issues include:

- Business Continuity Management
- partnerships and outsourcing
- surviving Change
- transformation of business practice through radical Change.

The Service Delivery book looks at what service the business requires of the provider in order to provide adequate support to the business Users. To provide the necessary support the book covers the following topics:

- Capacity Management
- Financial Management for IT Services
- Availability Management
- Service Level Management
- IT Service Continuity Management
- Customer Relationship Management.

The Service Support book is concerned with ensuring that the Customer has access to the appropriate services to support the business functions. Issues discussed in this book are:

- Service Desk
- Incident Management
- Problem Management
- Configuration Management
- Change Management
- Release Management.

The ICT Infrastructure Management book includes:

- Network Service Management
- Operations Management
- Management of Local Processors
- Computer Installation and Acceptance
- Systems Management. (covered here for the first time).

Lastly, the book on Applications Management will embrace the software development lifecycle expanding the issues touched upon in Software Lifecycle Support and Testing of IT Services. Applications Management will expand on the issues of business change with emphasis on clear requirement definition and implementation of the solution to meet business needs.

The major elements of the ITIL books can be likened to overlapping jigsaw puzzle pieces (or perhaps better as tectonic plates), some of which have a precise fit, and some of which overlap or do not fit together accurately. At the highest level, there are no strict demarcation lines. Indeed, if we consider further the analogy of tectonic plates, sliding over and under one another, joining and separating, then the earthly problem of points of instability or friction caused by the imprecise nature of the pieces has an IT Infrastructure Library equivalent. It is precisely where process domains overlap or where demarcation lines cannot be clearly drawn that many management problems arise. We cannot stop all the problems from occurring (just as we cannot stop earthquakes) but we can provide advice about how to prepare for and deal with them.

1.5   Why choose a jigsaw concept?

To clarify how the concepts within ITIL work together, CCTA produced a set of process models to describe the makeup of ITIL – a high-level process model for Service Support can be found at Appendix F. These process models have been used in practice and enhanced since first produced and now form the cornerstones of the ITIL core books. The process elements for management of services can be defined precisely. However, in practice, when analysing the processes in more detail, elements overlap. This situation illustrates the need for both consistency across the guidance, and advice on how to deal with management problems that may arise. The cause of these management problems may be the result of boundaries drawn that perhaps have more to do with the span of control than with logical grouping of related processes.

1.6   The Service Support book

Figure 1.2 expands the service support jigsaw puzzle pieces. Although obviously primarily centred on Service Support, the process elements pertaining to the business issue of Change to services (which is usually the signal for radical Change rather than Change due to faults or maintenance) and meeting Customer needs through Service Delivery are a major factor. The ITIL process elements covered in this book are also shown.

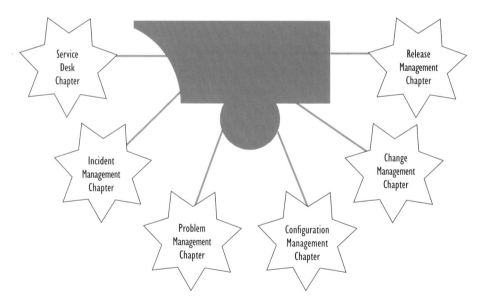

Figure 1.2 - Service Support; the coverage.

Note that all of the chapters relate to processes except Service Desk, which is a function that draws on all of the other processes.

1.7 Service Management

All the processes described in ITIL relate to each other. Half of these processes are detailed in this book, half in the book on Service Delivery. To better understand how these processes inter-relate, consider this example life cycle of an Incident:

1. A User calls the *Service Desk* to report response difficulties with the on-line service.

2. the *Incident Management* process deals with Incident.

3. the *Problem Management* process investigates underlying cause and calls in *Capacity Management* to assist in this process. *Service Level Management* alerted that the SLA. has been breached.

4. the *Change Management* process raises and co-ordinates a Request For Change (RFC)

5. the *IT Financial Management* process assists with the business case cost justification for the hardware upgrade.

6. the *IT Service Continuity* process gets involved in the *Change Management* process to ensure recovery is possible onto current back-up configuration.

7. the *Release Management* process controls the implementation of the Change by rolling out replacement hardware and software. Release Management updates Configuration Management with details of new Releases and versions.

8. the *Availability Management* process is involved in considering the hardware upgrade to ensure that it can meet the required availability and reliability levels.

9. the *Configuration Management* process ensures the CMDB information is updated throughout the process.

10. the *Customer Relationship Management* process liaises with Customer throughout the process to ensure he/she is kept abreast of progress.

1.8 Customers and Users

To avoid confusion regarding roles and terminology the terms 'Customer' and 'User' are used throughout the new books to differentiate between those people (generally senior managers) who commission, pay for and own the IT Services (the Customers) and those people who use the services on a day-to-day basis (the Users). The semantics are less important than the reason for differentiation. The primary point of contact for Customers is the Customer Relationship Manager, whilst the primary point of contact for Users is the Service Desk. A poorly functioning Incident Management process will affect the User population immediately. A service that is poor value for money will have a greater impact on the Customer.

It is therefore important that we distinguish the different, but related, needs of Users and Customers in the provision of services. Certainly, their goals may be at odds and need to be balanced; for example Users may demand high availability whereas Customers look for value for money at different levels of availability. There are information flows that should be maintained and key process elements that should be defined for use by both parties.

1.9 A Code of Practice for IT Service Management - PD0005

The British Standards Institute published 'A Code of Practice for IT Service Management (PD0005) which was based on the principles of the ITIL; the context diagram from the guide is reproduced below. The diagram is not a process model but simply a pictorial description. It can be viewed in the same way as Figure 1.1, i.e. the main principles (of Service Management in this instance) are placed in a coherent context, providing guidance that enables the reader to make links between related process elements.

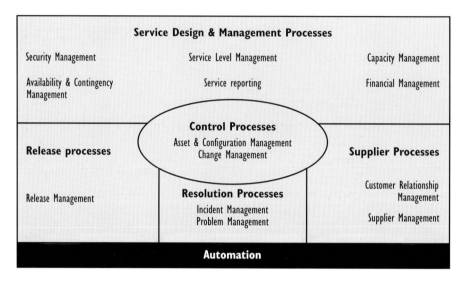

Figure 1.3 - PD0005 Service Management processes

If we now consider PD0005 in the context of Figure 1.3, it is obvious that the new IT Infrastructure Library models can be seen as an expansion of the BSI model, taking IT Service Management forward. The process elements are nearly the same, the principle of Change and Configuration Management as a linchpin is the same, the difference relates to the level of detail. Both BSI and CCTA espouse similar, if not identical, principles of best practice for IT Service Management.

1.10 Service Management: a process approach

The chapters in this book focus on Service Support as a set of integrated processes. Service Support focuses on processes in order to achieve goals; some managerial functions are required to enact the processes, but fundamentally it is the process and its suitability for purpose that is important.

More details about process theory and practice are provided in Appendix B to this book.

1.11 Recommended reading

These CCTA IS Management Guides are also related to Service Management and are recommended additional reading. They can be obtained from your ITIL bookseller or The Stationery Office:

Strategic Management of IS
Published by Format
1 90309 1 02 0
Approx 70 pages
October 1999
£25.00

This guide describes the context within which organisations in the public sector will need to think strategically about the exploitation of IS and IT, and the impact of current sector-wide policies and initiatives. It sets out the approach which senior business managers should take to the management of information systems and their IS strategy, together with guidance on managing the required changes.

Managing Change
Published by Format
1 90309 1 01 2
Approx 80 pages
September 1999
£25.00

This guide is intended for senior managers who are responsible for managing complex IS-related change. It investigates the issues associated with business transformation, organisational and cultural change. It provides practical advice on working across organisational boundaries and breaking the 'all pain, no gain' barrier. The guidance also provides clear interfaces to Programme Management and benefits realisation.

Acquisition
Published by Format
1 90309 1 03 9
Approx 70 pages
September 1999
£25.00

This guide focuses on business objectives and outcomes in making the right IT acquisitions. It explains the key issues relating to sourcing options and partnerships, together with procurement strategies for new ways of working and new kinds of contracts.

Managing Performance
Published by Format
1 90309 1 05 5
Approx 110 pages
September 1999
£25.00

This guide, developed in collaboration with NAO, focuses on three levels of performance management: business management; contribution of IS/IT to the business; and performance of the IS/IT function. It examines the role of the EFQM Excellence Model®, balanced scorecards, benchmarking and other widely adopted techniques.

Managing Services
Published by Format
1 90309 1 04 7
Approx 100 pages
February 2000
£25.00

This guide explains the foundations for effective service management, appropriate contracts and good working relationships. It helps the customer of IS/IT services to understand the providers' perspective on service delivery. It provides practical advice on how to achieve better performance from service providers and continuing value for money.

2 RELATIONSHIP BETWEEN PROCESSES

This book refers to the need for Configuration Management, Change Management, Incident Management, Problem Management and Release Management processes that are integrated. For example, the process of releasing components to the live environment (the domain of Release Management) is also an issue for Configuration Management and Change Management whilst the Service Desk is primarily responsible for liaison between IT providers and the Users of services. Whilst each component of Service Support is discussed separately in the book, the purpose of this section is to highlight the links and the principal relationships between all the Service Management and other infrastructure management processes.

2.1 Configuration Management

Configuration Management is an integral part of all other Service Management processes. With current, accurate and comprehensive information about all components in the infrastructure the management of Change, in particular, is more effective and efficient. Change Management can be integrated with Configuration Management. As a *minimum* it is recommended that the logging and implementation of Changes be done under the control of a comprehensive Configuration Management system and that the impact assessment of Changes is done with the aid of the Configuration Management system. All Change requests should therefore be entered in the Configuration Management Database (CMDB) and the records updated as the Change request progresses through to implementation.

The Configuration Management system identifies relationships between an item that is to be changed and any other components of the infrastructure, thus allowing the owners of these components to be involved in the impact assessment process. Whenever a Change is made to the infrastructure, associated Configuration Management records should be updated in the CMDB (see Figure 2.1). Where possible, this is best accomplished by use of integrated tools that update records automatically as Changes are made.

The CMDB should be made available to the entire Service Support group so that Incidents and Problems can be resolved more easily by understanding the possible cause of the failing component. The CMDB should also be used to link the Incident and Problem records to other appropriate records such as the failing Configuration Item (CI) and the User. Release Management will be difficult and error prone without the integration of the Configuration Management process.

The Service Delivery processes also rely on the CMDB data. For example:

- Service Level Management needs to identify components that combine together to deliver the service so that underpinning agreements can be set up
- Financial Management for IT needs to know the components utilised by each business unit especially when charging is in place
- IT Service Continuity and Availability Management need to identify components to perform risk analysis and component failure impact analysis

SLM is the hinge for Service Support and Service Delivery. It cannot function in isolation as it relies on the existence and effective and efficient working of other processes. An SLA without underpinning support processes is useless, as there is no basis for agreeing its content.

2.8   Capacity Management

Capacity Management is directly related to the business requirements and is not simply about the performance of the system's components, individually or collectively. Capacity Management is involved in Incident resolution and Problem identification for those difficulties relating to capacity issues.

Capacity Management activities raise Requests for Change (RFCs) to ensure that appropriate capacity is available. These RFCs are subject to the Change Management process, and implementation may affect several CIs, including hardware, software and documentation, requiring effective Release Management.

Capacity Management should be involved in evaluating all Changes, to establish the effect on capacity and performance. This should occur both when Changes are proposed and after they are implemented. Capacity Management should pay particular attention to the cumulative effect of Changes over a period of time. The negligible effect of single Changes can often combine to cause degraded response times, file storage problems, and excess demand for processing capacity.

2.9   Financial Management for IT Services

Financial Management is responsible for accounting for the costs of providing IT service and for any aspects of recovering these costs from the Customers (charging). It requires good interfaces with Capacity Management, Configuration Management (asset data) and Service Level Management to identify the true costs of service. The Financial Manager is likely to work closely with the Customer Relationship Manager and the IT Directorate during the negotiations of the IT department budgets and individual Customer's IT spend.

2.10   Availability Management

Availability Management is concerned with the design, implementation, measurement and management of IT services to ensure the stated business requirements for availability are consistently met. Availability Management requires an understanding of the reasons why IT service failures occur and the time taken to resume service. Incident Management and Problem Management provide a key input to ensure the appropriate corrective actions are being progressed.

The measurements and reporting of IT availability ensures that the level of availability delivered meets the SLA. Availability Management supports the Service Level Management process in providing measurements and reporting to support service reviews.

2.11   IT Service Continuity Management

IT Service Continuity Management is concerned with managing an organisation's ability to continue to provide a pre-determined and agreed level of IT Services to support the minimum business requirements following an interruption to the business. Effective IT Service Continuity requires a balance of risk reduction measures such as resilient systems and recovery options including back-up facilities. Configuration Management data is required to facilitate this prevention and planning. Infrastructure and business Changes need to be assessed for their potential impact on the continuity plans, and the IT and business plans should be subject to Change Management procedures. The Service Desk has an important role to play if business continuity is invoked.

2.12   Customer Relationship Management

Customer Relationship Management is about developing and nurturing a good professional working relationship between Customers and IT service providers. Customer Relationship Managers (CRMs) need to interface with all the other ITIL processes. For example, the CRM facilitates the interaction between the Customer and IT departments during the annual SLA/financial negotiations, and is involved in resolving Customer discontent with the service being provided.

2.13   ICT Infrastructure Management

ICT Infrastructure Management functions are involved in most of the processes of Service Support and Service Delivery where more technical issues are concerned.

2.14   Application Management

CCTA plans to produce guidance that discusses the major processes required to manage applications throughout their lifetime. Service Management is typically concerned with a product (software/hardware) at a particular point in time to support the service requirements of the business. But it should be more than this. It delivers a maintainable service for the business - this means delivering the skills, training, and communications with the application. Applications Management considers the issues from feasibility through productive life to final demise of the application.

2.15   Security Management

The Security Management function interfaces with IT Service Management processes where security issues are involved. Such issues relate to the Confidentiality, Integrity and Availability of data, as well as the security of hardware and software components, documentation and procedures. For example, Security Management interfaces with Service Management to assess the impact of proposed Changes on security, to raise RFCs in response to security problems; to ensure confidentiality and integrity of security data and to maintain the security when software is released into the live environment.

2.16 Environmental infrastructure processes

Changes to the environment may affect the quality of service, and Changes to the infrastructure may have implications for the environmental infrastructure. It is recommended that all relevant aspects of the environmental infrastructure be brought under Configuration Management control and subjected to the Change Management procedures described in this book.

2.17 Project Management

When implementing new processes in an organisation there are benefits to running the activity as a project. Accordingly, this book refers to Service Management Projects that are implemented to introduce new processes or to improve the current processes for the delivery or support of IT services.

There are a variety of structured project management methods that can be adopted. Within ITIL when we discuss project management if we need to draw on a particular method we will use PRINCE2 which is owned by CCTA and widely adopted throughout UK Government bodies, the Public and Private sectors, and internationally.

3 GETTING STARTED

Chapter 11 discusses how to set about planning and implementing the project of introducing Service Management. Within this chapter we look at how to build commitment from management so that they will provide the necessary funding and communicate support for the project.

What you need to know first is the benefit of using the method and how to market the message of those benefits to your organisation. These issues can form part of a business case for process implementation or improvement. An important part of the business case is likely to be concerned with articulating the problems with the current position and demonstrating the benefits of the new vision. A business case should look at the benefits, disadvantages, costs and risks of the current situation and the future vision so that management can balance all of these factors when deciding if the project should proceed. Appendix E provides some costed examples for developing a business case for introducing ITIL into an organisation.

3.1 Service Management benefits

It is important to consider the benefits for the organisation of having a clear definition of the Service Management function. Some of the benefits that could be cited include:

- improved quality of service - more reliable business support
- IT Service Continuity procedures more focused, more confidence in the ability to follow them when required
- clearer view of current IT capability
- better information on current services (and possibly on where Changes would bring most benefits)
- greater flexibility for the business through improved understanding of IT support
- more motivated staff; improved job satisfaction through better understanding of capability and better management of expectations
- enhanced Customer satisfaction as service providers know and deliver what is expected of them
- increased flexibility and adaptability is likely to exist within the services
- system-led benefits, e.g. improvements in security, accuracy, speed, availability as required for the required level of service
- improved cycle time for Changes and greater success rate.

The importance and level of these will vary between organisations. An issue comes in defining these benefits for any organisation in a way that will be measurable later on. Following ITIL guidance can help to quantify some of these elements.

3.2   A process led approach

Appendix B provides detailed information about using process models and definitions to complement a process led approach to implementing IT Infrastructure Library guidance in a programme of continuous improvement. Figure 3.1 represents a model that can be used by an organisation as the framework for process improvement.

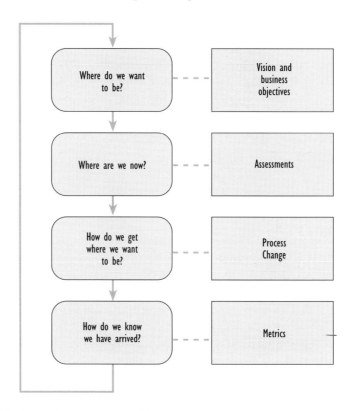

Figure 3.1 - Process improvement model

In short, if you can draw up a process model of best practice – or any practice in fact that is more effective than your current way of doing things – then you can compare that model with a description of your current practice and use it to define improvements. If you do this in the light of your business direction or critical success factors, you can define measures of how you can demonstrate improvements and achievements that are truly useful.

As a process based method, the IT Infrastructure Library is particularly suited to use in this way. Appendix B provides more information and a case study.

There are a number of different methods and notations by which processes can be defined and documented – each often associated with a specific design/modelling tool.

Taking a fairly generic view, Figure 3.2 illustrates the typical components one might find in a process definition.

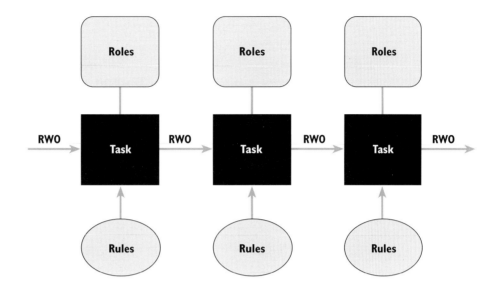

Figure 3.2 - Typical components in a process definition

Each process can be broken down into a series of tasks. For each task, there will be Inputs and Outputs (shown as **Real World Objects, RWO,** in the diagram). Whether these RWOs have a physical form, e.g. as a piece of paper, or are merely held as electronic information, is irrelevant.

Each task will be executed by a **role**. This may be embodied in a human being or performed by a piece of software. If human-centric, then there will be a set of competencies that an individual needs in order to perform the role.

The execution of the role is governed by a set of **rules**. These will range from the simple ("All boxes on the form should be completed") to the very complex ("Credit is only allowed if a set of criteria are met according to an algorithm").

Often, a process will span various organisational boundaries. It is important, therefore, that each process should have an **owner**. This is another **role**.

The process owner is responsible for the **process definition** itself, which should be treated as a CI, subject to all the usual Change control rigours. The process owner is responsible for ensuring that all that are involved in the execution of the process are kept informed of any Changes that occur.

3.3   Management commitment

Management commitment is about motivating and leading by example. If you or your managers do not support the use of best practice openly and demonstrably, or if you are not fully committed to Change and innovation, then staff cannot be expected to improve themselves, Service Management processes or service to Customers. Genuine management commitment is absolutely essential to 'staying the course' when implementing Service Management in an organisation.

3.3.1 Aspects of management commitment

Modern organisations require IT/ business alignment, and therefore a total quality approach to leadership is required from managers. The different aspects of management commitment can be found in commonly used Total Quality Models such as the EFQM (in Europe) or MBNQA (in North America) models.

3.3.2 Management commitment in the planning stage

Why do implementations fail?

This question has been asked many times in the past. If we examine the causes for failures at the highest level a pattern appears. Simply designing and implementing a new or updated process does not guarantee success. A number of factors could result in the process not realising its objectives. In most cases failure is caused by lack of attention to the 'process enablers'. It is not enough for management to provide the funds for the implementation process and then sit back expecting everything to work. Management should be committed during the entire *plan-do-check-act* cycle, and should also address all aspects of the Service Management framework. Other common reasons for failure include:

- lack of staff commitment and understanding
- lack of training
- the staff given the responsibility for implementation are not given sufficient authority to make the required decisions
- loss of the Service Management 'champion' (the person driving the implementation)
- loss of impetus after the initial hype
- lack of initial funding and lack of quantifiable long term cost benefits
- over-focus on tactical, isolated 'solutions' rather than a strategic solution, i.e., addressing individual elements of Service Management rather than the overall picture
- overly ambitious expectations of immediate benefits or try to do everything at once
- unrealistic implementation timetable
- no one accountable
- difficulties of changing the culture of the organisation
- tools unable to support the process, requiring tailoring of the process or of the tool
- inappropriate approach taken to implementation – not under Project Management controls
- inappropriate scoping of the process
- lack of appreciation for the hard work and discipline required to implement Service Management.

3.4 Cultural aspects

It would appear obvious that, in order to prosper, a business organisation should have Customer satisfaction as its prime objective. Unfortunately, until recently, many IT departments have been too obsessed with technology and flashing lights to recognise that they have Customers at all.

In recent years pressure has been put on IT service providers to become more aware of their role in supporting the business and to be run as accountable business units. This pressure has come from many quarters:

- outsourcing
- market testing
- compulsory competitive tendering
- the Customers themselves (who are, in increasing numbers, being given their own budgets and the freedom to use them where they see fit).

The days when staff in IT departments regarded their 'Customers' as a *necessary evil* or just *difficult colleagues* have (hopefully) passed. There is a growing awareness that in order to retain the in-house IT department they have to stay close to their Customers, understand and predict their requirements and satisfy them. IT departments are now raising the priority of Customer satisfaction from being merely 'nice to have' to 'essential'.

The provision of quality IT services with high levels of availability and performance can be achieved with the correct hardware, software and underlying support disciplines. This level of service may satisfy, but may not delight, the Customer! Extra effort is needed for the Customer to enjoy the experience and want to come back for more. The way in which the service is delivered is dependent on the people delivering the service. Customer delight will only be achieved if the people involved are responsive to their Customers' needs, are attentive, reliable, and courteous, delivering the service in the way they themselves would like to receive it.

We all know what a Customer is – someone who deals with a trader and habitually purchases from him. Similarly, we are all familiar with service – an act performed for the benefit or advantage of a person, institution or cause. Customer service therefore is concerned with performing acts that will benefit the Customer in a way that will encourage him to purchase service again and again.

3.4.1 What is culture?

It is important that all staff involved in delivering service are committed to the concept of Customer delight. This can only be achieved if the organisation's culture demands it. The prevalent culture within any organisation is a product of a variety of factors: the age and history of the organisation, its size, the technology in use, its objectives, the market as well as geography and the personalities and backgrounds of people employed.

There are many influencing factors and it is not reasonable to expect all organisations to have, or adopt, the same culture, organisational structure or systems. Despite the growing literature on the culture of organisations there is no textbook formula for organisational culture.

The term 'culture' is used in this context to refer to the values and beliefs of the organisation – the normal way of doing things. Component parts of the culture include:

- the way authority is exercised and people rewarded
- methods of communication
- the degrees of formality required in working hours and dress and the extent to which procedures and regulations are enforced.

An organisation's culture can be immediately recognised by an outsider by the staff's attitudes and morale; their vocabulary – the phrases and buzz words they use and the stories and legends they tell of the organisation's heroes.

3.4.2   Responsibilities

Most often, responsibility for creating and maintaining an organisation's culture should rest with its leaders. The prevailing culture will dictate the shape of the organisation's structure and the nature of the systems and procedures used.

In their best-selling book *In Search of Excellence*, a study of the best run American companies, Tom Peters and Robert Waterman noted

> …Without exception, the dominance and coherence of culture proved to be an essential quality of the excellent companies. Moreover, the stronger the culture and the more it was directed toward the market place, the less need was there for policy manuals, organisation charts, or detailed procedures and rules … people … know what they are supposed to do in most situations because the handful of guiding values is crystal clear

Procedures, therefore, should support the culture and not govern or influence it.

3.4.3   What is meant by 'service culture'?

In order to achieve business success the culture of every organisation should embrace the concept of service and Customer care.

The satisfaction of Customer requirements should be the number one priority – for everyone, whatever their role in the organisation. The concept of service should permeate through all layers of the organisation – from staff in the front line responsible for delivering service to those in a supporting role – either as managers or in the back room.

Service delivery should ensure that Customer requirements are met in a way that makes them feel that they are valued and respected – they should be made to feel good at every transaction. The aim should be to exceed Customers' expectations (not in *what* you deliver but in the *way* you deliver it) and give them confidence in your ability to satisfy all their future needs.

By taking the time and effort to listen to the Customers it is possible to understand the service being provided from their perspective. The key point about providing service is attention to detail; to go that little bit further to delight the Customer.

3.4.4   How is this relevant to IT service provision?

Achieving a service culture in an IT organisation should, in essence, be no different from achieving a service culture in a bread shop or a carpet wholesale business; the technology used and the product delivered may be different but the end result is the same – Customers receive service. Customers of IT services have come to expect the same levels of service at work as they receive at their local shopping mall – and they use the same criteria for choosing it.

If we accept that the quality of our IT service delivery is important then we should agree that the way we treat our Customers is an important part of service delivery.

3.4.5   What do Customers want?

Having recognised that IT departments are now in the business of service provision they should now adopt a whole new way of thinking and embrace the same business concepts as those used by all service providers. There is a lot of catching up to do.

Before any business goes into production of a new product or service it should perform some market research to find out what the Customers actually want and will buy.

So, what do Customers want?

- **Specification** – they want to know, up front, what they are going to get. The problem in IT service delivery is that Customers frequently don't know what they want – the 'IT experts' should translate their business requirements into solutions. Customers don't buy products or services, they buy solutions.

- **Conformance** to specification – once the appropriate IT solution has been found then it should conform to the specification. Customers want to know when they can receive it and should be satisfied that it will fulfil their business requirement.

- **Consistency** – they want it to be the same every time they come back for more.

- **Value for money** – the price they pay should be a fair one for the product or service they receive.

- **Communication** – they want to be told what they are getting, when, how and what to do if they have a problem with it.

Popular misconceptions about Customer care

Many people are cynical about the concept of Customer care and, in many cases, they have good reason to be. The following paragraphs describe areas of Customer care.

'The Customer Is King posters' (and other clichèd campaign material)

Allegedly witty and amusing posters proclaiming the virtues of Customer care can be a decorative addition to an office or corridor, on their own they achieve very little. If the same slogans are used continually on posters then they become part of the wallpaper and are ignored – be prepared to change them and beware of empty slogans that can be misinterpreted. Ensure that all staff are aware of the nature, scope and intention behind any Customer care promotion otherwise the material will be greeted by cynicism if it arrives unannounced.

A by-product of ITIL/BS5750/ISO9001/TQM

A service culture will not develop unaided. The adoption of the best practice in IT service delivery described in ITIL will help improve service quality. Improving the quality of procedures and obtaining quality certification will certainly focus the mind on service quality but these alone are not enough to ensure the IT department is truly Customer focused – a structured approach to cultural change is necessary.

Customer Charters and Service Level Agreements

Published guaranteed levels of service (such as SLAs) are worthless if the supplier consistently fails to meet the targets. The payment of recompense through penalty clauses is unlikely to satisfy the purchaser in the long term. These agreements tend to set targets for the tangible elements of service – availability, response times etc. and ignore the intangible elements, which are so crucial to Customers – the way in which service was delivered.

(Another) Management initiative

If Customer service is placed high on the agenda one month and then allowed to slip back, people will think that 'the management have been on another training course and have come back with some bright ideas and this actually has nothing to do with us'. Staff should be made to realise that Customer care is not management or technology driven – instead it is Customer driven, and that it makes sound business sense to adopt a Service Culture.

Someone else's responsibility

Where organisations have Customer Liaison departments or Customer Service Managers, staff may be tempted to relinquish the responsibility for Customer care, thinking it is someone else's job. The concept of Customer service should permeate throughout the whole organisation.

Something new

Although the concept of satisfying Customers' requirements is only now hitting some IT departments, it is nothing new. Man has been trading ever since he came down from the trees and learned how to make a surplus. Those men and women who produced something that wasn't marketable starved to death!

3.4.6 Common excuses for conducting 'business as usual'

Most of the Management Gurus preach what is little more than 'common sense' – to treat your Customers as individuals, to ask Customers what they want, listen to them and then provide what they want, to wander around amongst your Customers and staff and engender a feeling of trust. It sounds easy. So why do so many organisations still fail to provide consistent Customer satisfaction? Some of the common excuses include:

- *'We are increasing our market share and expanding our product portfolio'*
- *'Our Customers are happy – the number of Customer complaints is down on last year and the results of our Customer satisfaction survey show that we are improving our service'*
- *'We are the market leaders – we are the best'*
- *'Customer Service is an important issue, that is why we have a Customer service department – Customer satisfaction is their responsibility'*
- *'We are highly skilled IT people – we haven't been trained to deal with Customers'*
- *'We tried Customer Care before – it cost us a lot of money for little if any return'*
- *'We have always treated our Customers as Customers and always provided an excellent service'*
- *'We are not in a competitive situation – our Customers are tied to internal services. We are not a business unit – we run the IT department'.*

3.4.7 How much will all this cost?

Aiming to "exceed Customers' expectations" sounds very expensive. Indeed, if we promise to visit a Customer within four hours to fix a printer and we turn up in ten minutes with a brand-new replacement, we will certainly incur extra costs. The manpower overhead of having staff sitting around waiting for a call, the cost of having spare printers on-site etc. The Customer may very well be delighted with this level of service and will expect the same service every time – the Customer will certainly be disappointed if you take four hours next time.

Exceeding Customer expectations does not, therefore, mean 'giving away service'. In the example given above the Customer may have been quite happy with the four hour target and a ten minute response may actually in this case have been inconvenient to him – having arranged to do something else for the next four hours. The Customer may have been happy with the old printer and not want a new one – particularly if it is a different model or takes you some time to configure it.

The IT supplier could have delighted the Customer without incurring unnecessary cost by:

- logging and understanding the technical nature of the difficulty at the first point of contact
- responding in line with the urgency as stated by the Customer
- keeping the Customer informed of what will happen, when – and keeping the promise
- carrying out the work with the minimum level of disruption in a cheerful and professional manner
- reviewing the action taken to ensure that the difficulty has been fixed and that the Customer is happy.

Getting the job done in accordance with the Customers' wishes, correctly, first time, actually saves the cost of a potential repeat visit.

Implementing a Customer care programme *will* cost money – staff time, training, changes to operating methods, promotional material etc, but the cost of doing it should be weighed against the cost of not doing it – and the risk of losing dissatisfied Customers to a competitor. It will cost a lot more to find new Customers than to retain existing ones, so any money spent keeping existing Customers happy is going to be money well spent.

3.4.8   What are the potential benefits of Customer care?

Whatever the motivations behind the move towards a service culture the end result will be increased profitability:

- operating costs will decrease as less effort is wasted giving Customers products or services they don't want
- profits margins will improve as more repeat business is won – it is much cheaper to sell to an existing Customer than to court a new one
- efficiency will improve as staff will work more effectively as teams
- morale and staff turnover will improve as staff achieve job satisfaction and job security
- service quality will be constantly improving, resulting in an enhanced reputation for the IT department, which will tempt new Customers and encourage existing Customers to buy more
- the IT department will become more effective at supporting the needs of the business and will be more responsive to changes in business direction.

3.4.9   Service Management training

It is vitally important that the concepts of the IT Infrastructure Library are well known and understood in the Service Management function. ITIL foundation and management training is now widely available leading to an internationally recognised qualification developed by the EXIN and ISEB examination boards. At the turn of the Millennium, over 10,000 people now hold qualification in IT Service Management world wide, and many more have received training.

In addition it would be beneficial for the organisation to receive business-related training covering the broader aspects of infrastructure management. Far too often IT is accused of not knowing enough about the business and its needs; ITIL the business perspective series of books should be referred to for more information.

4 THE SERVICE DESK

This diverse chapter will concentrate on the IT Service Desk, and its function and position within the organisation. The advice, procedures, processes and guidelines described in this chapter are by no means definitive and may not apply to every type of organisational structure.

The chapter is broken down into the following sections:

- Overview
- Implementing your Service Desk infrastructure
- Service Desk technologies
- Service Desk responsibilities, functions, staffing levels etc
- Service Desk staffing skill set
- Setting up your Service Desk environment
- Service Desk education and training
- Service Desk processes and procedures
- Incident reporting and review
- Conclusion.

You will see that the structure of this chapter is different from that of the remainder of the book. Unlike the other disciplines, which are processes, the Service Desk is a function – a function that is crucial to the whole concept of Service Management. That is why the Service Desk is presented first in this book. The Service Desk is the point of contact between the customer and the service, and is responsible for the Incident Control provided by Incident Management. The chapter on Incident Management (Chapter 5) underpins the technical details mentioned in this chapter.

4.1   Overview

4.1.1   Why do we need a Service Desk?

With the ever-increasing demands of Customers and the globalisation of companies, the delivery of a world-class service is becoming the difference between success and failure and, without a doubt, a major competitive advantage, as illustrated in the 'Service-Profit Chain model' shown in Figure 4.1. By understanding its Customers and business needs clearly, an organisation can deliver that service.

Efficient, high-quality support of the computing infrastructure and Customers is critical for the achievement of corporate business goals. With disparate and distributed architectures put together, often in a piecemeal approach, the management and support of such an environment becomes very expensive, time-consuming and frequently an exercise in futility.

At ground level, the requirement is far simpler: what would we do *without* a Service Desk?

When a Customer or User has a problem, complaint or question, they want answers quickly. More importantly they want a result – their problem solved. There is nothing more frustrating than calling an organisation or department and getting passed around until you find the right person to speak to – provided, of course, that they are not out at lunch or on holiday or it's just after five o'clock.

The Service-Profit Chain

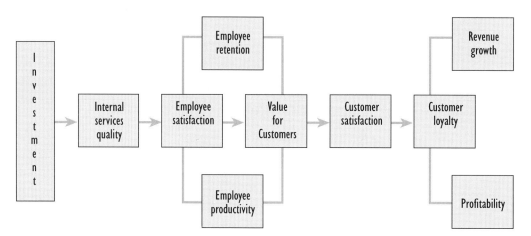

Figure 4.1 – The Service-Profit Chain model

4.1.2   The support problem

Many support departments are under pressure to improve service and reduce costs. They tend to work in reactive mode, as a loose collection of disparate groups, spending vast amounts of time fire-fighting and generally keeping their heads above water. The current situations in many companies include:

- no structured customer support mechanism in place
- low customer confidence/perception
- an outgrown customer support system
- support resource undermanaged
- continually fire-fighting
- the same problems being resolved repeatedly rather than eliminated
- continually interrupt-driven
- an overdependency on key staff
- a lack of focus
- uncoordinated and unrecorded change takes place
- an inability to cope with changes in the business
- staff resource/cost requirements being unclear
- an inconsistent quality of call response and response times
- no management information available – decisions being based on 'I think' rather than 'I know'.

To improve matters, a consolidated and team approach is required. More time is needed to plan, train, review, investigate, and work closer with Customers and Users – in short, to adopt proactive and structured working practices.

To meet both Customer and business objectives, many organisations have implemented a central point of contact for handling Customer, User and related issues. This function is known under several titles, including:

- Help Desk
- Call Centre
- Service Desk
- Customer Hot line.

There are many variants on these names, with the main generic descriptions being Call Centre, Help Desk and Service Desk.

4.1.3 Call Centre

The main emphasis on professionally handling large call volumes of telephone-based transactions for commodity telesales services (e.g. banking, insurance).

4.1.4 Help Desk

The primary purpose is to manage, coordinate and resolve Incidents as quickly as possible and to ensure that no request is lost, forgotten or ignored. Links to Configuration Management and knowledge tools are generally used as supporting technologies.

4.1.5 Service Desk

The Service Desk extends the range of services and offers a more global-focused approach, allowing business processes to be integrated into the Service Management infrastructure. It not only handles Incidents, Problems and questions, but also provides an interface for other activities such as customer Change requests, maintenance contracts, software licences, Service Level Management, Configuration Management, Availability Management, Financial Management for IT Services, and IT Service Continuity Management.

Many Call Centres and Help Desks naturally evolve into Service Desks to improve and extend overall service to the Customers and the business. All three functions share common characteristics:

- they represent the service provider to the Customer and to the User (internal or external)
- they operate on the principle that customer satisfaction and perception is critical
- they depend on blending people, processes and technology to deliver a business service.

In this chapter, the focus is on the Service Desk as the prime service function.

4.1.6 How can a Service Desk help my organisation?

The Service Desk provides a vital day-to-day contact point between Customers, Users, IT services and third-party support organisations. Service Level Management is a prime business enabler for this function. A Service Desk provides value to an organisation in that it:

- acts as a strategic function to identify and lower the cost of ownership for supporting the computing and support infrastructure
- supports the integration and management of Change across distributed business, technology and process boundaries
- reduces costs by the efficient use of resource and technology
- supports the optimisation of investments and the management of the businesses support services
- helps to ensure long term Customer retention and satisfaction
- assists in the identification of business opportunities.

Strategically, for Customers the Service Desk is probably the most important function in an organisation. For many, the Service Desk is their only window on the level of service and professionalism offered by the whole organisation or a department. This delivers the prime service component of '**Customer Perception and Satisfaction**'. Internal to the IT function, the Service Desk represents the interests of the Customer to the service team.

One key benefit of a Service Desk is the provision of management information, including information regarding:

- staff resource usage
- service deficiencies
- service performance and target achievement
- Customer training needs
- associated costs.

Are Service Desks only for larger organisations?

Providing a Service Desk for Customers will greatly benefit any size of organisation, whether the support staff is two or fifty, supporting ten or ten thousand Users. The basic premise of providing cost-effective Customer support is the same. For smaller organisations where staff resource and expertise is at a premium, issues such as resource management, staff dependency, documented solutions and procedures become significant.

4.1.7 Charging for support services

When designing your new Service Desk, it is important to consider the costs involved and, if 'charge-back' is required, how this is to be managed. Although charging methods are not covered in this book, the method adopted needs to be identified to ensure that the Service Desk system can both collect and pass on the required information and costings. From a practical perspective, it may be better simply to apportion the charges between all Customers on a fair and equitable basis, rather than using an explicit charging method.

Several methods are available, which may operate as individual items or be amalgamated to provide a single cost. These include:

- cost per call, which should vary depending on the type of Incident or service – some examples are:
  - desktop services (e.g. word processing)
  - application
  - installation/upgrade request
  - business service (e.g. payroll)
- cost of time and materials expended by support staff, for instance:
  - unit cost per time unit (e.g. per minute)
  - fixed charge
  - purchased number of support hours
- service entitlement based on a purchased maintenance contract:
  - gold, silver or bronze service levels
- cost apportioned as part of the overheads in providing IT services
- free service.

Rather than use actual cost values, it is common practice to use a 'charge unit', which has an associated value (e.g. 1 cost unit = 1 euro).

Caution

Charging per call can deter Customers from using the Service Desk, resulting in attempts to bypass the Service Desk or to resolve Incidents themselves before making a call. This could lead to increased diagnosis and resolution times at the Service Desk, because of the need to determine the action(s) that have been taken, which may have increased the complexity of the Incident.

4.1.8   Business and operational benefits

In overall terms, the introduction of a Service Desk can be expected to produce benefits both for the business and for the provision of the service, including:

- improved Customer service, perception and satisfaction
- increased accessibility through a single point of contact, communication, and information
- better-quality and speedier turnaround of customer requests
- improved teamwork and communication
- enhanced focus and a proactive approach to service provision
- a reduced negative business impact
- better managed infrastructure and control
- improved usage of IT support resources and increased productivity of business personnel
- more meaningful management information for decision support.

4.1.9   The role and direction of the Service Desk

The modern Service Desk is at once Customer-facing and focused on its main objectives, which are to drive and improve service to and on behalf of the business. At an operational level, its objective is to provide a single point of contact to provide advice, guidance and the rapid restoration of normal services to its Customers and Users.

Traditional IT departments who are technology driven, and often use the Service Desk function as a barrier rather than an enabler, are quickly becoming extinct. They are being replaced with a customer-focused 'Service Team' with technical expertise, business awareness and interpersonal skills, with support from a wide range of technological tools.

This new breed of service professional is well positioned to extended service provision to all aspects of the business, providing a consolidated and revenue-generating business activity, handling all aspects of service beyond the IT department. With good people, process and tools, the product or service being supported is, to a great extent, immaterial.

4.1.10   Customer interaction

Customer interaction is no longer restricted to the telephone and personal contact. Service can be greatly enhanced and extended to the Customer, Users and support staff by expanding the methods for registering, updating and querying requests (see Figure 4.2). This can be achieved primarily using email and the Internet/Intranet for remote offices, although fax can also be a valuable tool. These methods are best exploited for activities that are not business-critical, which include registering non-urgent Incidents or requests, such as:

- incident product purchases
- application queries
- requests for equipment moves, installations, upgrades and enhancements
- requests for consumables.

For the support team, a number of benefits are derived, including:-

- support personnel are freed from unnecessary telephone interruptions
- workloads are better managed.

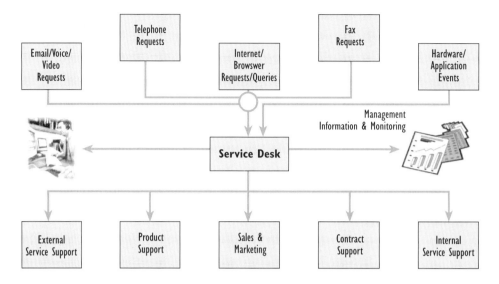

Figure 4.2 – Incident registration inputs

The usage of form-based inputs increases the integrity of the data supplied and assists in allocation to the best-suited support specialist, team or department. The Service Desk tool should automatically provide the Customer or User with a receipted unique reference number, which also allows for online querying of the request's progress.

4.1.11 Keeping the Customer and User informed

Providing Customers and Users with confirmation that their request has been accepted (see Figure 4.3), and its progress, is one of the most important roles of the Service Desk. Yet very few organisations have the staff resources to focus on and maintain this activity. As stated earlier, the use of technologies, such as email, will assist in this. However the real challenge is to create a personalised bond with customers, even through electronic communication.

Incident Confirmation Receipt

Dear Mr. Smith,

We are pleased to inform you that your reported Incident has been added into the ACME Service Desk. Your assigned Reference Number is **INC-22323**. This number should be retained for reference purposes. A support analyst will contact you before **Monday 12-Jan at 12:00 hrs**.

Reference No.	**INC-22323**
Description	Laser Printer not working
User Name	Mr. William Smith
Location	Library Rm. 34B
Telephone	0207 32324 ext. 2322
Mail address	Smith_W@EVE21
To be completed by	**Monday 12-Jan at 17:00 hrs**

Should there be any further questions or queries, please do not hesitate to contact the ACME Service Desk on 0207 333444, quoting your assigned Reference Number.

Yours sincerely,

John Jiles

(Service Support Specialist)

Figure 4.3 – Customer Incident Confirmation

 32

This same approach can be made for all correspondence with the Customer, such as:

- when an engineer has to be called out
- when a software enhancement request has been accepted
- when a request is completed
- when an installation is scheduled
- when further information is requested.

Such an approach is shown in Figure 4.4.

Installation Confirmation

Dear Mr. Smith,

We are pleased to inform you that your installation has now been scheduled. Your assigned Reference number is **CHG-22325**. This number should be retained for reference purposes

Description	Installation of New PC
Location	Library Rm. 34B
Telephone	0207 32324 ext. 2322
Mail address	jansen_w@eve21
Start Date	Tuesday 14-Jan 2000 at 09:00
To be completed by	**Wednesday 15-Jan 2000 at 12:00**

Should there be any further questions or queries, please do not hesitate to contact the ACME Service Desk on 0207 333444, quoting your assigned Reference Number.

Yours sincerely,

Jill Adams

(Service Support Installation manager)

Figure 4.4 – Scheduling confirmation

4.1.12 Physical attendance

When visiting a Customer location, the same personalised service can be provided to confirm that you have attended, especially if the Customer was not around at the time. Use a small form or business card, like the one shown in Figure 4.5.

> **Service Support Confirmation Receipt**
>
> Dear Mr. Jansen,
>
> A support specialist has been in attendance to your Incident.
>
> | | |
> |---|---|
> | **Reference Number:** | INC-23323 |
> | **Incident corrected:** | Yes [ ] No [ ] |
> | **Date/Time:** | Monday 12-Jan 2000 at 09:20 |
> | **Reported Symptom:** | unable to print |
> | **Solution:** | replaced faulty printer cable |
>
> Should there be any further questions or queries, please do not hesitate to contact the ACME Service Desk on 0207 333444, quoting your assigned Reference Number.

Figure 4.5 – Action confirmation

4.1.13 Monitored infrastructure events

Traditionally, the support function works in a reactive mode, responding to events, alarms and Incidents as they arise. In many cases, however, Incidents encountered with the infrastructure can be detected before they directly affect the Customer, or at least the support operation can be alerted immediately an Incident occurs.

Network and automated operations tools perform this function. In their simplest form they regularly monitor aspects of the infrastructure and upon detecting a non-standard condition automatically generate an Incident (also referred to as an Event). It is this Incident that can be automatically passed via the Service Desk to the required support team for action.

4.1.14 Actioned infrastructure Incidents

In addition to monitored Incidents, Incidents can be actioned from within scripts, applications and batch jobs. For example, when a backup fails, the Incident can be automatically registered in the support system, classified, prioritised and automatically forwarded via the Service Desk to the required support person or group.

4.1.15 Infrastructure Incident model

The 'Infrastructure Service Desk Incidents' diagram at Figure 4.6 demonstrates this overall strategy. When an Incident is registered from the infrastructure, it is automatically routed to the appropriate person or group. If however, the request has not been acknowledged, the escalation management process will take over alerting the Service Desk that an action is required.

Often, scripting can not only log the event but also recover the situation, by, for instance, restarting a back-up to alternative media or devices. These events need to be recorded because they are Key Performance Indicators (KPIs) on the success of an automated IT operation.

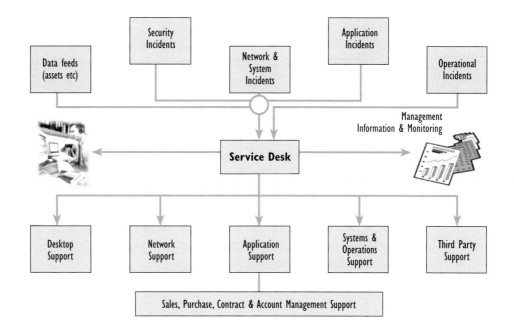

Figure 4.6 – Infrastructure Service Desk Incidents

4.1.16   Benefits

The following benefits can be expected from infrastructure monitoring and action:

- Customer impact and downtime are minimised
- repetitive manual tasks are performed automatically
- management information is automatically collected for analysis
- Incidents, once registered, will be under the control of escalation management
- the Service Desk attains a proactive position
- service availability and utilisation is extended
- operational and resource costs are reduced.

Advanced event management systems will attempt to correct failures and keep progress updated in the support system until the action is complete or requires manual intervention.

4.1.17   Use of Internet technology

Internet technology provides a number of useful facilities for supporting Service Management in global, local and distributed environments. These include:

- general marketing
- interact via email for less urgent requests
- provision of supplier program fixes and upgrades
- publishing of Known Errors
- 'instant' notification via Customer noticeboards
- a capability to perform knowledge searches
- management reporting
- importantly, a common cross platform User interface.

Allowing Internet access needs to be carefully considered and policed to ensure only **authorised** access is permitted and that, where applicable, only licensed and virus free software and other materials (e.g. pictures) are accessed. Care should be taken, when publishing or receiving any materials, that the content is both legal and accurate. Remember that legal consideration and copyright law differs from country to country.

The business benefits, costs and accessibility requirements of using Internet technology need to be fully understood, and an organisational policy defined to support Web usage.

4.2 Implementing a Service Desk infrastructure

Designing your Service Desk support infrastructure correctly is critical to success and should be done as a formal business improvement project with clear ownership, defined business goals, responsibilities, deliverables and management commitment.

However, before even starting to identify your needs, consider the basic premise of what you want to achieve. This is an opportunity to re-evaluate the whole way you have, to date, delivered service. Don't just think of automating current manual processes, using staff in the same way. Consider a rethink and redesign of the processes and activities in order to increase productivity, add value, reduce cost and improve the Customer's perception. Consider the question 'If this was your business, would you organise it, resource it, and run it, this way?'

4.2.1 Staff resourcing

An operational service needs to be maintained on a daily basis. It is not therefore always practical to expect 'business as usual' and still implement a successful service-improvement project. Additional resource is generally required to assist during the project set-up phase.

A major consideration is the skill sets available within your organisation to deliver this project successfully. It is essential that the project team involved has proven Service Management and implementation skills.

Where 'business as usual' cannot be maintained due to implementation of a service-improvement project, it is important, as well as acquiring additional resource, to communicate this fact to the Customer.

In situations where skilled resource is a problem, the usage of contract and outsourced services should be considered. Utilising and training by internal resources should also be investigated, for example by transferring staff from other teams in the department or releasing staff from non-critical projects.

4.2.2 Target effectiveness metrics

Decide and set targets for a manageable number of objective metrics for the effectiveness of the Service Desk. This task requires careful consideration, because the post-implementation and subsequent ongoing reviews will compare these targets with reality. Take the metrics into account during the technology-tool selection and design stages.

Guidelines for setting metrics include the following:

- do not set targets that cannot be measured
- maintain the metrics in the light of detailed design activities, ensuring their necessity and viability

- establish a baseline *before* discussing formal Service-Level Agreements (SLAs) with Customers
- general SLAs may be offered to provide a framework to start collecting metrics and using them to measure performance against the SLA criteria
- ensure that Customers are aware of what you are doing, and why.

In relation to SLA criteria, and subject to request volumes, baseline data should be collected for a period of approximately two months to ensure a viable sample is available for analysis. It is critical to understand the levels of service you are currently providing with the current resources available before making changes.

4.2.3 Key considerations

Here are some key points for consideration when setting up a Service Desk:

- first establish that the business need is clearly identified and understood
- make sure management commitment, budget and resource is made available before commencement
- ensure the proposed solution aligns with your Service Support strategy and vision
- identify, achieve and communicate **quick wins** (e.g. keeping customers informed, improved installation times)
- define clear objectives and deliverables
- start simple; don't try to do everything at once; **adopt a phased approach**
- involve/consult your Customers, especially critically important ones; don't use jargon
- involve/consult end Users
- sell the benefits to support staff
- train IT staff to be service staff
- educate/train Customers and Users in the use of the new service and its benefits
- advertise and 'sell' your service.

4.2.4 Selecting the right Service Desk structure

The type of Service Desk, skill level and organisational structure you choose is dependent on a number of important factors. There is no 'universal' configuration to suit all. As your business changes, so will your support operation; therefore flexibility is crucial to support future growth.

4.2.5 Types of Service Desk structure

Three types of structures should be considered for optimum usage:

1. local Service Desk
2. central Service Desk
3. virtual Service Desk.

These are each described in more detail below.

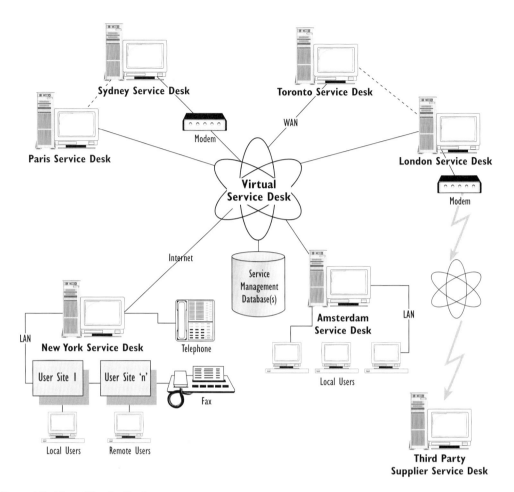

Figure 4.9 – Virtual Service Desk

Considerations when setting up a Virtual Service Desk include the following:

■ All persons accessing the Virtual Service Desk should use common processes, procedures and terminology.

■ A common, agreed-on language should be used for data entry.

■ Customers and Users still need to interact with a single point of contact. Consider global telephone numbers, local numbers that route to the Virtual Desk and Automatic Call Distribution (ACD) technology.

■ There will be the need for a physical presence on site by a specialist or maintenance engineer from time to time.

■ Network performance should be 'fit for purpose'. This should be reviewed in terms of forecast workloads. For example, if the local Service Desk in Holland is only handling ten requests a day, then network volume may not be a major consideration. However, a narrow bandwidth is not practical if several hundred requests are processed.

■ For the Virtual Desk, the support tools in place should allow for 'workload partitioning' and authorised views. (For example, if I am the person looking after local support in, say, Amsterdam, I only want to see requests for that location.) This should include other associated processes and related data, such as planned Changes, asset and configuration data.

■ Consistent ownership and management processes for Incidents should be used throughout the Virtual Service Desk, with automated transfers of Incidents and Incident views between local desks.

4.2.9   Service Desk Configuration considerations

The criteria to decide on the best configuration for your organisation are varied, but should include:

- business objectives and deliverables
- maturity and skill levels of the existing support organisation
- budget, costing and charge-back mechanisms
- levels and quality of the management information required
- size of organisation and nature of business
- political considerations
- organisational structure:
  - whether single location, multiple locations or a global location
  - number of Customers to be supported
  - working hours to be covered
  - language(s) spoken by both support staff and Customers
- range, number and type of applications to be supported:
  - standard
  - specialised
  - bespoke
- general business requirements (e.g. office tools)
- network infrastructure (local, wide-area)
- range, number and types of hardware/technology to be supported
- technology replacement cycle
- skill levels of Customers
- skill level of User base
- skill levels of support staff
- number of support staff (first and second-line)
- reliance on third-party organisations
- current call volumes.

4.2.10   Global 'follow the sun' support

When an organisation is providing 24-hour support, or extended cover, around the globe, the following points should be considered:

- the ability of telecommunications systems/switches to interact
- is time-zone support included in Service Level Agreements?
- is management reporting available in local and remote time zones?
- is local language support available?
- the need for multilingual support staff
- local considerations and cultural needs (e.g. in Spain, working days are often split between morning and early evening)
- localised SLAs and Operational-Level Agreements (OLAs) may need to be defined
- clear escalation channels and management-reporting chain
- all local desks should use consistent ownership and management processes for Incidents, with automated transfer of Incidents and Incident views between local desks.

Design Consideration

Furthermore, if you wish to pass requests between Service Desks or merge them in the future, consider agreeing unique identification, prefixing and number ranges for your global network, so as to avoid the problems that might arise if you have requests with the same number.

4.2.11   Incident classification

Classification is one of the most important attributes of an Incident to get right. Classification is used to:

- specify the service or equipment to which the Incident relates
- associate any Service Level Agreement or Operational Level Agreement in place
- select/define the best specialist or group to handle the Incident
- define the priority and business impact
- define a workload estimate
- define what questions should be asked or information checked
- act as a matching criterion for selecting solutions, Known Errors or Work-arounds
- summarise and define the final action taken (e.g. training required, no fault found)
- define a primary reporting matrix for management information.

The final classification(s) may vary from that initially reported. The Customer may have reported a 'symptom' of an Incident and not necessarily the root Problem. The levels of classification will vary depending on the detail required. For example, a top-level classification of 'Word Processing', or 'Payroll Service' is adequate for an overview; however, greater detail may then need to be obtained in areas such as:

- version number
- supplier
- software module (e.g. printing, bought ledger)
- grouping (e.g. business application).

When an Incident is completed, it is beneficial, for certain types of request, to enter a 'closure classification' or 'closure code'. This should state the actual cause, a summary conclusion, or a specific course of action. Examples include:

- Incident completed successfully
- Customer training required
- documentation needs reviewed
- no fault found
- monitoring required
- advice given
- Change request needs to be raised.

Detailed classification will ensure more effective management information.

4.2.12   Classification Process Review

The management information provided by reporting against classification should be reviewed regularly to ensure that meaningful, up-to-date, data is returned. However, one should not overcomplicate this process by adding too many classifications initially, because this may cause confusion when support staff are registering Incidents. It is also recommended that standard classifications such as 'Unknown' or 'Unable to classify' be included, as this will prevent support staff from making a 'best guess'. These Incidents can later be reviewed and classifications generated/amended, if required. In general, it is best to start simple and expand as business needs demand it.

Start simple and expand as the business needs demand it.

4.3 Service Desk technologies

A number of technologies are available to assist the Service Desk, each with its advantages and drawbacks. It is important to ensure that the blend of technology, process and Service Desk staff will meet the needs of both the business and the User. Selecting the latest – and often unproven – technology based on interesting, but less valuable, 'wow' features is to be avoided.

Technology investment is a long-term decision and your understanding of what is really important will increase your success in selection and implementation. Technology should be used to complement and enhance service, not replace it. The technology needs to support business processes, adapting to both current and future demands. It is also important to understand that with automation comes an increased need for discipline and accountability.

Service Desk technologies include:

- integrated Service Management and Operations Management systems
- advanced telephone systems (e.g. auto-routing, hunt groups, Computer Telephony Integration (CTI), Voice Over Internet Protocol (VOIP))
- Interactive Voice Response (IVR) systems
- electronic mail (e.g. voice, video, mobile comms, Internet, email systems)
- fax servers (supporting routing to email accounts)
- pager systems
- knowledge, search and diagnostic tools
- automated operations and Network Management tools.

It is important to appreciate that some Customer requests do not need 'live' Service Desk staff, while others need the personal touch.

4.3.1 The computerised Service Desk

Many support functions start as paper-based systems, with individuals recording and updating details and solutions. However well defined the processes, procedures and documentation are, though, it is not possible to do more than log Incidents and track them until they are completed. The use of a computerised Service Desk tool is essential for the modern support operation. Electronic management allows for improved efficiency, accuracy, and fast access to past solutions, Known Errors, call histories and management information. However, a great deal of effort is required in order to be able to access information that was not previously available.

Today's advanced Service Management systems will manage, track and monitor service requests, contractual obligations, staff resources and workflows. These systems will also integrate with the other essential service components (e.g. the management of Change control, Assets and Configuration, Cost, Business Continuity, Capacity Planning and a variety of automation and Network Management tools).

4.3.2 Computerised Service Desk benefits

Computerising the Service Desk will provide additional benefits, namely:

- everyone knows what's happening, because requests are accessible by all support staff
- the turnaround of Customer requests is faster, yielding improved efficiency
- request tracking, escalation and workflow is improved
- better information is available in the form of online access to:
    - Known Errors, solutions and request histories
    - external knowledge sources
- management information is more accessible and accurate
- duplicate, lost or forgotten requests are eliminated
- skilled staff and resources are better used
- complex support tasks and calculations are made easier.

4.3.3 Build or buy?

When deciding whether to build your own support tool or buy a commercial package, the most important thing to identify is who and what the tool is to be used by and for. While it is fairly straightforward to build a call-logging tool, capturing and updating the solutions may not be as straightforward. Some of the issues that will help you decide on build versus buy include the following.

- Do you have the Service Management and business expertise to design:
    - integration with email and other communication systems?
    - automated operations?
    - cross-platform and multilingual support?
    - integration with other support tools such as Asset Management and Configuration Management, Change control and automated operations?
- Do you have the resource, both now and in the future, to plan, implement, upgrade and maintain the system?
- Who will support it, how long will it take to develop, who is going to pay for it, when will it be ready?
- What if your 'experts' leave?

Unless your business requirement is very specific and unique, then the 'build your own' option is very expensive and will not deliver benefit in the short and medium term.

4.3.4 Running in a multiplatform environment

When selecting a software tool for use within a multiplatform environment, a number of key points require careful consideration:

- Does the tool provide the required functionality over all my hardware, network protocols and technology?
- Does the tool provide full functionality in all environments?
- Can I utilise my existing equipment (e.g. PCs and workstations)?
- Are the features available across my required platforms (e.g. if the tool is primarily PC based, will the features work on my UNIX workstations as well)?
- Can requests be passed between Service Desks running on different platforms?
- Does the tool provide full functionality over all network protocols and technology?

4.3.5   Running in a Wide-Area Network (WAN) infrastructure

Many of the tools available will operate effectively over a Local Area Network (LAN). However, when the tool is required to operate over a WAN, several key points should be considered:

- Has the tool been designed to operate over slower bandwidths?
- Does it support data transfer optimisation?
- Is its performance 'fit for purpose'?
- Does it provide full functionality over all network protocols and technology?

Ensure that part of your system acceptance criteria includes proven operation over your own network.

4.3.6   Intelligent phone systems, voicemail and email usage

The use of intelligent phone systems, voicemail and email can greatly benefit your Service Desk. It should however, not be used as an electronic barrier. The careful set-up of Interactive Voice Response systems is required so as to prevent the Customer being passed around. If voicemail and email *are* used, it is imperative that they are reviewed regularly and responses sent promptly to those leaving messages.

Put Service Level Agreements in place to maximise these technologies and ensure a consistent and high-quality service is maintained.

4.3.7   Deploying a self-service strategy

Self-service offers Customers a strategy that deploys tools to obtain support services without direct intervention from a support professional. It can be used as a method of reducing operating costs and improving Customer satisfaction by allowing them greater control over the transaction, especially out of normal support hours and for non-critical activities. Technologies such as the Internet, Interactive Voice Response systems, and mobile and wireless communications make self-service operations possible.

The primary characteristics of this model are:

- Customers determine the point of entry
- Customers have direct access to support information and knowledge
- Customers are able to manage support transactions themselves
- ease of access and speed of resolution is increased
- demand on support resources is reduced.

How self-service is implemented can vary significantly, depending upon what the organisation wants to achieve and the range of services it plans to offer. Examples of self-service include:

- Customers register their own requests and check on their progress
- Customers can search knowledge bases for solutions
- Customers can download program updates or bug fixes
- Customers can order goods or services.

4.3.8   Critical success factors

A successful self-service strategy depends on several important factors:

- **management commitment** – any initiative that entails change within an organisation requires management support and commitment to execute the initiative

- **a willingness to relinquish control** – it is essential to put the right processes and tools in place to ensure that while the Customer is in control, they are following a path that is carefully designed by the company

- **business metrics are collected and *used*** – to monitor the effectiveness of the service as provided, it is critical to know what self-help services are being requested, how often and what for

- **support processes are maintained** – it is important that none of the existing Change and Release processes is bypassed or invalidated

- **ease of use and quality content** – any system that is not easy to use or that does not contain high-quality content will fail, because if Customers are unable to get the information they need when they need it, they will immediately pick up the telephone next time they encounter a problem; indeed, in a worst-case scenario, the support team will find itself supporting yet another application – the self-service system itself

- **communication** – Customers need to know what self-service channels are in place, along with the value and responsibilities of using them.

There will always be Customers and Users who either need to, or prefer to, talk directly to a support specialist. The key is to provide choices in how to communicate with the support group. By incorporating self-service techniques into the traditional service model, companies add value in being more efficient and cost-effective, along with improved levels of Customer service.

4.3.9   Implementation considerations

Implementing new technologies and the supporting processes can represent major Change, and it is all too easy to underestimate the scale of work required. Support staff, Users and Customers will have to adopt new working practices. An important consideration is the key role that management has in avoiding the 'silver bullet' lifecycle, where new tools, processes and increased accountability are introduced and then abandoned at the first sign of difficulty.

When any new technology or process is introduced, if the introduction and awareness of the Change has been successful, then there is an initial enthusiasm for the new approach. However, once installed, there is a learning curve, unfamiliar working practices, potentially parallel running and teething troubles. The initial result of this is that, far from providing an immediately deliverable benefit, there is often a negative effect where the costs and additional workload appear to outweigh the benefits. This drop in benefit is soon matched by a fall in enthusiasm.

As familiarity with the technology or process begins to deliver visible benefits, enthusiasm for the Change rises too. It is essential for the management team to 'stick with it', and to encourage their staff to persevere and to work through any drop in enthusiasm. This progression is depicted in Figure 4.10.

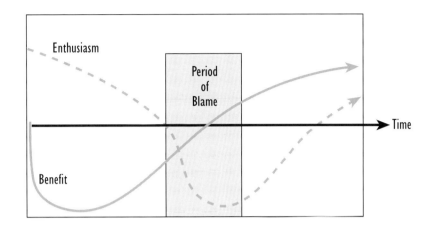

Figure 4.10 – The 'silver bullet' lifecycle
Source: BSI Code of Practice

4.3.10 Outsourcing a Service Desk

Careful consideration should be given to outsourcing your Service Desk, for viewing the Service Desk function purely as an overhead to the organisation is damaging. The Service Desk should be the 'window of service and professionalism offered by your organisation'. The intellectual capital in supporting your Customers is a valuable business asset and should not be discarded without a clear understanding of the business requirement.

Service Desk outsourcing considerations are as follows:

- have the outsourcer use *your* Service Desk tool, not the other way round – often internal support staff are involved in the support process and you do not want to retrain them each time you change supplier

- insist that you have complete access/ownership to management information at its source

- make sure the supplier is capable of supplying suitably skilled and qualified Service Management staff for holiday and sickness cover

- be sure to request details and previous experience of all supplied staff

- continually monitor 'value for money', deliverables and the business benefits derived

- regularly check for supplier dependencies – ensure all procedures, functions and processes are clearly documented, up-to-date and available

- make certain that the contractual terms, deliverables and chargeable activities are clearly understood and agreed by both parties

- seek professional and specialist assistance when negotiating contractual terms with a supplier.

Vendor partnership

You are buying a total solution and you should want your vendor to be a business partner. Utilise the vendor's expertise to help you implement any service-improvement project. A sign of a good working relationship between yourselves and a supplying organisation is that it is hard to tell the contracted staff from the full-time employees, in terms of their commitment and understanding of the Customers needs.

A professional vendor will seek a long-term relationship and repeat businesses in the form of additional product's upgrades, training and consultancy. Often buying the tool is the easy part; the costs of the software or other tools are generally the minority of the costs associated with an implementation project. Do not underestimate the cost of retraining your staff, the costs of changing procedures to maximise the benefits of the new tool, and the impact on Customers or secondary support organisations of the cost of expansion and additional software licenses.

4.4 Service Desk responsibilities, functions, staffing levels etc

Objective of the Service Desk:

- To provide a single point of contact for Customers

- To facilitate the restoration of normal operational service with minimal business impact on the Customer within agreed service levels and business priorities

The role and responsibilities of the Service Desk are dependent on the nature of the organisation's business and of the support infrastructure in place. For most organisations, a primary role is the recording and life-cycle management of all Incidents that affect the operational service delivered to the business and its Customers.

Incidents that cannot be solved quickly by the Service Desk should be passed to second-line or third-party support teams for diagnosis and resolution. If they remain unresolved beyond their SLA target, they may get referred to Problem Management. During this process, the Service Desk's role is to keep the Customer informed of progress or advise them of any Work-around that may allow them to continue working.

As a single point of contact, it is important that the Service Desk provides the Customer with, at a minimum, a status update on service availability and any request being managed by the service team, including the Incident number for use in future communication. Status update information might include:

- when their request is likely to be completed by

- when their equipment move or installation is scheduled for

- when a new Release is planned

- if their service enhancement request been accepted

- where to get further information on a subject

- if the computer systems are available at the weekend.

4.4.1 Service Desk functions

The common Service Desk functions include:

- receiving calls, first-line Customer liaison

- recording and tracking Incidents and complaints

- keeping Customers informed on request status and progress

- making an initial assessment of requests, attempting to resolve them or refer them to someone who can, based on agreed service levels

- monitoring and escalation procedures relative to the appropriate SLA

- managing the request life-cycle, including closure and verification
- communicating planned and short-term changes of service levels to Customers
- coordinating second-line and third-party support groups
- providing management information and recommendations for service improvement
- identifying Problems
- highlighting Customer training and education needs
- closing Incidents and confirmation with the Customer
- contributing to Problem identification.

4.4.2 Which Requests should be registered

Every Incident and question (Change requests should also be considered) reported by the Customer, its history and the solution given should be registered, whether it took one minute or one month to fix. The actual elapsed time is not a measure of its importance or business impact. For example:

- A colleague with years of experience in the relevant area may have made a 'one-minute-fix.' Without the information of what steps were performed to analyse the Problem and its solution, another colleague may spend days re-solving the same issue.

- If a Customer is not satisfied with the service provided and complains of having 'lots of problems this week', then it is important such a statement can be verified with the Service Desk records. If not, then the credibility of the Service Desk function can be greatly undermined.

- Other colleagues will be embarrassed if the Customer calls to ask for an update on a request and it has not been recorded, again undermining the Service Desk function and credibility of the department.

Every contact with the Customer provides an invaluable metric to assist in the understanding of Customer requirements.

4.4.3 Service Desk empowerment

It is important that the Service Desk is empowered to enforce agreed Customer service levels with second-line support and third-party suppliers. It is essential also that second-line support operations are clear on any agreed service levels (SLA/OLA) that they are required to support.

For the second-line support managers, it is not always practical for staff to 'drop' other work to support the Service Desk because they themselves may be on project deadlines. In these situations it is recommended that the second-line support team members, for whichever service is required, rotate support to the Service Desk. Even if the team consists of two members, it means that while one is supporting the Service Desk, the other can focus, uninterrupted, on project-based work.

With this method in place the Service Desk can provide second-line support managers with staff resource use figures to assist in overall staffing requirements, and clearly identify what is being done.

4.4.4 Escalation management

Telephone pick-up times

In many cases, organisations attempt to have Customers' telephone calls picked up within a specific number of rings (e.g. 3–10). The decision you make on the value set is dependent on the resources that you have available. However, the expected pick-up time should be clearly communicated to Customers and Users. The provision of self-help technologies and electronic Customer registration will greatly assist in freeing up telephone lines and resources to handle critical Incidents.

However, this contact point is a key influence on the Customer's perception of your service. Therefore getting the correct balance is critical to managing Customer satisfaction.

Telephone talk times

The time spent handling a Customer Incident on the telephone is dependent on available resources and their skill levels. Careful judgement is required to determine when to pass the Incident to second-line support or transfer it to another area in the support department. It is essential that the main support number(s) are kept available as much as possible, especially in the case of a major service failure when other Customers will be calling in.

Unless you have an advanced telephone system that informs you of queued calls, setting a staff 'talk time' maximum is advisable (e.g., 1–2 minutes) to ensure that all Customer Incidents are handled promptly and confidence is not lost.

Managing urgent Customer requests

In an ideal world, SLAs define the business need. However, when a Customer calls with a serious problem, they are only concerned with resolving the issue as quickly as possible. The Customer may be under pressure to get an important quotation out or may themselves have a Customer waiting. At this point, discretion and understanding is required. It is important that each Customer's individual situation is assessed and addressed, as this will ultimately define the Customer perception of your service.

If a Customer demands an action beyond the control of the Service Desk, the Service Desk staff should politely refer them to the duty Service Manager.

Managing service breaches

Even in the best-supported operations, services breaches will occur: another Incident requires urgent attention, staff are off sick, spare parts are not available, you are unable to diagnose the problem. What is then important is to successfully manage the service breach, by escalation to the Problem Management team, where appropriate.

It is also acceptable to have an 'agreed service breach' where the Customer has been informed of the probability of the breach and has agreed that this situation is acceptable. Key points to managing an agreed service breach are:

- informing the Customer in advance and explaining the reason for the likely breach
- informing the Service Manager (he/she doesn't want any surprises)
- agreeing on a course of action and follow through on it
- if/when the Incident has breached the agreed service level, documenting the event and stating the reason for it.

Managing Customer-initiated service breaches

It is often the case that a service breach occurs because the Customer is unavailable to get further information about a known Incident, or because the Customer's location is not accessible.

In this case it is necessary to document clearly that work could not progress because of this situation and how much SLA elapsed time was lost.

Recording service breach details

Recording service breach details is critical to understanding whether or not existing SLAs are practical. If an IT operation keeps breaching them or equally, consistently over achieves its targets, clearly the SLAs need to be reviewed and the area(s) causing the variation need to be identified.

It is equally essential to report on agreed and Customer-initiated service breaches. From a business perspective, the SLA has either been achieved or it has not.

4.4.5   Service Desk staffing levels

Defining full-time staffing levels is very difficult without a definitive way to predict the demand for service. The number of staff employed on the Service Desk is dependent on the needs of the business and is based on a range of important criteria, including:

- the business budget available/required
- Customer service expectations
- size, relative age, design, and complexity of the IT infrastructure and service catalogue – for example, the number of distinct hardware and software Incidents, the extent of customised versus standard off-the-shelf software deployed, etc.
- the number of customers to support, and associated factors such as
  - number of foreign-language Customers
  - skill level
  - Incident types
  - duration of time required for call types (e.g. simple queries, specialist application queries, hardware, etc.)
  - local or external expertise required
- the volume of Incidents
- the period of support cover required, based on
  - hours covered
  - out-of-hours support
  - time zone
  - location
  - travel time between locations
  - staff availability
- workload pattern of requests (e.g. daily, month end, etc.)
- the Service Level Agreement definitions in place (response levels etc.)
- the type of response required:
  - telephone
  - email/fax/voice mail/video
  - physical attendance
  - online access/control

- the level of training required
- the support technologies available (e.g. phone systems, Service Desk tools)
- the existing skill levels of staff
- the processes and procedures in use.

All these items should be carefully considered before making any decision on staffing levels. This should also be reflected in the levels of documentation required. Remember that the better the service, the more the business will use it.

4.4.6 Staff turnover considerations

Traditionally, first-line Customer interaction functions have a high staff turnover. This should be taken into account when reviewing the required resources and the training requirement to get staff up to speed and productive.

The 'Super User'

To keep deal with some of these staffing constraints, in some organisations it is common to use 'expert' Customers to deal with first-line support Problems and queries (commonly known as Super or Expert Users). This is typically in specific application areas, or geographical locations, where there is insufficient justification for full-time support staff. In this case, the User can be a valuable resource if use is properly coordinated, with:

- their roles and responsibilities clearly defined
- escalation channels clearly defined
- standard support processes defined and used
- all requests recorded and maintained, ideally in the main support system.

With all requests entered into the main Service Desk tool, valuable usage details can be provided to the local management to ensure that resource is focused in the correct areas and not misused.

4.4.7 Workload monitoring

From the above considerations, it is clear that a careful study of the workload mix is necessary to define the required staff levels, skill types and the associated costs. Such an analysis should include:

- the number of requests being handled by the Service Desk, with this initially needing to take into account requests passed directly to second-line support groups
- the types of request that staff are spending the most time on, such as
  - equipment failures
  - business application problems
  - telecommunications
  - Customer queries
  - installations/upgrades
- the types of request that are taking the longest time to turnaround to the Customer by:
  - first-line support
  - second-line internal support groups
  - third-party support groups
  - suppliers
- which Customers require the most support, and in which areas – this information can be used to develop training programmes for both Customer staff and Service Desk and support staff.

4.4.8   Customer satisfaction analysis and surveys

Aligning Customer perception and satisfaction is paramount to the success of any support operation. It is the Customers' perception that, in the end, defines whether the Service Desk is meeting their needs, rather than availability statistics or transaction rates. Satisfaction surveys are an excellent method of monitoring Customer perception and expectation and can be used a powerful marketing tool. However several key points should be addressed to ensure success:

- decide on the scope of the survey
- decide on the target audience
- clearly define the questions
- make the survey easy to complete
- conduct the survey regularly
- make sure the Customer understand the benefits
- publish the results
- follow through on survey results
- translate survey results into actions.

How often surveys are taken is a business decision, based on the rate of change within your organisation and other business drivers. To monitor satisfaction on a daily basis at source, your request closure process should be used for a detailed Customer satisfaction response on specific applications, Customers or services. To improve the speed of data capture and reduce the resource needed to analyse survey data, the usage of electronic based surveys should be considered.

Target Audience

It is important to define clearly the target audience for any surveys and the scope of the questions. For example, the questions you would ask of an accounts clerk in relation to the stability of the service provided would be different from those you would ask of an accounts director. From the clerk's perspective, their printer was unavailable 'several' times during the month, whereas the accounts director was only concerned that, at month end, he or she was unable to produce customer bills on time, which resulted in a financial loss.

4.4.9   Service Desk resourcing for smaller support units

For smaller support operations, the need for full-time support is often unclear. However, the need for a central point of contact for Customers is still essential. Methods for providing this central focus include:

- a single phone number with all staff being able to pick up - e.g. an ACD system
- staff rotating the job function on a daily/weekly basis
- investment in self-help technologies
- online bulletin/information boards.

4.4.10   Second-line staff awareness

It is often left up to the front-line, operational support staff to provide the Service Desk resource, with development and other such groups not being involved.

The involvement of second-line staff in the Service Desk is recommended, either on a full time or a rotational basis. These are generally the groups who provide operational documentation, introduce change, and provide training on new systems. Participating in the Service Desk is an excellent way for second-line staff to:

- better appreciate the Customers business needs and demands, first hand
- better empathise with first-line staff, minimising 'us and them' attitudes
- transfer knowledge about their speciality to other Service Desk personnel
- identify technical or procedural issues related to their speciality that would otherwise go unseen, and effect their remedy.

Second-line staff participation in the Service Desk is the first step to providing a truly business-focused service team. In particular, this approach is strongly recommended when a new service is going live, as the first weeks of implementation can be the most traumatic.

It is also recommended that Service Desk staff be given the opportunity to spend time working directly with Customers. The end in mind here is to ensure a better understanding of Customer requirements. Further, reciprocal arrangements where Service Desk staff work, on a seconded basis, with developers, support teams and project teams can also yield significant benefits.

4.4.11   Identifying training needs

From careful monitoring of the workload (as described in paragraph 4.4.7), Customer, User and support-staff training needs can be identified. By addressing Customer and User training needs effectively, call volumes and requests for assistance will be reduced, and both Users and support staff will be more productive.

4.4.12   Call rate reduction

Organisations may use 'call rate reduction' as a direct business benefit of introducing a Service Desk. However although call rates may drop initially upon the introduction of a Service Desk because of the improved service, they will typically start to rise again thereafter. This effect is due to improved Customer confidence, and will result in Customers using the Service Desk, not only for reporting Incidents, but also for advice and guidance and other support activities. This cycle should be carefully and continually monitored.

4.4.13   Workload definitions request types

When referring to Customer support workloads, many support departments define their performance based on very objective and simple statistics, such as:

- number of Incidents logged
- number of Incidents closed
- number of Incidents open at the end of a period
- number of Incidents resolved within a defined period.

However, best practice qualitative measures for a Service Desk in any given period include:

- number and type of Customer-reported Incidents
- number of business Problems identified for resolution, based on the Incident/request rate
- number of requested, planned and scheduled Changes.

In a Service Management framework these request types are specifically defined and managed as individual processes.

4.5   Service Desk staffing skill set

Objective:

■   To establish the profile of staff to work in the Service Desk

Because there are different types of Service Desk, each having its own requirements, particular attention should be paid to selecting the right type and calibre of staff.

Front-line Service Desk staff are generally the ones who are under the most Customer pressure and often take the brunt of Customer's sometimes unreasonable demands. It can be a seemingly thankless role, but it is also perhaps the most important and challenging role in IT. For many Customers, it is the relationship forged with the Service Desk that defines the perceived level of service and Customer satisfaction for the IT function as a whole. Having the right Service Desk staff skill set is therefore critical to the success, of not just the Service Desk, but the IT function as a whole.

The profile of staff working on the Service Desk should primarily be based on the considerations specified in para 4.6.1, Service Desk environment considerations . Regardless of whether technical staff work on the desk or not, a primary component for a successful implementation is interpersonal skills. These are skills, that cannot be acquired by just reading from a book; they require high levels of training and commitment. Interpersonal skills are essential for Service Desk personnel, as every contact with the Customer, is an opportunity to improve the Customers' perception of the IT function.

Consider how many of your technical staff are currently skilled and trained to manage the Customer interface for your department or organisation.

Support departments often mistake 'quick fixes' as good service. In some cases this is, of course, true. The Customer, wants a fix or response, but knows this is not always practical. It is important to engender in Customers and Users the confidence that once an Incident has been reported it will be professionally managed. If that confidence is not present, they may revert to calling their favourite support specialist and bypass the Service Desk. In some cases, they may stop calling on IT altogether.

4.5.1   Major Customer requirements

The major requirements that a Customer will have of a Service Desk are:

■   to provide a single point of contact

■   to communicate the level of service that will be provided, and when

■   to inform the Customer of the assigned priority of requests

■   to appraise the Customer of the progress of requests

■   to engender confidence that requests will not be lost or ignored.

4.5.2   Fix rates

As previously stated, the number of requests that the Service Desk should directly handle is dependent on a number of considerations. Defining expected fix rates is only practical in a stable environment and for specific areas. For example, it is *not* practical to state that a Service Desk will attempt to fix 85% of all requests, but it *is* practical to state that the Service Desk will attempt to fix 85% of all standard word-processing queries.

These statements demonstrate the importance of clearly understanding the Service Desk workload, and those areas that IT can effectively support. To state an 85% fix rate requires staff being trained to deliver at that level. If the primary role of the Service Desk is to support a major business application, then it is more practical to have staff trained in more detail for that application, and have additional material such as checklists and Known Errors available to them.

4.6 Setting up a Service Desk environment

Once you have decided to set up your Service Desk, you need to consider the environment that the Service Desk staff will be working in. Simply supplying desks and telephones is not enough.

If Customers visit your support centre, the image created is an important factor in the Customer's perception of the service and how seriously you take it. Many organisations use their Service Desk as a 'showcase' to demonstrate to Customers their commitment to quality service provision. In many cases, such organisations show Customers around their service function to demonstrate what happens when they call.

4.6.1 Service Desk environment considerations

When preparing to set up a Service Desk, bear in mind the following guidelines:

- if possible, provide a room/location away from the main support area with:
  - a pleasant and comfortable area for Customers and Service Desk staff
  - a low noise environment
  - privacy
- install a library of all your product, hardware and software documentation and reference material used by Customers
- ensure an up-to-date Service Catalogue is available at all times
- install conference phone facilities and hands-free units
- provide seating and desk space for round-table discussion – this helps defuse any 'them and us' situation
- provide beverage facilities to offer Customers, or at least easy access to them
- publish to the Customer base the location of the unit and its operating times.

When considering the level of service and the environment being provided , ask yourself '*Is this how I would like to be treated?*'

4.6.2 Defining your services

Although the Service Catalogue is part of Service Level Management, its understanding is fundamental to an effective Service Desk. The Service Catalogue defines the services available from your organisation to the Customer. It defines agreed expectations.

What you choose to define as a Service to your organisation is a business decision. Some examples are:

- payroll service
- printing service
- email service
- PC delivery and installation service.

Traditionally, computer departments have attempted to define services at a component level (e.g. server, network etc.). The problem with this approach to service definition is that it leads to confusion, because these elements are of no concern to Customers. At a component level, the service agreements are maintained by the 'back-to-back' Operational Level Agreements (OLAs) made with second-line support groups and third-party suppliers.

The major advantage of specifying a Service by application when registering a request, is that it allows instant classification of who should handle the activity, and how it should be handled. Using ITIL as a 'common language', support staff do not have to work out or translate the classification of the request, as this has already been agreed within the business.

4.6.3 Service Desk pre-Release requirements

It is essential that before any service or product is offered to a Customer (see Annex 4A for a sample Release document), the following is in place at the Service Desk and fully tested:

- an up-to-date Service Catalogue
- up-to-date processes, procedures and documentation
- training of Service Desk staff to the required level, including training on any technology support tools being used (Service Desk tool , email, knowledge tools)
- Customers are informed, in advance, of procedures for reporting Incidents with the new service and the direct benefits to them of doing so
- Service and Operational Level Agreements have been agreed by Service Desk management
- escalation procedures are in place
- Customer contact points (e.g. Super Users)
- required second-line checklists and Known Errors lists
- service availability schedules
- support staff skill lists
- details of related third-party support organisations
- details of all known bugs and Known Errors
- appropriate third-party contract and contact details
- involved third parties are aware of all procedures and processes in place
- details of third-party support and maintenance contracts.

Many organisations invest huge amounts of money and resource in developing, planning and training for a new Service. However, one of the most important deliverables of that service – support – is often neglected and added as an afterthought. This is a major cause for failure in a Release (and Customer perception of a new service). In contrast, it is good to use a new service as an opportunity to 'impress the business'. This is a 'moment of truth', which defines a mature and professional service operation.

User Handbook

A useful addition to your support arsenal is the 'User Handbook'. This should contain useful hints and tips for Problem solving on major applications and equipment and any preliminary checks or information that may be required before calling the desk (e.g. noting service name, screen numbers, error codes, etc). Importantly, it should tell the Customer what to expect when they call and what will happen. The provision of a quality service is only achievable when Customers and Service Desk staff work together.

A useful way of circulating and publishing the 'User Handbook' is online via Internet or intranet technology.

4.6.4   Advertising and selling the Service Desk

In addition to Customer feedback and management reporting, it is important that your Customers are aware in advance of any Changes affecting their service. Indeed, the introduction of the Service Desk should be viewed as an excellent public relations exercise to increase Customer awareness, and to **sell** the business benefits of that service.

Selling what you do to both the individual User and the whole business is essential for success. All too often, the only time the business is aware of what is being done is when someone complains or things go wrong. It is necessary to overcome these negative episodes and messages with positive ones. This is why it is so important to continuously communicate or 'sell' your achievement, successes and areas of improvement to your Customer as well as to IT Management.

Selling considerations are as follows:

- publish successes – show the business what you're doing *right*
- focus on general improvement:
    - publish newsletters
    - publish Customer satisfaction levels
- demonstrate cost savings based on improved service through:
    - purchase decisions
    - reduced maintenance costs
    - value for money
    - improved Customer response
- highlight areas for improvement and what you have done and intend to do about them
- create a marketing plan and follow through on it
- make public relations part of the Service Desk function, and assign someone responsibility for it.

Key success factors

The key success factors for implementing a successful Service Desk include:

- provide 'quick wins' to demonstrate the benefits
- start simple, adopting a phased approach
- involve Customers, especially those that tend to be outspoken and critical of your services
- explain the differences that will be seen by Customers
- involve third-party service suppliers
- make sure everyone involved or affected by the Service Desk knows what is being done and why – this also includes other support operations, such as telecommunications, building services)
- sell the benefits to support staff to avoid resistance to the changes – particularly important because support staff are generally cautious
- educate staff and managers to be 'Customer – and service-focused'.

4.6.5   Quick wins

Choosing your 'quick wins' should be based on what is important to your Customers and will yield a short-term service improvement and enhance Customer perception. Quick wins are essential to obtain Customer and business support during the initial phases of any service-improvement project.

Examples of possible quick wins are as follows:

- improvement in Customer and business perception
- provision of faster response to standard requests
- enhancement of the professionalism of the Incident registration and closure process
- keeping Customers better informed of progress
- allowing Customers to register and query their own requests
- publishing a Service Catalogue and User Handbook
- improving communications with the business
- development of better working relationships within the business
- reduced Incident-resolution times
- improvements to business reporting.

4.7   Service Desk education and training

Objectives:

- To improve Customer and support staff knowledge of available services and working practices
- To identify deficiencies in Customer and User training that either negatively impact the User's use of the service, or create an unnecessary workload for support staff
- To implement educational programmes that resolve deficiencies identified for Customers, Users and support staff

4.7.1   Soft skills

This section concentrates on the interpersonal skills, profile and personality required to interact with Customers and Users in order to manage and work on the Service Desk.

Everyone in the service business talks about Customer satisfaction, retention and long-term relationships. The big issues such as quality, consistency, reliability and value, build relationships. But it's often the small things that destroy relationships. When a Customer goes to a competitor or complains to management, it's usually a number of little things added to one final straw that breaks the relationship.

When considering how better to foster Customer relationships, you should consider the things you do *to* them, not just for them. Ask yourself whether everything you say you do, you actually do. Perhaps you are missing chances to turn business opportunities into clients and happy Customers for life. Start to look at the little things. They can keep your relationships from dissolving before your eyes.

4.7.2 Managerial focus

There are three aspects of management focus that need to be mentioned here:

- encouraging team working
- putting yourself in your team's shoes
- getting your hands dirty.

Encouraging team working

Service managers should encourage teamwork and participation. To many support staff, it seems that the only time a Customer speaks to them is when they want to complain. In today's environment, the rate of change can be very stressful. It is important to empower and involve the whole team, asking staff to regularly review and, if required, redesign processes. If a team member has an idea, encourage it. In many cases they are in a far better position to make a valid judgement than a manager is.

If the team is involved in the decision-making process, the members are more likely to buy into the final decision, and the success of the new process is almost guaranteed.

Putting yourself in your team's shoes

In a stressful support environment, it's not always easy to make the right decision. Managers tell staff that it's okay to make a mistake or not to know an answer. However, managers tend not to live by that advice themselves, often trying too hard to be the perfect manager. If we cannot be open and honest with our team, we can't expect the same from them. While this is extremely hard for many people, it is also extremely powerful. Not only does it create a good channel of communication, but it also builds a great deal of loyalty.

Getting your hands dirty

Managers' days are filled with meetings, reports and problems, and many do not have a spare minute to do another thing. Everyone knows this, especially your team, but you should make time to roll up your sleeves and participate in the handling of Customer requests. It doesn't have to be daily or even weekly, but the effort has to be sincere and frequent enough so that your team remembers it.

Be sure to strip yourself of your manager title and role when you participate so that you really experience their world.

4.7.3 Service Desk staff profile

Selecting and retaining the correct staff is critical to success. It is no longer enough to have 'technical skills'; professional skills are key. In fact, many successful service departments recruit staff from the 'business' or employ staff from other service-based industries who are then, if required, technically trained in the required areas. Today's Service Desk professional is master of many essential skills, with a mindset to match. A Service Desk member should be:

- Customer-focused
- articulate and methodical
- trained in interpersonal skills
- multilingual (if required)
- able to understand the business's objectives
- able to understand and accept that
  - the Customer's Problem affects the business
  - without the Customer there is no support department
  - the Customer is an expert in their own field
- genuinely wanting to deliver a first-class service.

4.7.4 Service staff responsibilities and mindset

Customer and Service Support is one of the most challenging roles in any organisation.

The primary role of Service Desk staff is to ensure that the services provided to the business are operational, exemplified by the attributes discussed below.

Teamwork

Teamwork is critical to success. Support staff are generally in the best position to review and/or amend processes and procedures and, most importantly, do the same with Customer perceptions.

Empathy with Users

In a stressful support environment, it's not always easy to look at things from your Customer's perspective. When seeking assistance, they may themselves be under stress, or up against a deadline. Your support and respect at this point is critical, and is often 'a moment of truth' for the support teams to deliver value to the business.

Professionalism

Because Customer support is a stressful activity, a clear and helpful frame of mind is essential. Customers quickly detect disinterest and respond accordingly.

Before you start a day's work, take a few minutes to leave your personal problems behind and get into the right mindset to act professionally – **smile**, and **be positive**,

4.7.5 Working with Customers

This sub-section describes some of the other skills involved when handling Customer requests.

First impressions count

When making contact with your Customer for the first time, take a moment to introduce yourself. Describe the approach you have planned to take to diagnose and resolve their issue. Rather than simply solve their problem, it is important to demonstrate your ability to reason and effectively troubleshoot. Through this, the Customer will become confident in and trust your ability, which will in turn provide you greater freedom in future interactions.

Let the Customer play a role in the solution, no matter how small. You will be viewed as 'here to help.' If you don't know the answer to a question, don't pretend to; you aren't necessarily expected to know everything about everything. Of course, saying 'this is outside the realm of my particular expertise, but I can look into it for you' might be better received than a simple 'I don't know', because the former at least demonstrates a definite focus and direction. **Always** be constructive; **never** be confrontational.

Accept ownership

Treat the Customer's concerns as if they were your own. Formulate a plan of action and keep the Customer updated on any developments, as they occur. This clearly demonstrates that the Customer's concerns are important to you, and whether the solution to their problem is simple or complex, you are 'here to help'.

In an environment where support is divided between different support groups, never simply pass on the Customer to a new team without first describing the process. It is imperative that you retain accountability, even when you delegate responsibility for the resolution of the Customer's problem. Explain that while your expertise is in this area, another team might be better suited to address the particular issue.

Speak in terms that a Customer can understand

It is important to identify quickly the level of expertise that your Customer has in the area they have reported. Leading questions such as 'Have you been using this application/equipment for a while?' will assist you in your approach. In many cases, especially business applications, the Customer may be more expert than your support staff.

When explaining or exploring a Problem with a Customer try to stay away from technical jargon; rather, use familiar analogies. Comparing a low bandwidth to a residential street and a high-speed connection to a motorway is one example. Comparing a Mini's performance to a Porsche 911 can be used as another. Do not, however, patronise your Customer.

Seemingly strange things may occur as part of your diagnosis of an Incident. Avoid saying 'This is strange' or 'I've never seen this before', or 'This doesn't happen on my machine', instead, refer to such occurrences as 'unique'.

Views things from the Customer's perspective

The Customer with a Problem is only concerned with getting back to work as quickly as possible. They are themselves probably under pressure to get a quotation out or working to a project deadline. Take this into account and remain composed if the Customer becomes anxious. If they demand an action beyond your control, politely refer them to the duty Service Manager.

4.7.6   Active listening

Some people, although they might talk well, simply talk too much – smothering others with words, and attempting to sweep them off their feet with one point or question after another. People like this probably cause more Customer upset and produce more frustrations than any other mistake that people can make.

In a support role, listening is a major skill to improve service – just as surely as speaking is a skill. Learning to do both is essential. Here are some points to remember:

- Keep in mind that there is more to listening than just standing still with your mouth shut. To be a good listener, you should be an *active* listener.

- You should be alert and interested. You should project yourself into the other person's mind to see the situation through their eyes.

- You should listen past the words to gain an understanding of why those words are being said.

For example, do not be too quick to jump on someone coming out with a statement such as 'Your service is awful'. If you handle this as a simple service objection, you may have missed the point. What is probably meant is 'I don't understand why I cannot access my application in the evenings'.

The best listeners are the ones who ask the most pertinent questions. Questions help the other person to say what they are trying to say, and they demonstrate that you are sincerely interested in the person as well as the Problems.

Listening can be divided into two forms, passive and active. A *passive* listener receives the other person's messages as they are transmitted, but takes no initiative to react to them or to seek amplification on any points that are not understood. An *active* listener takes the initiative in drawing out the other person and seeks clarification of the message being transmitted.

Active listening is an essential skill to learn and is highly recommended for all Service Desk staff.

4.7.7 Service Desk staff training

Service Desk training is often seen as something only for first-line support staff. However, to promote a professional and consistent approach to the Customer, all support staff, from the Service Desk to Computer Operations and Development should be trained in several important areas. Being technically competent is no longer enough in a modern service organisation. The ability to communicate and work with Customers is an essential skill and a worthwhile investment in developing:

- general interpersonal skills
- telephone techniques
- writing techniques (letter, email, voice)
- active listening and questioning
- stress and complaint management.

4.8 Service Desk processes and procedures

4.8.1 Considerations

When designing your processes and procedures, and taking the broad view, you will need to:

- review their validity on a regular basis, and update as required
- involve all relevant parties
- allocate sufficient time and resources
- consider alternatives (e.g. information being computerised rather than in printed form)
- provide new reference materials based on Incident and Problem trend analyses.

More detailed points are discussed in the remainder of this section.

4.8.2 Common structured interrogation technique

Providing a common structured dialogue to managing Customer requests is essential, no matter who in the support organisation responds to the Customer. The order in which questions and responses are required helps both the Customer and the support person to ensure nothing is forgotten. Using a common technique presents a professional and well-structured organisation to the Customer.

It is important to apply a common structured interrogation technique to establish and maintain:

- Customer 'pickup', i.e. response times
- contact identification (e.g. name, company, telephone)
- contact detail confirmation
- Customer response dialogue (e.g. Good morning, ACME Service Desk, Barry speaking. How can I help you?'), but done in a way that is as User-friendly as possible and not sound as if it is being read from a script.

4.8.3   Customer details and identification

Correct and unique Customer identification is essential to ensure that Customer details, existing requests and management information are uniquely and easily selectable.

The more we know about our Customers and Users, the better we can support them.

Example contact identification types include:

- name (e.g. SMITH_W)
- account code
- equipment/computer identity
- email/Internet identifier
- telephone number/extension
- personnel number
- location
- associated notes.

It should be possible to identify a Customer from one or two pieces of identification information and retrieve the rest of the information from the stored Customer database.

Providing a Customer-preferred greeting is important when corresponding with a Customer, whether orally or in writing. Many Customers and Users like to be referred to in a specific manner (e.g. Mr, Dr, Ms, Bill), and so your support systems should be designed to provide this. After all, 'Dear **Mrs. Smith**' or '**Dear Jill**' is much more preferable to 'Dear P123232' or 'Dear SMITH_J'.

The more criteria a Customer can be selected on the better. It may be that the Customer has forgotten their account code, but your support systems should be able to isolate Customer by other user-friendly means. Possible criteria include:

- Customer ID
- name
- department
- telephone
- post code
- address/location.

4.8.4   Maintaining the Customer database

Maintaining a single source of Customer and supplier details is a major issue for many organisations, because there are generally several sources:

- personnel department (e.g. name, department, NI number)
- IT department (e.g. computer id, email address, location)
- telephone switchboard (e.g. telephone no, fax no).

A process should be defined for maintaining Customer, support staff and supplier details that answers such questions as:

- what needs to be stored?
- what are the sources, and where are they?
- how do we consolidate them?
- how do we keep them up to date?
- who maintains the master source?

4.8.5 Marketing the Service Desk amongst Customers

Raising the profile of your support services, especially the Service Desk is critical to success. The Service Desk needs to attain its own identify in order to instil confidence and strengthen the Customer relationship. This can be done using the following techniques:

- invite Customers to visit your computer training and support facilities
- use advertising materials (e.g. mouse mats, screen savers, help cards, a bulletin board)
- provide service awareness seminars and workshops
- develop your own stationery and letterheads (if permitted by the organisation)
- get involved in company activities (hockey team etc).

Knowledge and procedures review

It is important that all reference materials and procedures used by Customers, Users and support staff are well maintained, kept up-to-date and regularly reviewed, including:

- standard checklists
- training manuals
- lists of Known Errors and solutions
- product and application documentation
- hardware documentation
- knowledge bases
- support specialists skill set
- command procedures, scripts and programs
- the Customer/Supplier database(s).

4.9 Incident reporting and review

Objective:

- To produce reports from which management can make decisions and measure performance based on agreed service levels and deliverables.

The ability to provide good-quality management information shows a level of maturity within your support organisation. When you first build a support organisation, you may have little formal reporting in place. As you mature in your support processes, you will see an expanding need to report on and clearly understand request histories, trends and workloads. Management information is often the only method available adequately to justify additional resources and expenditure.

Reporting, however, is often subjective and needs to be focused on business improvement. It is important that results are not just filed away but used as an essential business tool to justify, develop and continually improve the service.

Receiving reports is essential not only for Customers but also for all the teams contributing to the service-provision process, with each team requiring the information in different ways. For example:

- network support by Problems by location/zone
- PC support by desktop and hardware devices
- development group by application

- Service Desk by Customer and priority
- account management by Customer satisfaction
- management by business impact, service breaches, cost
- third parties by target achievement.

4.9.1   Effective workload analyses

The most valuable and expensive resource within your support operation is your staff. Optimising staff utilisation is of primary importance. Workload analysis can help determine staffing levels, when staff are needed, and how work patterns vary from day-to-day, or even week-to-week.

Accurate support-staff and third-party workload analyses need to take into account the complete request life-cycle and the time spent during each phase. For detailed analysis, support staff should enter the time they spend working on a request or any part of it. For example a request may be logged and closed by the Service Desk; however, during its life-cycle, persons from other support groups may have spent time working on the request. Therefore each individual's elapsed time and actual time spent needs to be accounted for and reported on.

Figure 4.11 gives an example of a single request, which took four hours to complete. In the given scenario, we may wish to know whether the 'Third-Party Engineer' exceeded his or her Service Level Agreement, as well as the actual Customer Incident. In the same situation we may also wish to know how long a request may spend in a specific status, priority etc.

Support Group	Duration
Service Desk	10 min
PC Support	1 hr 50 min
Third Party Engineer	1 hr 30 min
Service Desk	30 min

Figure 4.11 – Incident workload analysis

Workload analysis is an important tool for identifying SLA and OLA target achievement.

4.9.2   Frequency of reporting and review

An organisation should establish a suitable frequency of reporting and review, depending upon the importance of the review. Providing results in graphical form is useful for presenting management overviews on major areas of interest.

To provide a common service objective, it is important that all members of the service team are aware of the major issues, concerns, performance levels and achievements of the whole team and not just their specific group.

Suggested review periods and levels are set out below.

Daily reviews of individual Incident and Problem status against service levels

These should report:

- areas requiring escalation by group
- possible service breaches
- all outstanding Incidents.

Weekly management reviews

These should highlight:

- service availability
- major Incident areas that:
  - occur the most often
  - staff spend the most time working on
  - take the longest time to turn around to the Customer
- related Incidents that require Problem records to be generated
- Known Errors and required Changes
- service breaches
- Customer satisfaction
- trends, major services affecting the business
- staff workloads.

Monthly management reviews

These should report on:

- service availability
- overall performance, achievements and trend analyses
- individual service target achievements
- Customer perceptions and levels of satisfaction
- Customer training and education needs
- support staff and third-party performance
- application and technology performance
- content of review and reporting matrix
- cost of service provision/failure.

Proactive service reports

Reporting, whether online or in textual form, is also essential for proactive support at the Service Desk. Consider the following reports to aid this:

- planned Changes for the following week
- major Incidents/Problems/Changes from the previous week, along with any Work-arounds, fixes etc
- 'unsatisfied' Customer Incidents from previous weeks
- previous weeks' poorly performing infrastructure items (eg, server, network, application).

4.9.3 Archiving Service Desk records

As time progresses, the total number of Service Desk Incident records logged will increase. The question of when and what to archive is based on several considerations, including:

- the volume of requests
- the usefulness of the content
- whether it is still required at the Service Desk or online

- whether it is a type of request that needs to be archived
- whether the data is required as part of a relationship with another Customer Incident still being processed
- whether the requests pertain to monthly, quarterly, annual functions (e.g. accounts year end).

Retention of information relating to quarterly and annual Incidents should be carefully considered. It may be the case that the last time this job ran was a year ago, and therefore any Problems found and their solutions will only have been registered during that period, if not subsequently corrected via Change Management.

4.10 Conclusions

The successful implementation and ongoing support of the Service Desk process will return major business benefits to your organisation, expressed as cost reductions, Customer satisfaction, staff commitment and professionalism.

4.10.1 Critical success factors

To introduce and maintain a successful Service Desk, it is essential that:

- business needs are understood
- Customer requirements are understood
- investment is made in training for Customers, support teams and Service Desk staff
- service objectives, goals and deliverables are clearly defined
- service levels are practical, agreed, and regularly reviewed
- the benefits are accepted by the business.

4.10.2 Service Desk implementation guidance

Any Service Desk implementation should be carefully planned as a project, with frequent deliverables at each stage of the project and with regular stage reviews. You should:

- adopt a phased implementation approach
- involve your Customers, and ask them what they need
- involve/consult your support staff
- identify quick wins to implement first
- constantly measure progress
- don't expect too much too soon
- realise that its hard work – don't give up.

Annex 4A: SAMPLE RELEASE DOCUMENT

A sample Release document follows, to act as a template for informing Customers of a new or updated service being provided.

20 August 2000

Dear Customer,

Introduction of the New Service Desk At My Company Limited

My Company Ltd continually strives to improve the service it delivers to its customers. The IT Services Department, providing internal support for business applications and equipment, is no exception.

In order to understand more fully the services you require from us, we having undertaken a study to identify specific IT needs. From this have emerged several major areas where you feel improvement is required:

- general improvement in all areas of service provision
- provision of a single point of contact for all queries and problems
- to be kept informed of progress of problems you have encountered through to final resolution
- to know what services are available.

To ensure we can meet the increasing demands of the business with the available resources, we are introducing the MCL Service Desk. This will allow you, the customer, to register service problems, queries and requests, or maybe just talk something over. The initial benefits to you will be that:

- you will be kept **informed** at all times
- **training** needs will be highlighted
- **earlier** identification of problem areas affecting service
- **clear** understanding of available services you will receive.

Upon registering your problem or request, you may be asked for a few details, such as your name and a brief description of the request, and you will then be given an *Incident reference number*. Then, if you need to contact us again on the same matter, merely by quoting this number, we will be able to tell you quickly how matters are progressing. For non-urgent and out-of-hours requests, you can contact us by email, for which you will receive a receipted return email (support@mcl.co.uk) quoting your *Incident reference number*.

To support this change, we will also be introducing Service Level Agreements (SLAs). These are contracts specifying agreed levels of service that your department requires for *business-critical* activities. This will allow us to focus resource and costs more effectively and better identify areas for improvement. These SLAs will be continually monitored and reviewed for effectiveness.

When one of your requests is resolved, we will ask you to let us know how well we performed. This is your opportunity to state how you feel about the service and, most importantly, tell us where you believe we need to improve – and just as important, when we are doing a 'Good Job.'

The commencement date of the new service is scheduled for 1 October 2000. More details will be given nearer the start date.

I am in no doubt that there will be operational difficulties to overcome, but with your support, I am sure these will be resolved quickly. If in the meantime you have any questions regarding the new service, please do not hesitate to contact me on ext. 3333.

Bill Smith
MCL Customer Services Manager

5 INCIDENT MANAGEMENT

5.1 Goal of Incident Management

The primary goal of the Incident Management process is to restore normal service operation as quickly as possible and minimise the adverse impact on business operations, thus ensuring that the best possible levels of service quality and availability are maintained. 'Normal service operation' is defined here as service operation within Service Level Agreement (SLA) limits.

5.2 Scope of Incident Management

In ITIL terminology, an 'Incident' is defined as:

> *any event **which** is not part of the standard operation of a service and **which** causes, or may cause, an interruption to, or a reduction in, the quality of that service.*

Examples of categories of Incidents are:

- application
  - service not available
  - application bug/query preventing Customer from working
  - disk-usage threshold exceeded
- hardware
  - system down
  - automatic alert
  - printer not printing
  - configuration inaccessible
- service requests
  - request for information/advice/documentation
  - forgotten password.

A request for new or additional service (i.e. software or hardware) is often not regarded as an Incident but as a Request for Change (RFC). However, practice shows that handling of both failures in the infrastructure and of service requests are similar, and both are therefore included in the definition and scope of the process of Incident Management. The word 'Incident' in this chapter applies to both, if not explicitly stated otherwise, although organisations may decide to develop their own service-request procedures to isolate them from the more technical issues.

Within the more technically oriented systems-management function, an automatically registered event such as exceeding a disk-usage threshold, is often regarded as part of 'normal' operations. These events are included in the definition of Incidents even though service delivery to Customers is not affected.

Figure 5.1 shows the Incident Management process. These are split down as follows:

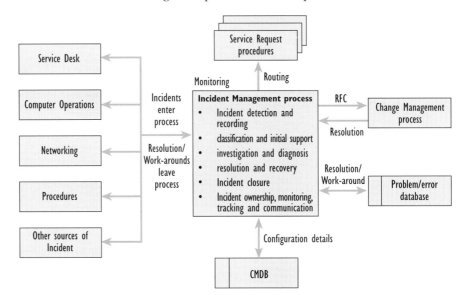

Figure 5.1 - Incident Management process

◆ Inputs:

- ■ Incident details sourced from (for example) Service Desk, networks or computer operations

- ■ configuration details from the Configuration Management Database (CMDB)

- ■ response from Incident matching against Problems and Known Errors

- ■ resolution details

- ■ response on RFC to effect resolution for Incident(s).

◆ Outputs:

- ■ RFC for Incident resolution; updated Incident record (including resolution and/or Work-arounds)

- ■ resolved and closed Incidents

- ■ communication to Customers

- ■ management information (reports).

◆ Incident Management activities:

- ■ Incident detection and recording

- ■ Classification and initial support

- ■ investigation and diagnosis

- ■ resolution and recovery

- ■ Incident closure

- ■ Incident ownership, monitoring, tracking and communication

The roles and functions related to the Incident Management process are:

- ■ first, second-and third-line support groups, including specialist support groups and external suppliers (roles)

- ■ Incident Manager (role)

- ■ Service Desk manager (function).

5.3   Basic concepts

5.3.1   Incident Handling

Most IT departments and specialist groups contribute to handling Incidents at some time. The Service Desk is responsible for the monitoring of the resolution process of *all* registered Incidents – in effect the Service Desk is the owner of all Incidents. The process is mostly reactive. To react efficiently and effectively therefore demands a formal method of working that can be supported by software tools.

Incidents that cannot be resolved immediately by the Service Desk may be assigned to specialist groups. A resolution or Work-around should be established as quickly as possible in order to restore the service to Users with minimum disruption to their work. After resolution of the cause of the Incident and restoration of the agreed service, the Incident is closed.

Figure 5.2 illustrates the activities during an Incident life cycle, with an alternative perspective provided in Annex 5E.

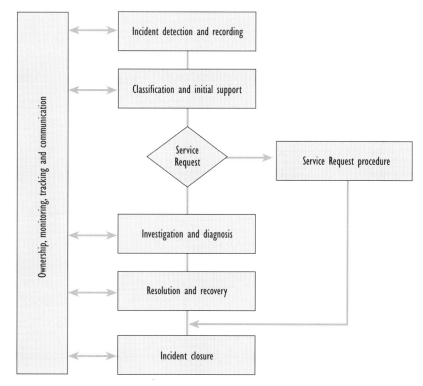

Figure 5.2 - The Incident life cycle

The status of an Incident reflects its current position in its life-cycle, sometimes known as its 'workflow position'. Everyone should be aware of each status and its meaning. Some examples of status categories might include:

- new
- accepted
- scheduled

- assigned/dispatched to specialist
- work in progress (WIP)
- on hold
- resolved
- closed.

Throughout an Incident life-cycle it is important that the Incident record is maintained. This allows any member of the service team to provide a Customer with an up-to-date progress report. Example update activities include:

- update history details
- modify status (e.g. 'new' to 'work-in-progress' or 'on hold')
- modify business impact/priority
- enter time spent and costs
- monitor escalation status.

An originally reported Customer description may change as the Incident progresses. It is, however, important to retain the description of the original symptoms, both for analysis and so that you can refer to the complaint in the same terms used in the initial report. For example, the Customer may have reported a printer not working, which is found to be have been caused by a network failure. When responding to the Customer it is better initially to explain that the printer Incident has been resolved rather than to talk about resolution of network Problems.

An audited history is essential when reviewing progress, and is especially important when resolving issues of SLA breaches. The following updates to the Incident record should be registered during the Incident life cycle:

- name of person who made the modification
- date and time of modification
- what the person modified (e.g. priority, status, history)
- why they made the change
- time spent.

If third-party organisations are not allowed to have access to allow them to update the Service Desk support records, which is a preferred option, then a process to update the records on behalf of the supplier is required. This will ensure that resource usage is properly accounted for. However, if the software allows partitioning of Incidents and screening of information, it could work quite well for some organisations to allow direct update by third parties. You need, in this decision, to consider what you are not prepared to allow your supplier to see, and how closely you need to be aware of what your supplier is doing.

The same situation may also exist when the Service Desk updates a request on behalf of a support person working in the field. Retrospective Incident update may be required for situations such as engineers working in the evening and the Service Desk having to update records on their behalf on the following morning.

5.3.2 First, second- and third-line support

Often, departments and (specialist) support groups other than the Service Desk are referred to as second- or third-line support groups, having more specialist skills, time or other resources to solve Incidents. In this respect, the Service Desk would be first-line support. Figure 5.3 illustrates how this terminology relates to the Incident Management activities mentioned in previous paragraphs.

Note that third- and/or *n*-line support may eventually include external suppliers, who may have direct access to the Incident registration tool (depending on safety rules and technical issues).

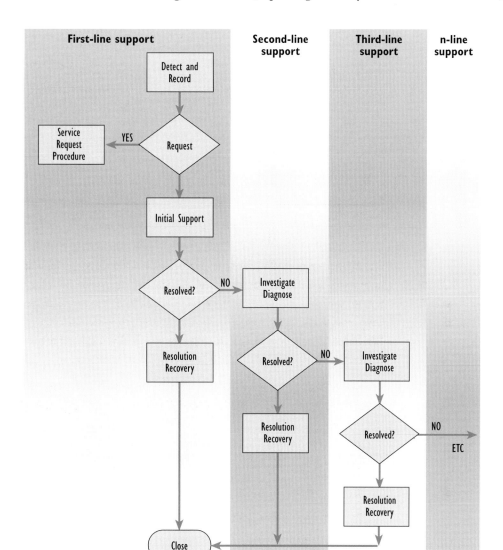

Figure 5.3 - First, second- and third-line support

5.3.3   Functional versus hierarchical escalation

'Escalation' is the mechanism that assists timely resolution of an Incident. It can take place during every activity in the resolution process.

Transferring an Incident from first-line to second-line support groups or further is called 'functional escalation' and primarily takes place because of lack of knowledge or expertise. Preferably, functional escalation also takes place when agreed time intervals elapse. The automatic functional escalation based on time intervals should be planned carefully and should not exceed the (SLA) agreed resolution times.

'Hierarchical escalation' can take place at any moment during the resolution process when it is likely that resolution of an Incident will not be in time or satisfactory. In case of lack of knowledge or expertise, hierarchical escalation is generally performed manually (by the Service Desk or other support staff). Automatic hierarchical escalation can be considered after a certain critical time interval, when it is likely that a timely resolution will fail. Preferably, this takes place long enough *before* the (SLA) agreed resolution time is exceeded so that corrective actions by authorised line management can be carried out – for example hiring third-party specialists.

5.3.4   Priority

The priority of an Incident is primarily determined by the impact on the business and the urgency with which a resolution or Work-around is needed. Targets for resolving Incidents or handling requests are generally embodied in an SLA. In practice resolution targets for Incidents are often related to categories. Examples of category and priority and coding systems are to be found in Annexes 5A and 5B respectively.

The Service Desk plays an important role in the Incident Management process, as follows:

- all Incidents are reported to and registered by the Service Desk – where Incidents are generated automatically, the process should still include registration by the Service Desk

- the majority of Incidents (perhaps up to 85% in a highly skilled environment) will be resolved at the Service Desk

- the Service Desk is the 'independent' function monitoring Incident resolution progress of all registered Incidents.

On receipt of an Incident notification, the main actions to be carried out by the Service Desk are:

- record basic details - this includes timing data and details of symptoms obtained

- if a service request has been made, the request is handled in conformance with the organisation's standard procedures

- from the CMDB, the Configuration Items (CI) reported as the cause for an Incident is selected, to complete the Incident record

- the appropriate priority is assigned and the User is given the unique system-generated Incident number (to be quoted at the beginning of all further communication)

- the Incident is assessed and, if possible, resolution advice is given: this frequently will be possible for routine Incidents or when a match to a known Problem/error is achieved

- following successful resolution the Incident record is closed: details of the resolution action and the appropriate category code are added

- the Incident is assigned to second-line support (i.e. a specialist group) following unsuccessful resolution or recognition that a further level of support is needed.

5.3.5   Relationship between Incidents, Problems, Known Errors and RFCs

Incidents, the result of failures or errors within the IT infrastructure, result in actual or potential variations from the planned operation of the IT services.

The cause of Incidents may be apparent and that cause can be addressed without the need for further investigation, resulting in a repair, a Work-around or an RFC to remove the error. In some cases the Incident itself, i.e. the effect or potential effect upon the Customer, can be dealt with quickly. Perhaps by rebooting a PC or resetting a communications line, without directly addressing the underlying cause of the Incident.

Where the underlying cause of the Incident is not identifiable, then it may be appropriate to raise a Problem record. A Problem is thus, in effect, indicative of an *unknown error* within the infrastructure. Normally a Problem record is raised only if investigation is warranted.

This impact will often be assessed via the impact, (both actual and potential), upon the business services, and the number of similar Incidents apparently sharing a common underlying cause that have reported. This may be appropriate even where the actual result of the Incident has been addressed. It can be seen therefore that a Problem record is independent of associated Incident records, and both the Problem record and the investigation into its cause can persist even after the initial Incident has been successfully closed.

Successful processing of a Problem record will result in the identification of the underlying error, and the record can then be converted into a *Known Error* once a Work-around has been developed, and/or an RFC. This logical flow, from an initial report to the resolution of an underlying Problem, is shown in Figure 5.4.

Figure 5.4 - Relationship between Incidents, Problems, Known Errors and RFCs

We thus have the following definitions:

- **Problem**   The unknown underlying cause of one or more Incidents.
- **Known Error**   A Problem that is successfully diagnosed and for which a Work-around is known.
- **RFC**   A Request For Change to any component of an IT Infrastructure or to any aspect of IT services.

A Problem can result in multiple Incidents, and it is possible that the Problem will not be diagnosed until several Incidents have occurred, over a period of time. Handling Problems is quite different from handling Incidents and is therefore covered by the Problem Management process.

During the Incident-resolution process the Incident is matched against the Problem and Known Error database. It should also be matched against the Incident database to see whether there is a similar Incident outstanding, or whether there has been resolution action taken for any previous similar Incident. If a Work-around or resolution is available, the Incident can be resolved immediately. If not, Incident Management is responsible for finding a resolution or Work-around with minimum disruption to the business process.

When Incident Management finds a Work-around it will be analysed by the Problem Management team who will update the associated Problem record (see Figure 5.5). Note that an associated Problem record may not exist at this time – for example, the Work-around may be to send a report by fax due to a communication line failure, but at this point there may not be a Problem record for the communication line failure, which the Problem Management team would have to create. The process is then that the Service Desk will link Incidents that are clearly the result of an existing Problem record.

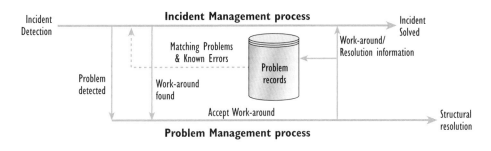

Figure 5.5 - Handling incident Work-arounds and resolutions

It is also possible that the Problem Management team, while investigating the Problem associated with the Incident, finds a Work-around or a resolution for a Problem and/or some related Incidents. In this case, the Problem Management team should inform the Incident Management process in order that open Incidents have their status changed to 'Known Error' or 'closed' as appropriate.

Where it is felt at Incident logging that an Incident should be treated as a Problem, then it should be referred immediately to the Problem Management process, where, if appropriate, a new Problem record will be raised. Incident Management will, as always, remain responsible for pursuing a resolution to the Incident with minimal possible disruption to the business processes.

5.4   Benefits of Incident Management

The major benefits to be gained by implementing an Incident Management process are as follows:

◆ For the business as a whole:

- reduced business impact of Incidents by timely resolution, thereby increasing effectiveness
- the proactive identification of beneficial system enhancements and amendments
- the availability of business-focused management information related to the SLA.

◆ For the IT organisation in particular:

- improved monitoring, allowing performance against SLAs to be accurately measured
- improved management information on aspects of service quality
- better staff utilisation, leading to greater efficiency
- elimination of lost or incorrect Incidents and service requests
- more accurate CMDB information (giving an ongoing audit while registering Incidents)
- improved User and Customer satisfaction.

In contrast, failing to implement Incident Management may result in:

- no one to manage and escalate Incidents - hence Incidents may become more severe than necessary and adversely affect IT service quality
- specialist support staff being subject to constant interruptions, making them less effective
- business staff being disrupted as people ask their colleagues for advice
- frequent reassessment of Incidents from first principle rather than reference to existing solutions
- lack of coordinated management information
- lost, or incorrectly or badly managed Incidents.

5.5   Planning and implementation

5.5.1   Timing and planning

Some guidelines for planning Incident Management are as follows:

- Do not plan to implement and operate Incident Management in isolation. If possible, the scope of planning should be extended to include the implementation, integration and operation of the Service Desk, Problem Management, Configuration Management, Change Management and Release Management processes.

- If resources are not available to implement all Service Support processes at the same time, begin by implementing the Service Desk function together with Incident Management. This will result in 'quick wins' and therefore acceptance of process implementation in general within the IT organisation and with Customers.

- Plan to create the Service Desk and to define Incident Management processes at the earliest opportunity. If a major new Customer IT service is being implemented with gradual User take-on, install the Service Desk from the outset. Do this even if the initial number of Users would normally fail to justify a desk. This approach allows the Service Desk to grow with the new service take-on.

- The planning phase for Incident Management could last from three to six months for a sophisticated, extensive solution. The implementation phase could last from three months to a year, although implementation and improvement should be considered as an ongoing activity.

- The procurement of hardware and software can be time-consuming. Start selection procedures as soon as possible, based on seeking those that support the ITIL processes, and provide the required level of flexibility to allow for organisation-specific needs.

- Keep closely linked systems, especially Configuration Management, in step. Plan for the creation of a Configuration Management Database (CMDB) and the conversion of existing equipment inventories. If no integrated Configuration Management system is in place, make this database part of the Incident Management system.

- Plan for an interface with the Problem Management system to assist Service Desk staff in recognising and giving advice on circumventing Known Errors. If such a system is scheduled for later implementation, consider the use of an interim paper-based or free-standing electronic solution (e.g. spreadsheet) to 'bridge the gap.'

5.5.2   Critical success factors

Successful Incident Management requires a sound basis, as highlighted by the following points:

- An up-to-date CMDB is a prerequisite for an efficiently working Incident Management process. If a CMDB is not available, information about Configuration Items (CIs) related to Incidents should be obtained manually, and determining impact and urgency will be much more difficult and time-consuming.

- A 'knowledge base' in the form of an up-to-date Problem/error database should be developed to provide for resolutions and Work-arounds. This will greatly speed up the process of resolving Incidents. Third-party Known Error databases should also be available to assist in this process.

- An effectively automated system for Incident Management is fundamental to the success of a Service Desk. Paper-based systems are not really practical or necessary, now that good and cheap support tools are available.

- Forge a close link with the Service-Level Management (SLM) process to obtain necessary Incident response targets. Timely Incident resolution will satisfy Customers and Users.

5.5.3 Possible problem areas

Be prepared to overcome:

- no visible management or staff commitment, resulting in non-availability of resources for implementation
- lack of clarity about business needs
- working practices not being reviewed or changed
- poorly defined service objectives, goals and responsibilities
- no provision of agreed Customer service levels
- lack of knowledge for resolving Incidents
- inadequate training for staff
- lack of integration with other processes
- lack of, or expense of, tools to automate the process
- resistance to change.

5.6 Incident Management activities

This section discusses in more detail the six activities encapsulated in Section 5.3 (Basic concepts), namely:

- Incident detection and recording
- classification and initial support
- investigation and diagnosis
- resolution and recovery
- Incident closure
- ownership, monitoring, tracking and communication.

Each of these is discussed in more detail below.

5.6.1 Incident detection and recording

Incident details from Service Desk or event management systems are the inputs for Incident Management. Resultant actions are to:

- record basic details of the Incident
- alert specialist support group(s) as necessary
- start procedures for handling the service request.

Outputs will be:

- updated details of Incidents
- the recognition of any errors on the CMDB
- notice to Customers when an Incident has been resolved.

All Incidents should be recorded: automatic generation of 'skeleton Incident records' in an Incident database by a system-monitoring tool is the ideal solution to this requirement. Symptoms, basic diagnostic data, and information about the related Configuration Item should be included in Incident records during detection and recording. Annex 5C illustrates the scope of data to be captured in records during the entire Incident Management process. This data is required both for Incident resolution/recovery and for management information on Incident types and trends.

In the past, it has been common practice for all Incidents to be reported to the Service Desk, where personnel manually created a record in the Incident database. Where this was not practical or possible support groups have been allowed to record Incidents manually; in this case the Service Desk received alerts so that they were informed about possible degradation of services. With modern technology, however, Incidents can nowadays be reported by various means, including the ability for Users to log Incidents directly to the system. But the fundamental requirement remains that these Incidents should still all reach the Incident Management database and that the Service Desk should receive appropriate alerts and maintain overall control – Incident monitoring remains the responsibility of the Service Desk.

An alert to the Service Manager is required in the case of serious degradation of service levels, in case it is necessary to take special action.

An Incident should be handled in conformance with standard SLM procedures. These specific procedures do not fall within the scope of the Incident Management process.

5.6.2   Classification and initial support

Inputs:

- recorded Incident details
- configuration details from the CMDB
- response from Incident matching against Problems and Known Errors.

Incident records raised in the previous activity are now analysed to discover the reason for the Incident. The Incident should also be classified, the process on which further resolution actions are based. Annex 5A provides some examples of classification codes.

Actions:

- classifying Incidents
- matching against Known Errors and Problems
- informing Problem Management of the existence of new Problems and of unmatched or multiple Incidents
- assigning impact and urgency, and thereby defining priority
- assessing related configuration details
- providing initial support (assess Incident details, find quick resolution)
- closing the Incident or routing to a specialist support group, and informing the User(s).

Outputs:

- RFC for Incident resolution
- updated Incident details, and
- Work-arounds for Incidents, or Incident routed to second- or third-line support.

Classification is the process of identifying the reason for the Incident and hence the corresponding resolution action. Many Incidents are regularly experienced and the appropriate resolution actions are well known. This is not always the case, however, and a procedure for matching Incident classification data against that for Problems and Known Errors is necessary. Successful matching gives access to proven resolution actions, which should require no further investigation effort.

Classification is one of the most important aspects of Incident Management (and often one of the most difficult to get right). The classification is used to:

- specify the service with which the Incident is related
- associate with an SLA where appropriate
- select/define the best specialist or group to handle the Incident
- identify the priority based upon the business impact
- define what questions should be asked or information checked
- determine a primary reporting matrix for management information
- identify a relationship to match against Known Errors or solutions.

The final classification(s) may vary from the initially reported classification because end Users are only able to report symptoms of the Incident rather than the root Problem. The levels of classification will vary depending on the detail required. For example, a top-level classification of 'Word Processing', or 'Payroll Service' is adequate for an overview; however, it may then be necessary to obtain greater detail in areas such as:

- version number (of application in use)
- supplier
- module (e.g. printing), or
- grouping (e.g. business application).

As much information as possible should be provided when classifying Incidents. Classification data contributing to the matching process includes:

- details of Incident symptoms
- initial Incident categorisation
- details of associated Configuration Items (CIs)
- the business impact.

The process of classification and matching allows Incident Management to be carried out with more speed and minimum recourse to support. The classification-matching process is an ideal application area for the use of so-called expert software.

The Service Desk collects information about affected CIs and therefore should be able to detect inconsistencies in the CMDB when asking a User for configuration id numbers, serial numbers and so on. If inconsistencies are discovered, an exception report should be raised and the Configuration Management process informed. This can take place automatically via the Incident Management software or by reporting on a daily basis.

One of the important aspects of managing an Incident is to define its priority: how important is it and what is the impact on the business. The responsibility for definition lies with Service Level Management within the parameters sets in the SLA. The priority with which Incidents need to be resolved, and therefore the amount of effort put into the resolution of and recovery from Incidents, will depend upon:

- the impact on the business
- the urgency to the business
- the size, scope and complexity of the Incident
- the resources availability for coping in the meantime and for correcting the fault.

'Impact' is a measure of the *business criticality* of an Incident or Problem, often equal to the extent to which an Incident leads to degradation of agreed service levels. Impact is often measured by the number of people or systems affected. Criteria for assigning impact should be set up in consultation with the business managers and formalised in SLAs.

When determining impact, information in the CMDB should be accessed to detect how many Users will suffer as a result of the technical failure of, for example, a hardware component. The Service Desk should have access to tools that enable it rapidly to:

- assess the impact on Users of significant equipment failures
- identify Users affected by equipment failure
- establish contact to make them aware of the Problem
- give a prognosis
- alert second-line (specialist) support groups.

'Urgency' is about the necessary *speed* of solving an Incident of a certain impact. A high-impact Incident does not, by default, have to be solved immediately. For example a User having operational difficulties with his workstation (impact 'high') can have the fault registered with urgency 'low' if he is leaving the office for a fortnight's holiday directly after reporting the Incident.

'Priority' is defined by *expected effort*. An Incident with a low impact and average urgency that can be resolved with minor effort will be resolved immediately in most organisations (e.g. a password reset).

Initial support involves resolution of the Incident to the satisfaction of the Customer by the Service Desk. The resolution may be derived from several areas, including:

- identification of a Known Error
- Service Desk staff expertise
- a knowledge search (with the help of expert software when possible).

After this, little further action is required by the Service Desk other than recording details of the resolution, the classification and Customer satisfaction.

Tip:

- The number of requests resolved directly by the Service Desk is an essential service-monitoring component and leads to contented Users!

In the event that classification matching is unsuccessful, or the resolution process is complex, investigation and diagnosis by a support group is the next step.

Although responsibility for resolution is handed over to another support group, the Service Desk should retain ownership of the Incident, and manage it until it is resolved to the Customer's satisfaction.

5.6.3   Investigation and diagnosis

Inputs:

- updated Incident details
- configuration details from the CMDB.

Actions:

- assessment of the Incident details,
- collection and analysis of all related information, and resolution
- (including any Work-around) or a route to n-line support.

Outputs:

- Incident details yet further updated, and a specification of the selection or required Work-around.

Wherever possible, the relevant User should be provided with the means to continue business, perhaps via a degraded service. An example could be that faulty printers might necessitate printing taking place at another more distant location. The effect of such a Work-around is to minimise the impact of the Incident on the business and to provide more time to investigate and devise a structural resolution. Temporary Work-arounds may have to be advised to other Users too.

Once the Incident has been assigned to a support group, it should:

- accept assignment of the Incident, specify the date and time (preferably automatically), ensuring:
  - the Incident status and its history are regularly updated
  - the Customer via the Service Desk is kept informed of progress towards resolution
  - the current status of the Incident is reflected (e.g. work in progress, and so on)
- advise the Service Desk/Customer of any identified Work-around, if it is possible to provide one immediately
- review the Incident against Known Errors, Problem, solutions, planned Changes or knowledge bases
- if necessary, ask the Service Desk to re-evaluate the assigned business impact and priority, adjusting them as required, based on agreed service levels
- record all details applicable to this phase of the Incident life cycle:
  - solution
  - classification added/updated
  - a update of all related Incidents
  - time spent
- reassign the Incident back to the Service Desk for closure action.

Investigation and diagnosis may become an iterative process, starting with a different specialist support group and following elimination of a previous possible cause. It may involve multisite support groups and support staff from different vendors. It may continue overnight with a new shift of support staff taking over the next day. All this demands a rigorous, disciplined approach and a comprehensive record of actions taken with corresponding results.

Tip:

If it is not clear which support group should investigate or resolve a User-related Incident, the Service Desk, as the owner of all Incidents, should coordinate the Incident Management process. If there are differences of opinion or there are any other issues arising, then the Service Desk should escalate the Incident to the Problem Management team.

Annex 5D shows a typical process of Incident investigation. Continual expansion of the Incident record should occur, with each progress point logging the action taken in a progress summary.

5.6.4 Resolution and recovery

Inputs:

- updated Incident details
- any response on an RFC to effect resolution for the Incident(s)
- any derived Work-around or solution.

Actions:

- ■ resolve the Incident using the solution/Work-around or, alternatively, to raise an RFC (including a check for resolution)
- ■ take recovery actions.

Outputs:

- ■ RFC for future Incident resolution
- ■ resolved Incident, including recovery details,
- ■ updated Incident details.

After successful execution of the resolution or some circumvention activity, service recovery can be effected and recovery actions carried out, often by specialist staff (second- or third-level support). The Incident Management system should allow for the recording of events and actions during the resolution and recovery activity.

5.6.5 Incident closure

Inputs:

- ■ updated Incident details,
- ■ resolved Incident.

Actions:

- ■ the confirmation of the resolution with the Customer or originator
- ■ 'close' category
- ■ Incident.

Outputs:

- ■ updated Incident detail,
- ■ closed Incident record.

When the Incident has been resolved, the Service Desk should ensure that:

- ■ details of the action taken to resolve the Incident are concise and readable
- ■ classification is complete and accurate according to root cause
- ■ resolution/action is agreed with the Customer – verbally or, preferably, by email or in writing
- ■ all details applicable to this phase of the Incident control are recorded, such that:
  - – the Customer is satisfied
  - – cost-centre project codes are allocated
  - – the time spent on the Incident is recorded
  - – the person, date and time of closure are recorded.

Tips:

- ■ This process is essential in resolving disputes between a service provider and a Customer over the validity of closure.
- ■ It is important that there should be **restricted** access to the Incident closure routine, and this should be controlled by the Service Desk Manager.
- ■ Incidents should be matched with the corresponding Problem/Known Error record, where one exists.

- If a closed Incident is reopened, it is important to record the reason and adjust the workload values assigned if further work is required – if not, a new Incident should be raised and linked to the original one.

5.6.6 Ownership, monitoring, tracking and communication

Inputs:

- Incident records.

Actions:

- monitor Incidents
- escalate Incidents
- inform User.

Outputs:

- management reports about Incident progress
- escalated Incident details; and
- Customer reports and communication.

The Service Desk is responsible for owning and overseeing the resolution of *all* outstanding Incidents, whatever the initial source, by the following procedure to:

- regularly monitor the status and progress towards resolution and against service levels of all open Incidents
- particularly note Incidents that move between different specialist support groups, as this may be indicative of uncertainty and, possibly, a dispute between support staff (in excessive cases, Incidents may be referred to Problem Management)
- give priority to monitoring high-impact Incidents
- keep affected Users informed of progress
- check for similar Incidents.

Following this procedure will help to guarantee that each individual Incident will be resolved within agreed timeframes or, at least, as soon as possible. Larger Service Desks should consider the establishment of a dedicated team for Incident monitoring and tracking.

In the event that an Incident fails to achieve satisfactory progress, the Service Desk should act in accordance with well-defined escalation procedures. These procedures should be agreed on by all support groups. In practice, it is important to be aware of support staff becoming too engrossed in an Incident, spending much time on diagnostics gathering, and consequently losing sight of the immediate User need; in all circumstances, when agreed escalation thresholds have been exceeded (which are defined in SLAs), action should be taken to escalate the matter regardless of the views of support staff.

Tips:

- Identify Incidents that are liable to breach agreed service level targets and inform the assigned solver.
- Make individuals who are identified as escalation contacts aware of any Incidents that are likely to breach service levels.
- Record in the Incident history any information regarding escalation of an Incident at the Customer end, and bring this to the attention of the escalation contacts.

- Agree on escalation values and processes such as:
  - when 75% of the agreed time for resolution has elapsed and the request is still unresolved, the Service Desk should consult with the assigned solver on progress
  - when 90% of such time has elapsed and the request is still unresolved, the Service Desk should consult with the line manager of the assigned solver.

5.7 Handling of major Incidents

Major Incidents are those for which the degree of impact on the User community is extreme. Incidents for which the timescale of disruption – to even a relatively small percentage of Users – becomes excessive should also be regarded as major.

The Problem Manager should in these circumstances be notified (if not already aware) and should arrange a formal meeting with interested parties (or regular meetings if necessary). These should be attended by all key in-house support staff, vendor support staff and IT services management, with the purpose of reviewing review progress and determining the best course of action. The Service Desk representative should attend these meetings and ensure a record of actions/decisions is maintained, ideally as part of the overall Incident record.

5.8 Roles of the Incident Management process

Processes span the organisation's hierarchy. Therefore it is important to define the responsibilities associated with the activities that have to be performed in the process. To remain flexible, it is advisable to use the concept of roles; in many organisations roles may be combined because of the small size of the organisation or because of cost. For example, many organisations combine the roles of Change Management and Configuration Management. A role embraces a set of responsibilities, tasks and levels of authorisation.

5.8.1 Incident Manager

An Incident Manager has the responsibility for:
- driving the efficiency and effectiveness of the Incident Management process
- producing management information
- managing the work of Incident support staff (first-and second-line)
- monitoring the effectiveness of Incident Management and making recommendations for improvement
- developing and maintaining the Incident Management systems.

In many organisations, the role of Incident Manager is assigned to the (function) Service Desk Supervisor.

5.8.2 Incident-handling support staff

First-line support (Service Desk) responsibilities include:
- Incident registration
- routing service requests to support groups when Incidents are not closed
- initial support and classification

- ownership, monitoring, tracking and communication
- resolution and recovery of Incidents not assigned to second-line support
- closure of Incidents.

Second-line support (specialist groups that may be part of the Service Desk) will be involved in tasks such as:

- handling service requests
- monitoring Incident details, including the Configuration Items affected
- Incident investigation and diagnosis (including resolution where possible)
- detection of possible Problems and the assignment of them to the Problem Management team for them to raise Problem records
- the resolution and recovery of assigned Incidents.

Ownership, monitoring, tracking and communication tasks cover:

- monitoring the status and progress towards resolution of all open Incidents
- keeping affected Users informed about progress
- escalating the process if necessary.

5.9   Key Performance Indicators

To judge process performance, clearly defined objectives with measurable targets – often referred to as Key Performance Indicators (KPIs) – should be set. The following metrics are examples for the effectiveness and efficiency of the Incident Management process:

- total numbers of Incidents
- mean elapsed time to achieve Incident resolution or circumvention, broken down by impact code
- percentage of Incidents handled within agreed response time (Incident response-time targets may be specified in SLAs, for example, by impact code)
- average cost per Incident
- percentage of Incidents closed by the Service Desk without reference to other levels of support
- Incidents processed per Service Desk workstation
- number and percentage of Incidents resolved remotely, without the need for a visit.

Reports should be produced under the authority of the Incident Manager, who should draw up a schedule and distribution list, in collaboration with the Service Desk and support groups handling Incidents. Distribution lists should at least include IT services management and specialist support groups. Consider also making the data available to Users and Customers, for example via SLA reports.

5.10   Tools

Tool requirements specific to the Incident Management process are thus:

- automatic Incident logging and alerting in the event of fault detection on mainframes, networks, servers and so on (possibly through an interface to system management tools) all modifications to the Incident record being registered in order to keep control

■ automatic escalation facilities so as to facilitate the timely handling of Incidents and service requests

■ highly flexible routing of Incidents as a basic requirement, because control staff may be located in multiple sites or they may be co-located in an operations bridge, and such a physical distribution may vary depending on the time of day

■ automatic extraction of data records from the CMDB of a failed item and affected items

■ specialised software: speed and effectiveness are major objectives of handling Incidents, and because achievement depends upon a very accurate level of Incident classification and successful matching at the point of alert, it is the classification-matching process that is an ideal application area for the use of software

■ ACD (telephone) systems integration for automatically registering names and phone numbers of Users

■ the presence of diagnostic tools/modules (i.e. Case-Based Reasoning) can help the diagnostic process.

Annex 5A: Example coding system for Incident/request classification

Type of Incident	Main Category	Sub-category	Indication Priority
Failure	Software	Wordprocessing	2
		Spreadsheet	2
		Business application	1
	Hardware	Mainframe	1
		Midrange	1
		Workstation	2
	Etc...		
Service request	Password reset		1
	Change toner cartridge		3
	Help User	Office software	3
		Business application	2
	Etc...		

Note: 'Priority' order to handle Incidents is primarily defined by impact and urgency. Depending on the type of call, an indication of impact and urgency (and thus priority) can be given in advance. Thus priority is often based on experience or agreements/expectations with the Customer.

Linking an 'indication priority' to a 'type of Incident' also speeds up the classification process and helps the Service Desk staff to be consistent in assigning priorities.

Annex 5B: Example of a priority coding system

		Impact		
		High	*Medium*	*Low*
	High	1	2	3
Urgency	Medium	2	3	4
	Low	3	4	5

Priority code	*Description*	*Target resolution time*
1	Critical	1 hour
2	High	8 hours
3	Medium	24 hours
4	Low	48 hours
5	Planning	Planned

Note: A third aspect defining priority, namely expected effort, is not incorporated in this model.

Annex 5C: Data requirements for service Incident records

The following data should be recorded during the Incident life-cycle:

- unique reference number
- Incident classification
- date/time recorded
- name/id of the person and/or group recording the Incident
- name/department/phone/location of User calling
- call-back method (telephone, mail etc.)
- description of symptoms
- category (often a main category and a subcategory)
- impact/urgency/priority
- Incident status (active, waiting, closed etc.)
- related Configuration Item
- support group/person to which the Incident is allocated
- related Problem/Known Error
- resolution date and time
- closure category
- closure date and time.

To have control during the complete Incident life-cycle, for every action is recorded:

- name/id of the support group or person recording the action
- type of action (routing, diagnose, recovery, resolving, closing etc.)
- date/time of action
- description and outcome of action.

Annex 5D: The process of Incident investigation

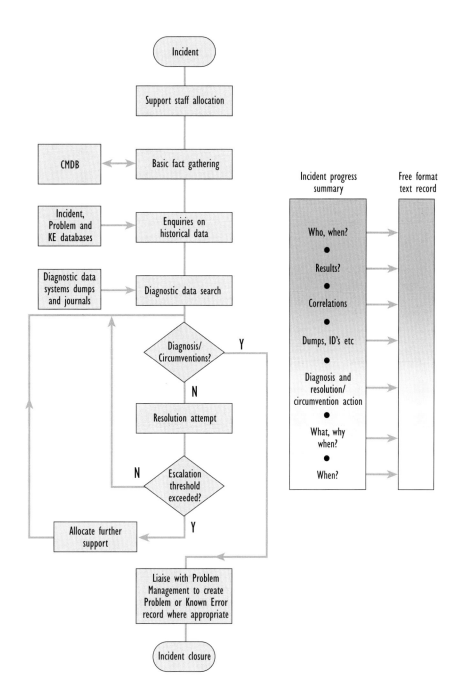

Annex 5E: Incident handling on the Service Desk (flow)

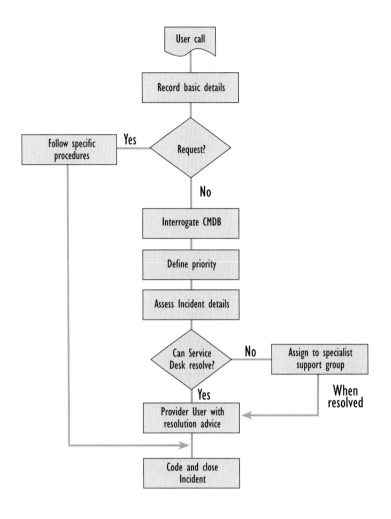

6 PROBLEM MANAGEMENT

6.1 Goal of Problem Management

The goal of Problem Management is to minimise the adverse impact of Incidents and Problems on the business that are caused by errors within the IT Infrastructure, and to prevent recurrence of Incidents related to these errors. In order to achieve this goal, Problem Management seeks to get to the root cause of Incidents and then initiate actions to improve or correct the situation.

The Problem Management process has both reactive and proactive aspects. The reactive aspect is concerned with solving Problems in response to one or more Incidents. Proactive Problem Management is concerned with identifying and solving Problems and Known Errors before Incidents occur in the first place.

6.2 Scope of Problem Management

Problem control, error control and proactive Problem Management are all within the scope of the Problem Management process. In terms of formal definitions, a 'Problem' is an unknown underlying cause of one or more Incidents, and a 'Known Error' is a Problem that is successfully diagnosed and for which a Work-around has been identified.

Inputs to the Problem Management process are:

- Incident details from Incident Management
- configuration details from the Configuration Management Database (CMDB)
- any defined Work-arounds (from Incident Management).

The major activities of Problem Management are:

- Problem control
- error control
- the proactive prevention of Problems
- identifying trends
- obtaining management information from Problem Management data
- the completion of major Problem reviews.

Outputs of the process are:

- Known Errors
- a Request for Change (RFC)
- an updated Problem record (including a solution and/or any available Work-arounds)
- for a resolved Problem, a closed Problem record
- response from Incident matching to Problems and Known Errors
- management information.

6.3 Basic concepts

The availability of relevant and easily applied advice in the early stages of an Incident is central to an organisation's ability to resolve Incidents effectively; very few Incidents that are received at the Service Desk are new or mysterious to the support staff. Similarly, specialists within second-line or third-line support staff will have already resolved many difficult and 'original' Incidents and Problems. The best use of the resources expended on these resolutions is to document them in such a way that frontline staff can apply them.

The Problem Management process is intended to reduce both the number and severity of Incidents and Problems on the business. Therefore, part of Problem Management's responsibility is to ensure that previous information is documented in such a way that it is readily available to first-line and other second-line staff. This is not simply a matter of producing documentation. What is required includes:

- the information to be indexed so that it is easily referenced by simple and detectable triggers from new Incidents
- regular inspection to ensure the continued relevance of documentation in the light of changing
  - technology
  - available external solutions
  - business practices and requirements
  - in-house skills
  - frequency and impact of recurring Incidents
  - interpretation of internal best practice
- that the process should be subject to a detailed review
- staff using the information to be trained to understand the depth and power of the information available, how to access and interpret it, and their role in providing feedback on its relevance and ease of use
- a suitable repository for the information – typically based on an integrated Service Management tool which can capture it at logging or first-analysis stage of the Incident handling process.

It is common to make use of 'expert system' software to facilitate the Problem Management process. However, it is important that it includes expert knowledge, updated with feedback from those staff who use the system.

Problems and Known Errors can be identified by:
- analysing Incidents as they occur (reactive Problem Management)
- analysing Incidents over differing time periods (proactive Problem Management)
- analysing the IT Infrastructure
- the provision of a knowledge database
- developers/vendors when new products are introduced.

A Problem is a condition often identified as a result of multiple Incidents that exhibit common symptoms. Problems can also be identified from a single significant Incident, indicative of a single error, for which the cause is unknown, but for which the impact is significant.

A Known Error is a condition identified by successful diagnosis of the root cause of a Problem, and the subsequent development of a Work-around.

Structural analysis of the IT infrastructure, reports generated from support software, and User-group meetings can also result in the identification of Problems and Known Errors. This is proactive Problem Management.

Problem control focuses on transforming Problems into Known Errors. Error control focuses on resolving Known Errors structurally through the Change Management process.

6.3.1 What is the difference between Incident Management and Problem Management?

Problem Management differs from Incident Management in that its main goal is the detection of the underlying causes of an Incident and their subsequent resolution and prevention. In many situations this goal can be in direct conflict with the goals of Incident Management where the aim is to restore the service to the Customer as quickly as possible, often through a Work-around, rather than through the determination of a permanent resolution (for example, by searching for structural improvements in the IT infrastructure, in order to prevent as many future Incidents as possible). In this respect, therefore, the speed with which a resolution is found is only of secondary (albeit still of significant) importance. Investigation of the underlying Problem can require some time and can thus delay the restoration of service, causing downtime but preventing recurrence.

6.3.2 Problem control

The Problem control process is concerned with handling Problems in an efficient and effective way. The aim of Problem control is to identify the root cause, such as the CIs that are at fault, and to provide the Service Desk with information and advice on Work-arounds when available.

The process of Problem control is very similar to, and highly dependent on, the quality of the Incident control process. Incident control focuses on resolving Incidents and on providing Work-arounds and temporary fixes for specific Incidents. If a Problem is identified for an Incident or a group of Incidents, available Work-arounds and temporary fixes are recorded in the Problem record by the Problem control process. Problem control also advises on the best Work-around available for the Problem.

Because Problem control is concerned with preventing the recurrence of Incidents, the process should be subject to an approach that is carefully managed and planned. The degree of management and planning required is greater than that needed for Incident control, where the objective is restoration of normal service as quickly as possible. Priority should be given to the resolution of Problems that can cause serious business disruption.

Activities recognised in Problem control are:
- Problem identification and recording
- Problem classification
- Problem investigation and diagnosis.

6.3.3 Error control

Error control covers the processes involved in progressing Known Errors until they are eliminated by the successful implementation of a Change under the control of the Change Management process. The objective of error control is to be aware of errors, to monitor them and to eliminate them when feasible and cost-justifiable.

Error control bridges the development (including applications development, enhancement and maintenance) and live environments. Software errors introduced during the development phase can affect live operations; therefore, Known Errors identified in the development or maintenance environment should be handed over to the live environment.

Activities recognised in error control are:

- error identification and recording
- error assessment
- recording error resolution (investigation of solution, the raising of an RFC)
- error closure
- monitoring Problem and error resolution progress.

In practice, each of these processes of Problem Management requires careful management and control. Different operational objectives apply during each of these control processes.

6.3.4 Proactive Problem Management

Proactive Problem Management covers the activities aimed at identifying and resolving Problems before Incidents occur. These activities are:

- trend analysis
- targeting support action
- providing information to the organisation.

By redirecting the efforts of an organisation from reacting to large numbers of Incidents to preventing Incidents, an organisation provides a better service to its Customers and makes more effect use of the available resources within the IT support organisation.

6.3.5 Completion of major Problem reviews

Feedback from these reviews is a major contributor to the continual process of improvement.

6.4 Benefits of Problem Management

The benefits of taking a formal approach to Problem Management include the following:

- *Improved IT service quality.* Problem Management helps generate a cycle of rapidly increasing IT service quality. High-quality reliable service is good for the business users of IT, and good for the productivity and morale of the IT service providers.
- *Incident volume reduction.* Problem Management is instrumental in reducing the number of Incidents that interrupt the conduct of business.
- *Permanent solutions.* There will be a gradual reduction in the number and impact of Problems and Known Errors as those that *are* resolved *stay* resolved.
- *Improved organisational learning.* The Problem Management process is based on the concept of learning from past experience. The process provides the historical data to identify trends, and the means of preventing failures and of reducing the impact of failures, resulting in improved User productivity.

■ *Better first-time fix rate at the Service Desk.* Problem Management enables a better first time fix rate of Incidents at the Service Desk, achieved via the capture, retention and availability of Incident resolution and Work-around data within a knowledge database available to the Service Desk at call logging.

In contrast, the costs of not implementing a Problem Management process may include:

■ a purely reactive support organisation, facing up to Problems only when the service to Customers has already been disrupted

■ an IT User organisation, confronted with recurring Incidents, losing faith in the quality of the IT support organisation

■ an ineffective support organisation, with high costs and low employee motivation, since similar Incidents have to be resolved repeatedly and structural solutions are not provided.

6.5 Planning and implementation

6.5.1 Timing and planning

Timing and planning are important because:

■ Good Problem Management relies to a great extent on an implemented and efficient Incident Management process. So it is sensible to implement Problem Management either in parallel with, or after Incident Management processes.

■ If resources are scarce, it is advisable to concentrate in the first instance on the implementation of Problem and error control (reactive Problem Management). When these activities reach maturity, resources can be directed to proactive Problem Management. The quality of proactive Problem Management depends largely on successful implementation of service monitoring activities and the base data thereby captured.

■ Smaller organisations can introduce reactive Problem Management by focusing daily on the 'top ten' Incidents of the previous day. This can prove to be effective, since experience shows that 20% of Problems cause 80% of service degradation!

6.5.2 Key success factors

Points to consider include:

■ An effective automated registration of Incidents, with an effective classification, is fundamental for the success of Problem Management.

■ Setting achievable objectives and making use of the Problem-solving talents of existing staff is a key activity. Consider 'part-time' Problem Management, whereby staff set aside periods when they will look at Problems away from the daily fire-fighting pressures.

■ In view of the potentially conflicting interests between Incident Management and Problem Management (paragraph 6.3.1), good cooperation between both processes is essential. Both also have enormous synergy, which can help. Support staff, often involved in both processes, should be aware of the importance of balancing activities between the two.

6.5.3 Risks

The benefits of Problem Management can be weakened by:

- Absence of a good Incident control process, and thus the absence of detailed historical data on Incidents (necessary for the correct identification of Problems).

- Failure to link Incident records with Problem/error records, means a failure to gain many of the potential benefits. This is a key feature in moving from reactive support to a more planned and proactive support approach.

- Lack of management commitment, so that support staff (usually also involved with reactive Incident control activities) cannot allocate sufficient time to structural Problem-solving activities.

- The undermining of the Service Desk role. Problem Management staff should accept support requests only from authorised sources. Difficulties will arise if the process deals with requests from many sources since multiple reports of Incidents with the same cause may not be interpreted in the same way.

- Failure to set aside time to build and maintain the knowledge base will restrict the delivery of benefits.

- An inability to determine accurately the business impact of Incidents and Problems. Consequently the business-critical Incidents and Problems are not given the correct priority.

6.6 Problem control activities

The occurrence of some Incidents is, for all practical purposes, unavoidable. Computer equipment and telecommunications lines fail occasionally. Many other Incidents are caused, not by random failures, but by errors somewhere in organisations' increasingly complex IT infrastructures. Even *anticipated* failures of computing or telecommunications equipment can increase in impact to unacceptable levels because of an error in a vendor product.

Reactive Problem control (Figure 6.1) is concerned with identifying the real underlying causes of Incidents in order to prevent future recurrences. The three phases involved in the (reactive) Problem control process are:

- Problem identification and recording
- Problem classification – in terms of the impact on the business
- Problem investigation and diagnosis.

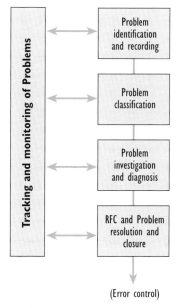

Figure 6.1 - Problem control

When the root cause is detected the error control process begins.

6.6.1   Problem identification and recording

Problem identification takes place when:

- matching the process to existing Problems and Known Errors is not successful during the stage of Incident initial support and classification

- analysis of Incident data reveals recurrent Incidents

- analysis of Incident data reveals Incidents that are not yet matched to existing Problems or Known Errors

- analysis of the IT infrastructure indicates a Problem that could potentially lead to Incidents

- a major or significant Incident (serious and adverse impact on services to the Customer) occurs for which a structural solution has to be found.

It should be noted that some Problems may be identified by personnel outside the Problem Management team, e.g. by Capacity Management. Regardless, all Problems should be notified and recorded via the Problem Management process. Much of the Availability Management process is concerned with the detection and avoidance of Problems and Incidents to the IT infrastructure; a synergy between the two areas is thus an invaluable aid to improving service quality.

Tips:

- Problem Management requires effort and resources and therefore can be expensive. The organisation may decide that the efforts and costs are not justifiable in certain types of unmatched Incidents – perhaps for Incidents with a quick resolution, low impact or low possibility of recurrence. In such cases, a dummy Problem record can be introduced in the CMDB, related to all connected Incidents, Known Errors, RFCs and CIs.

Problem records need to be recorded in a database (ideally the CMDB) and are very similar to Incident records. They usually exclude some of the standard Incident data (e.g. User data) that is inappropriate. However, Problem records should be linked to all associated Incident records. The solution and Work-arounds of Incidents should be recorded in the relevant Problem records for others to access should other related Incidents occur.

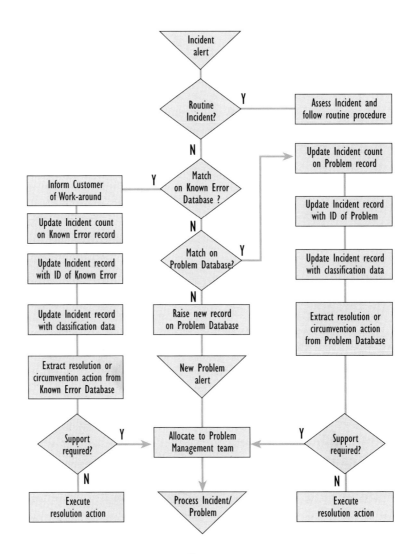

Figure 6.2 - Incident-matching process flow

The process of Problem identification, illustrated in Figure 6.2 includes the basic classification of Problems. Data on affected CIs should be accurately appended to this basic classification data. Ideally, these CIs are the lowest level of item capable of discrete amendment – for example, a module of applications code or hardware component. Identification of a Problem CI to this level is, however, often impossible at the Problem identification stage.

6.6.2 Problem classification

When a Problem is identified, the amount of effort required to detect and recover the failing CI(s) has to be determined. Therefore it is important to be aware of the impact of the Problem on existing service levels. This process is known as 'classification'. In practice, support effort is allocated to only a small proportion of Problems linked to a single Incident.

The steps involved in Problem classification are similar to the steps in classifying Incidents; they are to determine:

- category
- impact
- urgency
- priority.

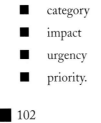

Problems are categorised into related groups or domains (e.g. hardware, software, support software, whatever is appropriate). These groups could match the organisational responsibilities, or the User and Customer base, and are the basis for allocating Problems to support staff. Annex 6A gives an example of a simple but effective structure for categorising Problems.

Identification of a new Problem should be followed by an objective analysis of its impact (that is, its effect on the business). The relationships between components in the IT Infrastructure registered in the CMDB can be of great help when determining the impact of a Problem.

Organisations should design their own impact coding system in relation to their business needs. Impact coding is a most useful mechanism for the effective allocation of support effort. The further inclusion of a simple priority rating, subordinate to impact, provides a total control mechanism.

When determining the impact of a Problem, the relations between components in the IT infrastructure registered in the CMDB can be of great help. By interrogating the CMDB, it is possible to identify CIs that are dependent on part of, or identical to, the CI in the IT infrastructure to which the Incident is applied.

Urgency is the extent to which resolution of a Problem or error can bear delay; it should not be confused with priority. Priority indicates the relative order in which a series of items – be they Incidents, Problems, Changes or errors – should be addressed. This will be influenced by considerations of risk and resource availability but is primarily driven by a combination of urgency and impact. Despite a low business impact, something that requires urgent resolution will often be dealt with before something of very high potential business impact but that has lower urgency. It sometimes helps to allocate numerical values to each, in order to derive from them a numerical priority; but, as with all Service Management, such numbers should be modified by human common sense and business awareness. However, a useful and simple starting point is to assign numerical values from 1 to 4 to each of urgency and impact and sum these for any one Problem to give a relative priority. That done, an organisation should monitor and examine critically the resulting priorities and monitor the function to reflect their requirements. Both 'urgency' and 'priority' are listed in Appendix A (Glossary of Terms). Aspects influencing urgency are, for example:

- the availability of a temporary fix
- the existence of a Work-around
- the possibility of planned delay of resolution
- an awareness of future impact upon the business, e.g. equipment required to support month-end processes.

Every Incident, Problem and Change will have both an impact on the business services and an urgency:

- impact describes the *potential* to which the business stands vulnerable
- urgency illustrates the time that is available to avert, or at least reduce, this impact.

Tips:

- Assign an impact code to all Problems at the earliest opportunity. When this has been done, it is important to make all Problems subject to a managed staff-assignment process before detailed investigations begin. The person assigned assumes responsibility for the Problem and becomes the focal point for all communications and for coordinating resolution activity on that Problem. Schedule effort according to impact, with major Problems receiving immediate attention. Make certain this resource-control process allows for low-impact Problems that have exceeded their specified time threshold.

■ The process of impact analysis suffers from one major constraint: it reflects a snapshot view. Although a Problem may be correctly assigned a low impact code, the sheer number of subsequent Incidents later attributed to it may demand that the Problem receives immediate attention. Incident thresholds should be set to address this difficulty. As illustrated in Figure 6.2, the Problem Management process can be designed to maintain a count of matched Incidents in Problem (and Known Error) records. The Problem and error control systems periodically scan this count, comparing it with a predetermined threshold value. When the count equals or exceeds the threshold, such Problems/Known Errors should be escalated to receive immediate attention. However, beware that the number is not always equal to the importance: a Problem that prevents the posting of 0.5% of orders can be suddenly and rightly recognised as critical when you find you can't enter order values exceeding £999,999.99!

6.6.3 Problem investigation and diagnosis

The process of Problem investigation is similar to that of Incident investigation (see Chapter 5) - but the primary objective of each process is significantly different. Incident Management's aim is rapid restoration of service, whereas Problem Management's aim is diagnosis of the underlying cause. Investigation activities should include available Work-arounds for the Incidents related to the Problem, as registered in the Incident record database. Problem Management activities should include updating recommended Work-arounds in the Problem record, to support Incident control.

Diagnosis frequently reveals that the cause of a Problem is not an error in a registered CI (hardware, software item, documentation or procedure) but is procedural. Incorrect release of a version of a program is one example. These situations result in Problem closure with an appropriate categorisation code. Problems of this type do not automatically achieve the formal status of Known Error. To ensure that these Problems are followed up and that action is taken to address them, consider creating a dummy CI record for the offending procedure and re-classifying the Problem as a Known Error, or raise an RFC.

Diagnosis showing the cause to be a fault in a registered CI should automatically change the status of the Problem into a Known Error. At this point the error control system and procedures take over.

As indicated earlier, the objectives of Problem investigation frequently conflict with those of Incident resolution. For example, Problem investigation may require detailed diagnostics data, which is available only when an Incident has occurred; its capture may significantly delay the restoration of normal services. Be sure to liaise closely with Incident control and the computer operations or network control functions to get a balanced view of the right time for such actions.

Methods of Problem analysis

Literature provides many methods for structural Problem analysis and diagnosis. Some available methods are:

■ Kepner and Tregoe (see Annex 6B)
■ Ishikawa diagrams (see Annex 6C)
■ brainstorming sessions
■ flowchart methods.

Problem Management should select methods that best fit the organisation's purposes.

6.6.4 Tips on Problem control

The following are points worth remembering in relation to Problem control:

- The categorisation of Incidents can produce a first step towards Problem definition. Problem Management therefore should closely relate with Incident Management with regard to establishing common Incident and Problem categories. Appropriate categories should be created both for recording reported Incidents, which should be in 'Customer terms', and for recording the finally detected causes, more likely to be expressed in 'IT terms'.

- If possible, establish a multidisciplinary team with, for instance, Problem Management, as coordinator, in order to involve as many different perspectives as possible in the investigation.

- Ensure that support specialists involved have adequate tools and diagnostic aids in order to be able to carry out their tasks effectively.

- If a Problem does not involve an error in a system component but is caused by say, a general lack of User training, execute any resolution action and close the Problem record. Alternatively, a new CI record can be created – in this example for 'training Problems' – and the Problem can then be converted into a Known Error in the usual way. Ensure that the detected cause reflects the situation, e.g. lack of user knowledge, training.

- Investigation procedures during the Incident or Problem control process require that documentation on all products in the IT infrastructure is available to the process and to support staff for reference purposes. This includes documentation on the following:
  - application systems
  - systems software
  - in-house utility routines
  - networking hardware and software
  - overall configuration/network diagrams.

- In addition to product information, it is also necessary to have effective procedures to collect diagnostic data for Problem resolution. It is particularly important that support staff are familiar with these procedures, as any inappropriate use during an Incident can delay the resumption of normal IT services. So you also need procedures that support and enforce your process requirements – and those procedures might include adequate training, qualifications etc.

- Often, support specialists are involved in both the Incident Management process and the Problem Management process. Keeping in mind the different goals of these processes (quick resolution versus structural resolutions), it can prove useful to assign specialists to both processes for a fixed percentage of their time, perhaps 80% to Incident Management and 20% to Problem Management. This prevents support specialists becoming fully absorbed by reactive Incident Management.

- During Incident and Problem investigations, Problem Management staff also require accurate records of recent Changes, because these may provide pointers to the cause.

6.7 Error control activities

Error control covers the processes involved in successful correction of Known Errors. The objective is to change IT components to remove Known Errors affecting the IT infrastructure and thus to prevent any recurrence of Incidents.

Many IT departments are concerned with error control, and it spans both the live and development environments. It directly interfaces with, and operates alongside, Change Management processes. Figure 6.3 shows the three phases of the error control process. The monitoring and tracking phase covers the entire Problem/error life-cycle.

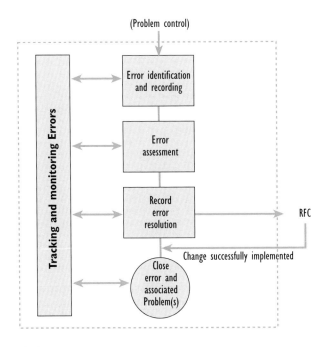

Figure 6.3 – Error control

6.7.1 Error identification and recording

An error is identified when a faulty CI (a CI that causes, or may be likely to cause, Incidents) is detected. A Known Error status is assigned when the root cause of a Problem is found and a Work-around has been identified.

There are two sources of Known Error data that feed the error control system. One is the Problem control subsystem in the live environment and the other its equivalent in the development environment. Errors found during live operations are identified and recorded as described in Problem control activity investigation and diagnosis. In this case, the Problem record forms the basis of the Known Error record (indeed, it really involves only a change of status).

The second source of Known Errors arises from development activity. For example, implementation of a new application or packaged Release is likely to include known, but unresolved, errors from the development phase. The data relating to Known Errors from development needs to be made available to the custodians of the live environment when an application or a Release package is implemented.

Many IT departments are involved in this sequence of events. The Problem Management system should provide a record of all resolution activity and provide monitoring and tracking facilities for support staff. It should also provide a complete audit trail navigable in either direction, from Incident to Problem to Known Error to Change request to Release or urgent Change implementation.

6.7.2   Error assessment

Problem Management staff perform an initial assessment of the means of resolving the error, in collaboration with specialist staff. If necessary, they then complete an RFC according to Change Management procedures. The priority of the RFC is determined by the urgency and impact of the error on the business. The RFC identifier should be included in the Known Error record and vice versa in order to maintain a full audit trail, or the two records should be linked.

The final stages of error resolution – impact analysis, detailed assessment of the resolution action to be carried out, amendment of the item in error, and testing of the Change – are under the control of Change Management. In extreme circumstances, authorisation and execution of an urgent resolution may be necessary.

Errors in third party products

Problems in vendor-maintained products may be identified by Problem Management or specialist support teams and should be reported to the person responsible for vendor support. Vendor support should be monitored to ensure that responses to Problem reports are received in a reasonable time.

Where software maintenance targets – e.g. mean and maximum time to repair and associated IT infrastructure reliability and serviceability – are specified in a contract or in licence conditions, remedial action should be initiated with the third party organisation in cases of non-compliance. The possibility of specifying maintenance targets should be borne in mind when procuring software, particularly when there is competition for the business. Note that Changes necessary to resolve software errors should be subject to the same Change Management procedures as for internal products.

Error control in the software environments

The processes of Problem and error control are essentially the same in the live and development environments. The support tools described earlier for Problem Management in the live environment are precisely those required in the development environment. Figure 6.4 shows how there is a cyclical relationship between error control in the live and development environments. Interworking and integrated Problem Management systems facilitate the handling of this situation.

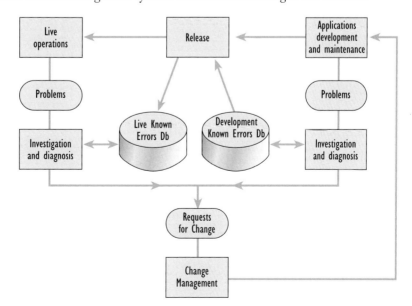

Figures 6.4 – The error cycle in the live and development environments

Errors found during live operations result in an accumulation of RFCs. The Release strategy (see Chapter 9 – Release Management) allows for the eventual creation of a Release to incorporate authorised Changes for the amendment of system facilities. Development staff should be aware of all Known Errors and Problems that are associated with the package Release. They are required to delete Known Errors as they are corrected, but they add any newly introduced errors from the development activity itself, to a revised errors database (or CMDB).

Upon implementation of a new Release, this revised errors database replaces the database of the previous Release as the live version. The cycle then repeats itself as new errors are discovered in live operation.

6.7.3 Error resolution recording

The resolution process for each Known Error should be recorded in the Problem Management system. It is vital that data on the CIs, symptoms, and resolution or circumvention actions relating to all Known Errors is held in the Known Error database. This data is then available for Incident matching, providing guidance during future investigations on resolving and circumventing Incidents, and for providing management information.

6.7.4 Error closure

Following successful implementation of Changes to resolve errors, the relevant Known Error record(s) is closed, together with any associated Incident or Problem records. Consideration should be given to inserting into the process an interim status, on the Incident, Known Error and Problem records, of 'Closed pending PIR' to ensure that the fixes have actually worked. A Post-Implementation Review (PIR) can then confirm the effectiveness of the solution prior to final closure.

For Incidents, this may involve nothing more than a telephone call to the user to ensure that they are now content. For more serious Problems and Known Errors, a formal review may be required.

6.7.5 Problem/error resolution monitoring

Change Management is responsible for processing RFCs, whereas error control is responsible for monitoring progress with regard to resolving Known Errors. Throughout the resolution process, Problem Management should obtain regular reports from Change Management on progress in resolving Problems and errors.

Problem Management should monitor the continuing impact of Problems and Known Errors on User services. In the event that this impact becomes severe, Problem Management should escalate the Problem, perhaps referring to the Change Advisory Board to increase the priority of the RFC or to implement an urgent Change as appropriate.

The progress of Problem resolution should be monitored against SLAs. Typically, SLAs stipulate that there should not be more than a certain number of outstanding errors per severity level during each measurement interval (generally a rolling four-week period). If the number of Problems or errors at a severity level reaches a predefined threshold that looks likely to cause non-conformance to the SLAs, escalation should be invoked.

6.7.6 Tips on error control

The following are points worth remembering in relation to error control:

- Not all Known Errors need to be resolved. An organisation can decide to allow Known Errors to remain – for instance because the resolution is too expensive, technically impossible, or requires too much time to resolve. In practice, error control is concerned with selecting justifiable investments to resolve a Problem.

- Preparing an RFC is one of the responsibilities of error control. Resolutions are often found in technical adjustments. Don't forget that these RFCs may also need to include amendments to procedures, working methods and/or organisational structures.

- Consider creating standard error records, by specific device (CI) or by device category, for routine hardware failures. Use these to maintain a quick guide to the failure rate – although most information, such as mean time between failures (MTBF) and downtime, is produced from Incident data.

- The rectification of many hardware faults is carried out under Incident control, and not via error control and Change Management. Any Changes to the specification of hardware should, however, be subject to the normal Change Management procedures.

- Ideally, common tools should be used for Incident, Problem and error control in live and development environments. If this is not possible, because of the use of specific CASE tools in the development environment, it will be necessary to design and produce a viable transfer mechanism.

- In practice, the level of detail usually required for development Configuration Management often precludes a viable shared system. The key thing is to share the data, especially in terms of passing to the live environment information on Problems, Known Errors and ongoing Changes that are being handed over with any new or changed software.

6.8 Proactive Problem Management

The activities described so far in Problem and error control are mainly reactive. Proactive Problem Management activities are concerned with identifying and resolving Problems and Known Errors *before* Incidents occur, thus minimising the adverse impact on the service and business-related costs.

Problem prevention ranges from prevention of individual Problems, such as repeated difficulties with a particular feature of a system, through to strategic decisions. The latter may require major expenditure to implement, such as investment in a better network. Problem prevention also includes information being given to Customers that obviates the need to ask for assistance in the future. Analysis focuses on providing recommendations on improvements for the Problem solvers, e.g. provision of online technical tools may reduce the time taken to resolve Problems, thereby reducing the length of time that calls are outstanding.

The main activities within proactive Problem Management processes are trend analysis and the targeting of preventive action.

6.8.1 Trend Analysis

Incident and Problem analysis reports provide information for proactive measures to improve service quality. The objective is to identify 'fragile' components of an IT infrastructure and investigate the reasons for the fragility – in this context 'fragility' is proportional to the impact to the business should the CI fail.

Incident and Problem analysis can identify:

- trends, such as the post-Change occurrence of particular Problem types
- incipient faults of a particular type
- recurring Problems of a particular type or with an individual item
- the need for more Customer training or better documentation.

Categorisation of Incidents and Problems and creative analysis may reveal trends and lead to the identification of specific (potential) Problem areas that need further investigation. For instance, analysis may indicate that Incidents related to the usability of recently installed client–server systems is the Problem area that has the most growth in terms of negative impact on business.

Analysis – for example of events from System Management tools, literature, conferences and feedback from User groups – can also reveal possible Problems deserving further investigation. Organising workshops with prominent Customers or conducting Customer surveys can also lead to the identification of trends and (potential) Problem areas.

Analysis of Problem Management data may reveal:

- that Problems occurring on one platform may occur on another platform – for example, a Problem concerning network software on a midrange system may well be of significance on a mainframe system
- the existence of recurring Problems – for example, if three routers are substituted serially, because of the same failure, it may indicate that the router-type concerned is not appropriate and should be replaced by another type, or when a software application is involved then complete redevelopment might be necessary which would be classed as a major Change.

6.8.2 Targeting preventive action

Trend analysis can lead to the identification of faults in the IT infrastructure, which can then be analysed and corrected as described in the Problem and error control sections. Trend analysis can also lead to the identification of general Problem areas needing more support attention. It should be possible to make meaningful comparisons by expressing this in terms of financial cost to the organisation.

In order to direct scarce resources for Service Support most effectively (i.e. to gain the most business benefit from it), it is worthwhile investigating which Problem areas are taking up most support attention. This is typically a task for proactive Problem Management. In order to be able to estimate the business-related impact of Incidents in a specific Problem area, it can prove useful to introduce the concept of the 'pain factor' of Incidents as a measure. With this concept, a pain value is given to each Incident category on the basis of a formula, taking into account, for instance:

- the volume of Incidents
- the number of Customers impacted
- the duration and related costs of resolving the Incidents
- the cost to the business – this being perhaps the most important factor of all.

This approach avoids concentrating effort on a group of Incidents, that may be relatively large in number but do not cause a high impact on the level of service provided, instead indicating that it may be more profitable to investigate a small number of Incidents, that are having a very high impact on the business of the organisation.

After the Problem areas that need most attention have been identified, Problem Management should initiate appropriate actions. These may include:

- raising an RFC
- providing feedback regarding testing, procedures, training and documentation
- initiating Customer education and training
- initiating Service Support staff education and training
- ensuring adherence to Problem Management and Incident Management procedures
- process or procedural improvement.

6.8.3 Tips on proactive Problem Management

The following points are worthy of particular note:

- The added value of trend analysis in CI robustness is rather limited until sufficient historical data has been accumulated.
- Engineering reports from many manufacturers' operating systems provide information on inherent Problems. These reports should be examined on a regular basis to identify potential hardware Problems before they occur. Ideally, vendor staff should do this (perhaps remotely) but, in any event, it is the responsibility of Problem Management to ensure that it is done. These reports can be used to trigger the repair or replacement of hardware CIs before any fault actually occurs.
- Proactive Problem Management does not necessarily need to be a full-time task. For smaller IT service organisations, assigning a support specialist for a period of two weeks every six months to analyse Incident and Problem data, and for a further two weeks to initiate RFCs, could suffice.

6.8.4 Major Problem reviews

On completion of the resolution of every major Problem, Problem Management should complete a major Problem review. The appropriate people involved in the resolution should be called to the review to determine:

- what was done right
- what was done wrong
- what could be done better next time
- how to prevent the Problem from happening again.

6.9 Providing information to the support organisation

Problem Management provides information on identified Problems, Known Errors and Requests for Change issued. This information can be on an ad-hoc or a periodic basis. Often, the information and reports are aimed at management in order to monitor the quality of the Problem Management process. However, it is also a useful for the management reports to be presented to the business and IT management in such a way that they can use the reports to inform the decision-making process within the organisations. Besides this, reports can also be relayed to other processes and the Service Desk.

6.9.1   Providing management information

Management information should provide insight into the effort and resources spent by the organisation on investigating, diagnosing and resolving Problems and Known Errors. Besides this, it is important to provide insight in the progress made and the results obtained as a result. Metrics have to be selected carefully. Only through careful and meaningful measurement can management form an opinion on the quality of the process.

6.9.2   Cascading information

Temporary Work-arounds, permanent fixes or simply information on the progress of resolutions should be cascaded to the people who reported the Problem. This information may also have to be cascaded to other Customers as a Problem affecting many people may only be reported by one person.

Disseminating this information is primarily a task of the Service Desk. Problem Management should provide sufficient information and support to the Service Desk for this task. Relevant information can be distributed by Problem Management to the Service Desk and the support organisation by feeding this information into existing Service Management tools and databases.

To disseminate information effectively, the Problem Management process should have access to Configuration Management information such as who uses what, when they use it, and where they are, plus all the necessary contact details. Some of the details required for Problem Management can be obtained from the call logging part of the Incident Management process. However, for Problem Management it is often more effective to use contact maps and formal communication routes agreed in advance of Problems occurring. This type of information is often obtained when negotiating (or renegotiating) SLAs. Another source is the regular service reviews that form part of Service Level Management.

6.10   Metrics

By maintaining historical information from Incident control and Problem/error control, it is possible to derive measures that are indicative of the quality of service and the performance of the process.

6.10.1   Problem/error control reporting

Management information on this subject includes:

- the number of RFCs raised and the impact of those RFCs on the availability and reliability of the services covered
- the amount of time worked on investigations and diagnoses per organisational unit or supplier, split by Problem types
- the number and impact of Incidents occurring before the root Problem is closed or a Known Error is confirmed
- the ratio of immediate (reactive) support effort to planned support effort in Problem Management
- the plans for resolution of open Problems with regard to resources:
  - people
  - other used resources
  - costs (against budget)
- a short description of actions to be undertaken.

Information about weak components in the IT Infrastructure and breaches of agreed service levels with the business and by suppliers are of concern to Availability Management. The frequency and duration of Problems is a measurement of performance against agreed service levels. Information required will include:

- the number of Problems and errors split by:
  - status
  - service
  - impact
  - category
  - User group
- the total elapsed time on closed Problems
- the elapsed time to date on outstanding Problems
- the mean and maximum elapsed time to close Problems or confirm a Known Error, from the time of raising the Problem record, by impact code and by support group (including vendors)
- any temporary resolution actions
- the expected resolution time for outstanding Problems
- the total elapsed time for closed Problems.

6.10.2 Periodic audits

Process control requires periodic audits of all operations and procedures. These audits are intended to confirm that the Problem Management and support teams are adhering to defined procedures. The audits should analyse major problem reviews, and check:

- that reports are produced and analysed according to the agreed schedule
- a representative sample of Incidents, to verify that related Problems have been correctly identified and recorded
- a representative sample of Problems, to verify that Problems are diagnosed correctly and diagnosed within the prescribed period
- a representative sample of Known Errors, to verify that Known Errors are cleared by authorised Changes to CIs and within the prescribed period
- that thresholds for escalation have been adhered to
- a representative sample of records, for correctness and completeness
- that documentation is being maintained correctly – updates being distributed by Problem Management staff and executed by recipients
- that management reports are produced regularly and are meaningful
- for evidence of trend analyses and the identification of preventive actions
- staff training records.

6.10.3 Tips on metrics

The following are important points to bear in mind with regard to metrics:

- Define, during the specification stage, target effectiveness metrics for the process. Plan to use them as a control when Problem Management operations commence in order to assess effectiveness and evaluate trends objectively. Set actual targets in advance, if possible, or during the first few weeks of operation. If possible, obtain statistics from current support activities as a basis for the targets. These will be useful later in identifying the benefits accrued from the introduction of Problem Management.

■ Do not set targets that cannot be measured.

■ When purchasing support tools, take relevant metrics into account during the product evaluation and system-design stages and try to obtain tools that can provide the necessary statistics.

■ Develop procedures to produce reports on key effectiveness criteria. Problem Management should review actual achievements against all targets on a regular basis, once a month. Record the results of each review and keep for audit purposes. If targets have to been relaxed, make sure the cause is overambitious targeting and not poor operations. Any deficiencies in the operation of Problem Management should be traced back and put right at source.

■ Plan to establish formal effectiveness and efficiency reviews of the process, paying particular attention to the requirements of Customers. Ensure support requirements are fully satisfied by the process when it is in operation.

■ Plan to set progressively more difficult targets, in line with the benefits planned from the introduction of Problem Management processes.

■ Monitor the effect of a successful Problem Management system on the workloads of staff. Experience suggests that an effective process, particularly when working alongside effective Change Management and Release quality control, quickly reduces the incidence of Incidents and Problems. This reduced number of Incidents and a consequential reduction in the number of support requests can result in a reduction in staff numbers. New applications and new Users can increase Problem and Incident workloads. Problem Management should, therefore, be informed of any anticipated Changes that may affect these workloads, so that plans can be made, not only in relation to staffing levels and staff accommodation, but also to other resources such as database and other IT capacity.

■ Sometimes an audit carried out in another Service Management process may uncover something that could indicate a Problem. Ensure that the relevant details are passed to Problem Management for any necessary corrective action.

6.11 Roles within Problem Management

Processes tend to span functions within the organisation. Therefore it is important to define the responsibilities associated with the activities in the process that have to be performed. To remain flexible, it is advisable to use the concept of roles. A role is defined as a set of responsibilities, activities and authorisations. In this chapter, very brief examples of relevant roles within the process are defined.

Roles should be assigned to people or groups within an organisation. This assignment can be full-time or part-time, depending on the role and the organisation.

6.11.1 Problem Manager

The Problem Manager has the responsibility for all Problem Management activities and has the following specific responsibilities:

■ developing and maintaining the Problem control process

■ reviewing the efficiency and effectiveness of the Problem control process

■ producing management information

■ managing Problem support staff

- allocating resources for the support effort
- monitoring the effectiveness of error control and making recommendations for improving it
- developing and maintaining Problem and error control systems
- reviewing the efficiency and effectiveness of proactive Problem Management activities.

It is recommended that the Service Desk Manager and the Problem Manager roles are not combined because of the conflicting interests inherent in these roles.

6.11.2 Problem support

Problem support has both reactive and proactive responsibilities, as follows:

◆ reactive responsibilities:
- identifying Problems (by analysing Incident data, for example)
- investigating Problems, according to impact, through to resolution or error identification
- raising RFCs to clear errors
- monitoring progress on the resolution of Known Errors
- advising Incident Management staff on the best available Work-arounds for Incidents related to unresolved Problems/Known Errors
- assisting with the handling of major Incidents and identifying the root causes.

◆ pro-active responsibilities:
- identifying trends and potential Problem sources (by reviewing Incident and Problem analyses)
- raising RFCs to prevent the recurrence of Problems
- preventing the replication of Problems across multiple systems.

Annex 6A: An example of a coding structure for Problems/error categorisation

Code Structure	Category Code	Description	Comments
A		**NON-CI CAUSES**	
A1	A10	HUMAN ERROR	*Consider creating CIs*
	A11	Computer Operations	*for these items*
	A12	Network Management	
	A13	User Support	
	A14	Problem Management	
	A15	Specialist Support	
	A16	Application Development	
	A17	Administration	
A2		PROCEDURAL FAILURE	*Consider creating CIs*
	A20	Change Management	*for these items*
	A21	Software Control & Distribution	
	A22	Other	
B		**APPLICATIONS CIs (internal)**	
B1		APPLICATION 1	
B10		Module 1	
	B100	Transaction type 1	
	B1000	Update Fails	
	B1001	Page Lock	
	B1002	Dual Update	
	B101	Transaction type 2	
B11		Module 2	
	B110	Job 1	
	B111	Job 2	
B12		Documentation	
	B120	Computer Operations Manual	
	B121	User Procedures Manual	
B2		APPLICATION 2	
Etc.			
C		**APPLICATIONS CIs (external)**	
C1		PACKAGE 1	
C10		Module 1	
	C100	Job 1	
	C101	Job 2	
C11		Documentation	
	C110	Module 1 manual	
	C111	Module 2 manual	
C2		PACKAGE 2	
Etc.			
D		**UTILITY SOFTWARE CIs (internal)**	
D1		JCL	
	D10	Application 1	
	D20	Application 2	

D2		DATABASE MAINTENANCE AND SUPPORT	
D3		SOFTWARE LIBRARY MAINTENANCE	
E		**SYSTEMS SOFTWARE CIs (external)**	
E1		MAINFRAME SYSTEMS SOFTWARE	
	E10	Operating system	
	E11	Transaction processing	
	E12	Data management	
	E13	Communications / networking	
	E14	Data Centre management	
	E15	Applications Generator	
E2 Etc.		MINICOMPUTER SYSTEMS SOFTWARE	
F Etc.		**COMPUTER HARDWARE CIs**	
G Etc.		**NETWORKING HARDWARE CIs**	

Note: The descriptions in this Annex are of causes. It is important not to confuse the causes and how to categorise them for future meaningful analysis with the initial descriptions of Incidents and Problems, which will be described much more in Customer/business terms – for example as a Problem with a particular service, or as unavailability of a PC or LAN.

Annex 6B: Kepner and Tregoe analysis

Charles Kepner and Benjamin Tregoe developed a useful method to analyse Problems. In this Annex, their method is presented as an example of a Problem analysis method.

Kepner and Tregoe state that Problem analysis should be a systematic process of Problem solving and should take maximum advantage of knowledge and experience. They distinguish the following five phases for Problem analysis (described further below):

1. Defining the Problem
2. Describing the Problem with regard to identity, location, time and size
3. Establishing possible causes
4. Testing the most probable cause
5. Verifying the true cause.

Depending on time and available information, these phases can be realised to a greater or lesser extent. Even in situations where only a limited amount of information is available, or time pressure is high, it is worthwhile adopting a structured approach to Problem analysis to improve the chances of success.

Defining the Problem

Because the investigation is based on the definition of the Problem, this definition has to state precisely which deviation(s) from the agreed service levels have occurred.

Often, during the definition of a Problem, the most probable Problem cause is already indicated. Take care not to jump to conclusions, which can guide the investigation in the wrong direction from the beginning.

In practice, Problem definition is often a difficult task because of a complicated IT infrastructure and non-transparent agreements on service levels.

Describing the Problem

The following aspects are used to describe the Problem, i.e. what the Problem *IS*:

- Identity. Which part does not function well? What *is* the Problem?
- Location. Where does the Problem occur?
- Time. When did the Problem start to occur? How frequently has the Problem occurred?
- Size. What is the size of the Problem? How many parts are affected?

The 'IS' situation is determined by the answers to these questions,. The next step is to investigate which similar parts in a similar environment are functioning properly. With this, an answer is formulated to the question 'What COULD BE but IS NOT?' (Which parts could be showing the same Problem but do not?).

It is then possible to search effectively for relevant differences in both situations. Furthermore, past Changes, which could be the cause of these differences, can be identified.

Establishing possible causes

The list of differences and Changes mentioned above most likely hold the cause of the Problem so possible causes can be extracted from this list.

Testing the most probable cause

Each possible cause needs to be assessed to determine whether it could be the cause of all the symptoms of the Problem.

Verifying the true cause

The remaining possible causes have to be verified as being the source of the Problem. This can only be done by proving this in one way or another – for example by implementing a Change or replacing a part. Address the possible causes that can be verified quickly and simply first.

Annex 6C: Ishikawa Diagrams

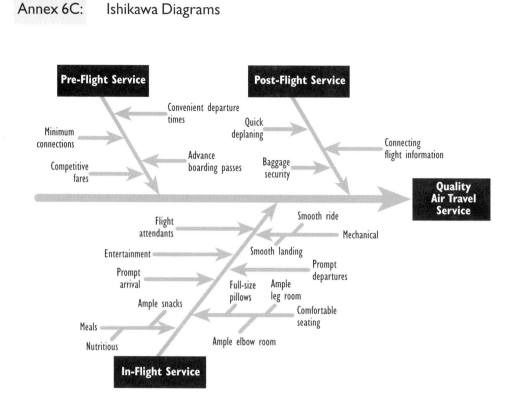

Figure 6C.1 – Example Ishikawa diagram

The Ishikawa diagram, also referred to as a cause-and-effect diagram, tree diagram, or fishbone diagram, displays the factors that affect a particular quality characteristic, outcome, or Problem. The diagram is named after its developer, Kaoru Ishikawa (1915-1989), a leader in Japanese quality control. An example is shown in Figure 6C.1.

An Ishikawa diagram is typically the result of a brainstorming session in which members of a group offer ideas on how to improve a product, process or service. The main goal is represented by the trunk of the diagram, and primary factors are represented as branches. Secondary factors are then added as stems, and so on. Creating the diagram stimulates discussion and often leads to increased understanding of a complex Problem. Japanese Circle members often post Ishikawa diagrams in a display area where they are accessible to managers and other groups. In the United States, Ishikawa diagrams are included in presentations by plant personnel to management or Customers.

Extracted from the SAS web site http.//www.sas.com/

7 CONFIGURATION MANAGEMENT

7.1 Goal of Configuration Management

Businesses require quality IT services provided economically. To be efficient and effective, all organisations need to control their IT infrastructure and services. Configuration Management provides a logical model of the infrastructure or a service by identifying, controlling, maintaining and verifying the versions of Configuration Items (CIs) in existence.

The goals of Configuration Management are to:

- account for all the IT assets and configurations within the organisation and its services
- provide accurate information on configurations and their documentation to support all the other Service Management processes
- provide a sound basis for Incident Management, Problem Management, Change Management and Release Management
- verify the configuration records against the infrastructure and correct any exceptions.

7.2 Scope of Configuration Management

Configuration Management covers the identification, recording, and reporting of IT components, including their versions, constituent components and relationships. Items that should be under the control of Configuration Management include hardware, software and associated documentation.

Given the definition above, it should be clear that Configuration Management is not synonymous with Asset Management, although the two disciplines are related. Asset Management is a recognised accountancy process that includes depreciation accounting. Asset Management systems maintain details on assets above a certain value, their business unit and their location. Configuration Management also maintains relationships between assets, which Asset Management usually does not. Some organisations start with Asset Management and then move on to Configuration Management.

The basic activities of Configuration Management are as follows:

- **Planning.** Planning and defining the purpose, scope, objectives, policies and procedures, and the organisational and technical context, for Configuration Management.
- **Identification.** Selecting and identifying the configuration structures for all the infrastructure's CIs, including their 'owner', their interrelationships and configuration documentation. It includes allocating identifiers and version numbers for CIs, labelling each item, and entering it on the Configuration Management Database (CMDB).
- **Control.** Ensuring that only authorised and identifiable CIs are accepted and recorded, from receipt to disposal. It ensures that no CI is added, modified, replaced or removed without appropriate controlling documentation, e.g. an approved Change request, and an updated specification.
- **Status accounting.** The reporting of all current and historical data concerned with each CI throughout its life cycle. This enables Changes to CIs and their records to be traceable, e.g. tracking the status of a CI as it changes from one state to another for instance 'under development', 'being tested', 'live', or 'withdrawn'.

■ **Verification and audit.** A series of reviews and audits that verify the physical existence of CIs and check that they are correctly recorded in the Configuration Management system.

Configuration Management interfaces directly with systems development, testing, Change Management and Release Management to incorporate new and updated product deliverables. Control should be passed from the project or supplier to the service provider at the scheduled time with accurate configuration records.

7.3 Basic concepts

7.3.1 Configuration Management planning

Configuration Management planning consists of agreeing and defining:

■ the strategy, policy, scope and objectives of Configuration Management

■ the analysis of the current position of assets and configurations

■ the organisational context, both technical and managerial, within which the Configuration Management activities are to be implemented

■ the policies for related processes such as Change Management and Release Management

■ interfaces, e.g. between projects, suppliers, application and support teams

■ the relevant processes, procedures, guidelines, support tools, roles and responsibilities for each of the Configuration Management activities

■ the location of storage areas and libraries used to hold hardware, software and documentation.

The Configuration policy/strategy sets the objectives and key success factors (KSFs) of what should be achieved by Configuration Management. The detailed activities and resources required to achieve the objectives and KSFs in the Strategy may be documented in a project plan. The milestones are often summarised in the Configuration Management Plan.

7.3.2 Configuration identification and CIs

Configuration identification is the selection, identification and labelling of the configuration structures and CIs, including their respective 'owner' and the relationships between them. CIs may be hardware, software or documentation. Examples include services, servers, environments, equipment, network components, desktops, mobile units, applications, licences, telecommunication services, and facilities. Configuration identification includes allocating identifiers for CIs, including individual versions of the CI and their configuration documents. Other records and data associated with a CI include Incidents, Known Errors and Problems, and corporate data about employees, suppliers, locations, business units, and procedures.

An important part of Configuration Management is deciding the level at which control is to be exercised, with top-level CIs broken down into components which are themselves CIs, and so on. This matter is covered in more depth in Paragraph 7.6.2, but to provide an illustration, Figure 7.1 shows example System A – which is an assembly of components A1, A2, A3. Each of these components can be broken down into smaller components. Each of the components shown is a CI, including the total system.

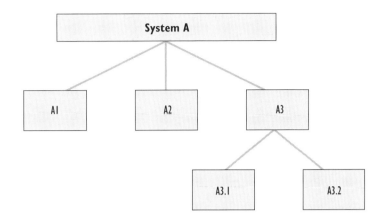

Figure 7.1 - Configuration breakdown

In distributed environments, individual components occur within many different services and configuration structures. For example, a person may use a desktop computer that is on the network for a building but may be running a central financial system that is linked to a database on the other side of the world. A Change to the network or the financial system may have an impact on this person and his/her business process. Correct configuration identification and documentation enables Change Management to be effective by knowing fully the potential impact of a particular change.

7.3.3   Configuration control

Configuration control is concerned with ensuring that only authorised and identifiable CIs are recorded from receipt to disposal. It ensures that no CI is added, modified, replaced or removed without appropriate controlling documentation e.g. an approved Change request.

7.3.4   Configuration status accounting

Configuration status accounting is the reporting of all current and historical data concerned with each CI throughout its life-cycle. It enables tracking of changes to CIs and their records, e.g. tracking the status as a CI changes from one state to another, e.g. 'development', 'test', 'live' or 'withdrawn'.

7.3.5   Configuration verification and audit

Configuration verification and audit comprises a series of reviews and audits that verify the physical existence of CIs and check that the CIs are correctly recorded in the CMDB and controlled libraries. It includes the verification of Release and configuration documentation before changing the live environment.

7.3.6   Configuration baseline

A configuration baseline is the configuration of a product or system established at a specific point in time, which captures both the structure and details of a configuration. It serves as reference for further activities. An application or software baseline provides the ability to change or to rebuild a specific version at a later date.

A configuration baseline is also a snapshot, or a position, that is recorded. Although the position may be updated later, the configuration baseline remains fixed as the original state and is thus available to be compared with the current position. A configuration baseline is used to assemble all relevant components in readiness for a Change or Release, and to provide the basis for a configuration audit and regression, e.g. after a Change. The Configuration Management system should be able to save, protect and report on a configuration baseline, its contents and documentation.

7.3.7 Configuration Management Database

Many organisations are already using some elements of Configuration Management, often using spreadsheets, local databases or paper-based systems. In today's large and complex IT infrastructures, Configuration Management requires the use of support tools, which includes a Configuration Management Database (CMDB). Physical and electronic libraries are needed along with the CMDB to hold definitive copies of software and documentation. The CMDB is likely to be based upon database technology that provides flexible and powerful interrogation facilities. A few examples of its potential use are to list:

- Release contents, including component CIs and their version numbers
- component CIs and their version numbers in the test and live environments
- CIs affected by a scheduled (authorised) Change
- all Requests for Change (RFCs) relating to one particular CI
- CIs purchased from a particular supplier within a specific period
- CI history
- equipment and software at a given location, for example to assist in an audit
- CIs that are scheduled to be upgraded, replaced or decommissioned
- Changes and Problem records associated with a CI
- all CIs affected by a Problem.

The CMDB should hold the relationships between all system components, including Incidents, Problems, Known Errors, Changes and Releases. The CMDB also contains information about Incidents, Known Errors and Problems, and corporate data about employees, suppliers, locations and business units.

Automated processes to load and update the Configuration Management database should be developed where possible so as to reduce errors and reduce costs. Discovery tools, inventory and audit tools, enterprise systems and network management tools can be interfaced to the CMDB. These tools can be used initially to populate the CMDB, and subsequently to compare the actual 'live' configuration with the records stored in the CMDB.

The CMDB may also be used to store and control details of IT Users, IT staff and business units, although the legal implications of holding information about people in the CMDB should be considered. Storing such information in the CMDB would allow personnel Changes to be related to Changes in CI ownership.

In addition to storing personnel information, the CMDB is often used for Service Level Management to hold details of services and to relate them to the underlying IT components. The CMDB is also used to store inventory details of CIs, such as supplier, cost, purchase date and renewal date for a licence. An additional bonus is the use of the CMDB to cover the legal aspects associated with the maintenance of licences and contracts.

7.3.8 Software and document libraries

A controlled library is a collection of software or document CIs of known type and status. Access to items in a controlled library should be restricted. Software libraries are used for controlling and releasing software throughout the systems development life-cycle, e.g. in development, building, testing and operations.

7.3.9 Definitive Software Library

The Definitive Software Library (DSL) is the term used for the library in which the definitive authorised versions of all software CIs are stored and protected. It is a physical library or storage repository where master copies of software versions are placed. This one logical storage area may in reality consist of one or more physical software libraries or filestores. The libraries should be separate from development, test or live filestore areas. The DSL may also include a physical store to hold master copies of bought-in software, e.g. a fireproof safe. Only authorised software should be accepted into the DSL, strictly controlled by Change and Release Management.

The DSL is a common foundation for the Release Management and Configuration Management processes. For details see Chapter 9 - Release Management.

7.3.10 Licence management

Company directors, senior managers, and others, are liable to face imprisonment and fines if illegal software is found to be in use within their enterprise. Configuration Management enables an enterprise to monitor and control software licences, from purchase to disposal. Software licence structures, and corporate and multi-licensing schemes, need to be understood and communicated to service-provider staff and Customers.

Responsibility for controlling and auditing software licences should be unambiguous and should involve purchasing and Asset or Configuration Management. This may be difficult when Users find it so easy to purchase and download software from the Internet, but this can be resolved by links to disciplinary procedures detailed within the organisation's Security Policy (see the ITIL book on Security Management – ISBN 0-11-330014-x).

7.4 Benefits and possible problems

7.4.1 Benefits

The real value of IT assets is generally much greater than their capital value because of the part these assets play in supporting the provision of quality IT services. The consequential loss to the organisation if these services are not provided can be very great.

Configuration Management contributes to the economic and effective delivery of IT services by:

- *Providing accurate information on CIs and their documentation.* This information supports all other Service Management processes, such as Release Management, Change Management, Incident Management, Problem Management, Capacity Management and Contingency Planning. For example, if a new product is available that requires a minimum configuration, Configuration Management can provide information for upgrade planning and replacements.

- *Controlling valuable CIs.* For example, if a computer were stolen then it would have to be replaced. Configuration Management helps IT management to know what its assets are supposed to be, who is responsible for their safekeeping, and whether the actual inventory matches the official one.

- *Facilitating adherence to legal obligations.* Configuration Management maintains an inventory of all items of software within an IT infrastructure. CIs that come to light, via configuration audits or calls to the Service Desk, that are not on this list are not authorised and may well have not been paid for. Illegal copies can easily be identified, for erasure or destruction.

- *Helping with financial and expenditure planning.* Configuration Management provides a complete list of CIs. It is easy to produce from this list expected maintenance costs and licence fees; maintenance contracts; licence renewal dates; CI life expiry dates; and CI replacement costs (provided that this information is stored). By providing this information Configuration Management contributes to IT directorates' financial planning.

- *Making software Changes visible.* Such Changes can be used to trigger investigations by IT management into possible Changes that may be needed for data protection, licence management and regulatory compliance.

- *Contributing to contingency planning.* The CMDB and secure libraries facilitate the restoration of IT service in the event of a disaster, by identifying the required CIs and their location (provided, of course, that they are themselves properly backed-up – see Paragraph 7.6.6.).

- *Supporting and improving Release Management.* Configuration Management information supports the roll-out across distributed locations by providing information on the versions of CIs and Changes incorporated into a Release.

- *Improving security by controlling the versions of CIs in use.* This makes it more difficult for these CIs to be changed accidentally, maliciously, or for erroneous versions to be added.

- *Enabling the organisation to reduce the use of unauthorised software.* Unauthorised software and non-standard and variant builds all increase complexity and support costs, and so any reduction in their occurrence should bring benefits to the organisation.

- *Allowing the organisation to perform impact analysis and schedule Changes safely, efficiently and effectively.* This reduces the risk of Changes affecting the live environment.

- *Providing Problem Management with data on trends.* Such data will relate to trends in Problems affecting particular CI types, e.g. from particular suppliers or development groups, for use in improving the IT services. This information on Problem trends supports the proactive prevention of Problems.

7.4.2   Possible problems

Possible problems faced in Configuration Management are:

- CIs are defined at the wrong level with too much detail (so that staff become involved in unnecessary work) or too little detail (so that there is inadequate control).

- Implementation is attempted without adequate analysis and design. The end result is, consequently, not what is required.

- Tactical schedules are over ambitious. Configuration Management may be perceived as a bottleneck if adequate time is not built into schedules to allow staff to carry out their duties. When Changes and Releases are being scheduled, past experience of the time taken to complete Configuration Management activities should be taken in to account. IT management needs to be proactive in providing automated facilities for activities on the critical path and to make it clear that time should be allowed for Configuration Management.

- Commitment is lacking. Without a firm commitment to the processes from managers, it is difficult to introduce the controls that some staff would prefer to avoid. Examples of poor Change Management and Configuration Management can often convince managers of the need for better control.

- The process is perceived to be too bureaucratic or rigorous. Consequently, individuals and groups use this as an excuse for not following the process.

- The process is routinely circumvented. Some people will try to circumvent Configuration Management in the interests of speed or with malicious intent. Attempts should be made to overcome this problem by making such people aware of the benefits of Configuration Management.

- Processes are inefficient and error-prone. This is often the case where manual processes are in use. In almost all cases it is advisable to choose an automated solution from the outset.

- Expectations of what the tool can do are unrealistic. Staff and managers may expect a Configuration Management tool to deliver a total solution and end up blaming the tool for processes or people that appear insufficient for the task.

- The chosen tool may lack flexibility. Problems can occur when the Configuration Management tool does not allow for new requirements or does not support all CI categories.

- Configuration Management has been implemented in isolation. If Configuration Management is implemented without Change Management or Release Management, it is much less effective and the intended benefits may not be realised.

- Expectations of what the Configuration Management process can do are unrealistic. Asset and Configuration Management cannot and should not be expected to make up for poor project management or poor acceptance testing. Poorly controlled installations and test environments will affect the quality of Releases and result in additional Incidents, Problems and Changes, which will in turn require additional resources.

- Proper configuration control is not in place. For example, Configuration Management may be difficult where Users have the ability to purchase, download and install software from the Internet.

7.5 Planning and implementation

Many enterprises implement Asset Management before implementing Configuration Management. The processes in this section apply to both Asset Management and Configuration Management.

Controlling IT infrastructure and services across distributed systems across multiple locations and support groups requires careful planning. This planning should include the Change Management, Configuration Management and Release Management processes, as there are many interdependencies among them. The planning and implementation of a central function for Change Management, Configuration Management and Release Management should be considered, together with support from distributed specialist teams (see Annex 7A).

7.5.1 Initial planning

The initial project planning activities for Configuration Management include:

- gaining agreement on the purpose, objectives, scope, priorities and implementation approach for Configuration Management

- assigning a person to be responsible for the Configuration Management processes and systems

- analysing existing Configuration Management systems, data and processes

- developing a high-level Configuration Management plan (which may be included in the organisation's Change Management and Configuration Management plans) and a design for the Configuration Management system

- planning for, and obtaining, finances for Configuration Management tools and commitment for extra resources

- agreeing on the corporate policy and processes, and defining what is 'tailorable' during the rollout.

For all but the smallest systems, Change Management and Configuration Management support tools are essential, as paper-based systems are impractical. Computer hardware and storage resources are required to accommodate Configuration Management tools and, in particular, the CMDB. Support tools should, as a minimum, allow data to be transferred from separate 'project Configuration Management' systems without the need for rekeying. Ideally, the Configuration Management tools for a live system and for development projects should work together in an integrated way.

Once the high-level Configuration Management plan is agreed and signed off, implementation can be planned. A phased implementation is recommended, starting with a well-defined service and the corporate data. This enables the benefits to be demonstrated early and the implementation activities tuned for more effective implementation during subsequent stages.

7.5.2 Agreement on purpose, objectives, scope, priorities and implementation approach aligned with business objectives

The purpose, objectives, scope and priorities for Configuration Management should be agreed with the Services Manager and other managers and be aligned to the business requirements. There should be an agreement on whether it is to be incorporated into a central function that includes Change Management and Release Management.

The purpose and scope might be:

> *To implement consistent Configuration Management, Change Management and Release Management processes for operational environments, package applications and business systems.*

The objective might be:

> *To bring all IT services and infrastructure components, with their associated documentation, under control, and to provide an information service to facilitate the effective and efficient planning, release and implementation of Changes to the IT services.*

Detailed objectives for Configuration Management should include:

- providing everyone working in Service Management and support with correct and accurate information on the present configurations with their physical and functional specifications
- defining and documenting the procedures and working practices to be followed
- identifying, labelling and recording the names and versions of the CIs that make up the IT services, infrastructure and their relationships
- controlling and storing definitive, authorised and trusted copies of specifications, documentation and software
- reporting the current status and history of all items on the IT infrastructure
- ensuring that all Changes to CIs are recorded as soon as practicable
- tracking and reconciling the actual state of the IT infrastructure against the authorised configuration records and data
- educating and training the organisation in the control processes
- reporting metrics on CIs, Changes and Releases
- auditing and reporting exceptions to infrastructure standards and Configuration Management procedures.

For many organisations, some form of phased implementation, including Change Management, is essential. The implementation approach may be on an organisational, geographical, Customer group, support group or other basis. Some organisations prioritise the CI types to be controlled.

The highest priorities might be:

- infrastructure servers
- mainframes
- Customer and supplier databases
- operational environments and applications supporting regulated business systems
- mission-critical services
- desktop builds and software licences
- networks.

Any such priorities have to be balanced with the change in procedures and practices within different groups. It is difficult for teams to implement a mix of processes for Change Management and Configuration Management other than for a short period of time.

The cost of support tools, together with any hardware requirements, needs to be planned. Although tools that integrate support for Incident Management, Change Management, Configuration Management, Release Management, Problem Management and Service Desks are likely to be more expensive than 'simple' Configuration Management tools, the additional cost will often be justified based on what the additional degree of integration makes possible. For larger organisations, these management processes are virtually impossible without adequate support tools.

7.5.3 Appointment of a Configuration Manager and planning a Configuration Management team

A central function may be set up to be responsible for managing Changes to hardware, communications equipment and software, system software, live applications software, and all documentation and procedures that are relevant to the running, support and maintenance of live systems. Guidance on setting up a central function is described in Annex 7A.

Configuration Management requires staff who will adopt a painstaking approach and pay due attention to detail. Central support staff are required, other than in very small installations. The following factors should be considered when planning staff numbers for Configuration Management:

- whether Configuration Management can be assigned with other responsibilities, or whether it requires the undivided attention of specific individuals

- whether the Configuration Management team is to be responsible for projects as well as the IT infrastructure and services

- whether the group is to be part of a joint Change, Configuration and Release Management team

- the size of the IT infrastructure, the level at which control is to be maintained, and hence the number of CIs to be controlled

- the number of staff who will be performing control activities in other groups and projects

- the extent to which support tools will be available

- the size, frequency and complexity of Changes and Releases.

A role specification for the Configuration Management team needs to be developed. Examples of the responsibilities are shown in Annex 7B. Typical roles include the Configuration Manager and the Configuration Librarian. Assign the Configuration Manager and other key roles as early as possible, because assigned individuals can then be involved in the implementation as key business Users.

7.5.4   Analysis of existing systems

From organisations having no processes at all, some organisations now have many Configuration Management processes and procedures. These may be embedded in other procedures or be specific to one team. If one of the objectives is to introduce a common Configuration Management system with consistent processes, an important activity is to identify and analyse the following:

- owners of high-level CIs

- current scope and resources (people and tools)

- current Change Management and Configuration Management practices, processes and procedures

- high-level configuration data held in current inventories, hard copy, local spreadsheets or databases

- roles, responsibilities and capabilities of staff involved in Configuration Management.

7.5.5   Developing Configuration Management plans and systems design

For some technologies and platforms, Configuration Management may be distributed across the organisation e.g. mainframe, physical networks and desktops. Some organisations devolve control to support groups that have expertise in a particular technology or platform, because it may not be cost-effective to train central staff in specialist areas. In these cases, the support group manager is responsible for the control of CIs owned and maintained by the group. The organisation's procedures for Change Management, Configuration Management, Release Management and a centralised CMDB should be adopted wherever possible. These may be defined in a Change and Configuration Management plan for the organisation (see Annex 7A) and be supported by functional and design documents for the Configuration Management system. The relationships between the plans should be documented to help staff see the context of Configuration Management within their group, with the manager of each group signing off its plan. An example relationship is shown in Figure 7.2.

Lower-level plans should align with, and refer up to, the higher-level plans so as to avoid duplication.

Although there will be situations where organisations' Configuration Management responsibilities will be devolved to individual areas with specific expertise, the ideal is to have a centralised function if resources permit; this ensures common processes and procedures. Devolution, on the other hand, needs careful management and regular auditing for compliance. It is always imperative that there is only one process owner – and this is even more important if there are a number of disparate groups performing Configuration Management.

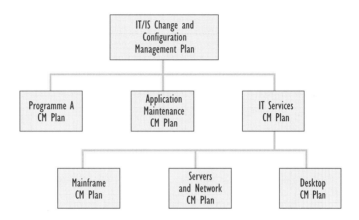

Figure 7.2 - Examples of Configuration Management plans for an organisation

The Configuration Management plans define the scope of Configuration Management, which is valuable input into system design and the next planning stage.

7.5.6 Detailed planning for implementation

Once the fundamental decisions on the scope of Configuration Management are made and the planning activities are completed, it is time to devise a plan for implementing Configuration Management. Unless the area is a greenfield site, procedures and records will probably already exist; clearly, there will be a need to plan the implementation with this in mind.

Key activities are as follows:

- analyse relevant existing Configuration Management practices in more detail and their interfaces to the Service Management processes, procurement and development
- analyse the capability of existing functions and staff involved in Configuration, Change and Release Management
- review configuration data held in hard-copy form, in local spreadsheets or in databases, and develop a conversion/loading strategy
- gather, refine, and gain agreement on requirements and functional requirements specifications
- develop vendor selection criteria for Configuration Management automation
- evaluate and select the CMDB and Configuration Management automation tools
- purchase and install the CMDB and other Configuration Management tools
- design the Configuration Management system in detail, including interfaces to Change Management, Release Management, other Service Management processes, procurement and development

- set up CI types, attributes, types of relationships, high-level CIs
- develop Configuration Management business processes and procedures that are integrated with the Configuration Management tools
- test the CMDB and other support tool(s) allowing sufficient time to rectify any problems even though Problems that are minor and will not affect the successful operation of the system need not be fixed before Configuration Management is implemented
- plan and provide secure storage areas to manage CIs (e.g. cabinets, controlled libraries and directories) in conjunction with Release Management
- develop and obtain agreement on roles, responsibilities and training plans
- communicate and train staff in both the importance and use of Change Management and Configuration Management.

Extra staff may be required for implementing Configuration Management, auditing the current infrastructure and populating the CMDB. Sometimes managers will assign staff to assist if they see the benefits of Configuration Management and their staff resources are scheduled in advance.

Planning to implement Configuration Management in stages will help to deliver early benefits and establish the need to provide funding and resources for future stages. For each stage, the following activities should be planned:

- schedule awareness training for key staff involved in Configuration Management
- define or develop Configuration Management plans for each group or technology and create local procedures where required
- analyse, design and build modules of the Configuration Management system to support Configuration Management processes and any related processes, interfaces and data
- assess and establish updated staff roles and responsibilities to include Configuration Management
- develop and plan for the registration procedures for new CIs to be brought into effect as soon as possible, preferably before the data on existing CIs is collected
- load the initial configuration and related records into the Configuration Management system
- train staff just before starting to use the new procedures and tools
- go live and support the implementation
- continue taking on IT infrastructure CIs – the most time-consuming part of the implementation is conducting the CI inventory and populating the CMDB and DSL
- monitor progress to ensure that the new procedures and tools are being used effectively and efficiently.

If Configuration Management is used to underpin other processes, such as Incident Management, further planning is required to roll out the systems in parallel. Local Configuration Management plans may define the CI identification and control processes for specific technology groups. The group manager may assign a Configuration Manager to own the local Configuration Management plan, to liaise with the central Configuration Management staff, and to be a member of the main CAB(s).

Plan to populate the CMDB as the inventory is carried out for each stage of implementation. Time should be allowed to do this correctly. Consider using temporary, but skilled, data-entry staff for this task, although if time allows it may be an opportunity for Configuration Management staff to become familiar with the support tool. If any of the data is already electronically stored for other purposes, consider reformatting and transferring the data.

Ideally the state of CIs should be frozen or held in a low-volatility period during CMDB population, but this may not be practical. However, once Configuration Management data is captured for particular CIs, these CIs should be bought immediately under Configuration Management control. In that case, it may be possible to populate the CMDB in a phased way (e.g. start with the hardware and then gradually progress to software, networks) – see Paragraph 7.5.7.

It may not be possible to bring items under Configuration Management control as the inventory is taken. In this case, plans should be made for procedures to track and record any Changes that occur between the time the inventory is taken and the start of Configuration Management control (e.g. when CMDB population is complete).

When all of the preparation has been completed, the actual switchover will require people to start using the new procedures at the agreed date and time. Publish the implementation date and time for the new procedures to those who are affected – in particular all IT services staff, external suppliers and service providers. Staff should be reminded of their responsibility to adhere to the new procedures from the outset.

7.5.7 Populating the CMDB and DSL

CIs should be brought under Configuration Management control as soon as the CI data has been collected. No new items that are in scope should be added to the IT infrastructure outside the control of Configuration Management.

An ideal option for CMDB population is to freeze Changes as the CMDB is being populated. Then every Change has to come under Configuration Management. This may not always be practicable but it is still worth consideration. Configuration Management and Change Management work very closely together – in fact, you cannot really have one without the other. As soon as the CMDB is populated, there has to be some level of Change Management in place to ensure that the configuration records and data are kept up to date.

If this approach is *not* possible, it is essential to record Changes that occur between collecting CI data, putting the data in the CMDB, and bringing the CIs under Configuration Management control. To do this, the time interval between these phases should be kept to a minimum for each CI. RFCs and Release records corresponding to Changes that are not yet implemented should be captured first. All RFCs from then on should be included in the CMDB. With this approach, the CMDB can be used to record all subsequent Change activity, including authorisation and implementation. The capture of any required historic records can be deferred until it is convenient.

Release Management should populate the Definitive Software Library in parallel with the implementation of the CMDB. Procedures are required to ensure that:

- only authorised and legally licensed software is accepted into the DSL
- this software is protected whilst resident in the DSL
- software is only checked out or copied from the DSL by authorised staff.

When the necessary staff, hardware and support tools are in place and all necessary training has been completed, the DSL and build environment(s) should be physically created. Security permissions should be established to limit access to authorised staff only. The DSL and build environments should be tested in accordance with criteria defined at the planning stage.

Project and applications staff should be told when to start delivering material and whom to send it to for inclusion in the DSL. Arrangements should be made for appropriate commercial off-the-shelf software to be housed in the CMDB and DSL with their associated documentation (e.g. licences).

Implementation of build management, distribution, and population occur sometime after creation of the DSL. These procedures should be tested before they are brought into use. If a gradual approach has been adopted, the first Release build will be when the deliverables from the selected project or supplier are to be subject to operational acceptance-testing. By the time Releases to the live environment are needed, the build and Release control procedures will have been used for putting software into the operational acceptance-testing environment, thereby providing another chance for many classes of potential problems with procedures and tools to be found and corrected.

Contingency plans should, however, be made in case the new procedures or tools fail. If software Releases are urgently required, it may be necessary to revert temporarily to previous procedures until the new procedures are corrected. Where possible, it is recommended that the procedures or tools for distributing software to sites are tested separately from those for installing and testing the software at the sites, thereby allowing problems with each of these phases to be isolated and corrected separately.

Although the procedures should be thoroughly tested before being brought into live use, time should be allowed to resolve any teething problems in the early stages of live use.

7.5.8   Cutover to new processes

The cutover to the new processes can take place in parallel with CMDB and DSL population. CIs can be gradually brought under Configuration Management control as the CI data is gathered and the information is recorded on the CMDB. Any Changes to CIs that are not yet under Configuration Management control should be communicated to the central function. If possible, CIs affected by Change should immediately be brought under control. All CIs that are new after the Configuration Management system has been switched on should be immediately brought under control.

In many cases, procedural measures and the use of tools to automate some configuration control, Release, distribution and audit processes can prevent – or at least detect – reversion to any previous procedures or practices.

Once the new Configuration Management system is in operation, it is vital that no new items are added to the IT infrastructure without Configuration Management authority. Interfaces to development or procurement, and incoming-goods processes are required to make this happen. Existing items to which Configuration Management control applies (i.e. all CIs other than those temporarily excluded to accommodate a phased implementation) should not be changed without authorisation. All unauthorised CIs/CI versions should be either expunged or brought under Configuration Management control.

7.5.9   Other implementation considerations

Configuration Management for infrastructure and services requires good planning and design to ensure that the objectives and expected benefits can be delivered.

The long-term commitment of management and staff is required for Configuration Management to work effectively. A successful implementation depends on having enough trained staff. If the Configuration Management function is understaffed or staffed by people who have not been adequately trained, it can become a bottleneck. Understaffing can also lead to critical errors, which can cost more to put right than the cost of adequate staffing in the first place. Additional staff may be required for a short period at implementation time (e.g. to assist with the CI inventory and/or populating the CMDB).

It is advisable to implement Configuration Management gradually, starting with those types of CI, or with those parts of the IT infrastructure, where control is perceived as most important or in the greatest need of improvement, and then expanding the system to encompass other areas.

With complex IT systems and services, it is essential to ensure that the Configuration Management system is maintained or the Configuration data will become out-of-date and fall into disrepute. Review and audit activities should be planned to ensure that:

- Configuration Management activities are audited against the Configuration Management plans

- the selection of CIs under Configuration Management is sufficient (but not too detailed) to provide control and to support effective Problem Management, Change Management and Release Management

- resources are available and staff are trained to perform the Configuration Management activities effectively

- there are appropriate levels of automation to reduce time-consuming and error-prone activities

- IT Service Management staff continue to have access to up-to-date, accurate and complete configuration records and data.

7.5.10 Costs

The costs of implementing Configuration Management will be outweighed by the benefits. For example, many organisations cannot function satisfactorily unless they can handle a high volume of software and hardware Changes without sacrificing quality. Without adequate control, organisations are at risk from such things as computer fraud, inadvertent software corruption, software viruses and other malicious software. The damage caused by these can cost an enormous sum to rectify.

The costs associated with implementing a Configuration Management function include staff salaries and overheads, support tools, accommodation costs for the team and training costs. The initial operating costs may be slightly greater than normal, while the staff are learning the procedures.

The practical application of Change Management and Configuration Management will result in a better quality of service, which will more than repay any overhead costs. Overhead costs depend on many factors, including:

- staff costs to develop and run the procedures
- hardware and software configuration identification and level of control
- hardware and software for the CMDB and DSL, including licences and maintenance costs
- specialist software Configuration Management tools for each platform, including the associated hardware and software
- the number of Users who are to have access to the Configuration Management system, and those Users' locations
- whether the Configuration Management system should be tailored to the needs of the organisation
- whether to integrate the Configuration Management and Service Management tools
- the diversity and quality of existing information that is to be loaded into the CMDB.

There may be an increase in staff costs during the initial data-capture exercise. However, do not make the mistake of categorising Change and Configuration staff as an overhead! If Configuration Management is not performed, there is likely to be a net increase in staffing requirements. Time will have to be spent in correcting things that would not have gone wrong if the disciplines had been in operation, and it will take more staff to handle Changes and Problems.

Other costs for implementation of Configuration Management will depend on:

- staff training and education
- staff costs to develop and run the procedures
- the number of Users who are to have access the Configuration Management system
- the diversity and quality of existing information that is to be loaded into the CMDB and DSL, and the effort required to reconcile and load it
- the time and resources needed to clean up poor-quality data
- the impact of existing commitments.

7.6 Activities

7.6.1 Configuration Management planning

The planning of Configuration Management should reference existing procedures and plans wherever possible, in order to keep things simple and to avoid duplication. A Configuration Management plan should define:

- the purpose, scope and objectives of Configuration Management (and how it fits in with the organisation's overall Change Management and Configuration Management plan)
- related policies, standards and processes that are specific to the support group
- Configuration Management roles and responsibilities
- CI naming conventions
- the schedule and procedures for performing Configuration Management activities: configuration identification, control, status accounting, configuration audit and verification
- interface control with third parties, e.g. Change Management, suppliers
- Configuration Management systems design, including scope and key interfaces, covering:
  - CMDB
  - locations of Configuration Management data and libraries
  - controlled environments within which CIs are manipulated
  - links and interfaces to other Service Management systems
  - support tools (e.g. build and installation tools)
- housekeeping, including licence management, archiving and the retention period for CIs
- planned configuration baselines, major Releases, milestones, workload and resource plan for each subsequent period.

Plan the first three to six months in significant detail and the following twelve months in outline. Performance relative to the plan should be reviewed regularly – at least every six months – and should include the Configuration Management workload for the period and the resources needed to service it. Checks should be made to ensure that the staff, IT resources, and support tools – including the size of the CMDB to be made available to Configuration Management – are likely to be adequate.

Where deficiencies are identified, steps should be taken to obtain further resources or procure enhanced support tools.

It is generally a fact that Configuration Management activity grows with the passage of time. The number of CIs under control and the frequency of Changes affecting them will vary. Information on growth should be available from the organisation's IT service, workload and capacity plans. IT Service Management may also decide to implement Changes in the light of management reports, efficiency/effectiveness reviews, and audits of the Configuration Management function.

At each review point, Configuration Management plans for the preceding period should be compared with actual events. Any deficiencies in the planning process should be rectified to improve future planning.

In considering the future work of the Configuration Management group, IT Service Management should ensure that only required Configuration Management data is handled; redundant data should be purged. The cost of keeping and capturing CI details should be compared with current and potential benefits; if the current level of detail is costing too much, do not store it!

7.6.2   Configuration identification

The IT infrastructure configuration should be broken down and uniquely identified to enable effective control, recording and reporting of CIs to the level that the business requires. As a rough guide, this could be to the level of 'independent Change'. The scope should include the hardware, and software used to build, release, verify, install, distribute, maintain, recover and decommission CIs. This includes any environments and software tools used to build a CI. Examples of the components that should be identified are:

- hardware (including network components where relevant)
- system software, including operating systems
- business systems – custom-built applications
- packages – commercial off-the-shelf packages, standard products, and database products,
- physical databases
- environments
- feeds between databases, applications and EDI links
- configuration baselines
- software releases
- configuration documentation, e.g. system and interface specifications, licences, maintenance agreements, SLAs, decommissioning statement
- Change documentation, deviations and waivers
- other resources e.g. Users, suppliers, contracts
- other documentation e.g. IT business processes, workflow, procedures
- network components
- Service Management components and records such as capacity plans, IT service continuity plans, Incidents, Problems, Known Errors, RFCs, etc.

It is important to consider the degree of granularity that is required. Is it sufficient, for example, to merely register a PC at 'PC' level or to go deeper so as to consider the monitor, the base unit, the keyboard and the mouse – or even register the network card, the type of hard disk, and so forth. The same question can be applied to software (on module, submodule, or whatever level). Besides discussing the level of granularity required, a lot of discussion in practice is about scope: are telephones included, should SLAs, and so forth.

Consider the size of database to be created and the problems of maintenance and audit – is it really necessary to open up each PC and check each component at each audit? Before deciding on these issues, consider how to plan maintainance of the database and what to do with the information being maintained. How, for example, will one thousand PCs be updated to show that a new software Release has been installed on each one? Is the database to be used to estimate the financial value of the infrastructure for audit purposes? What is the value to the business of holding low level data?

Configuration structures and the selection of CIs

Configuration structures should describe the relationship and position of CIs in each structure. In addition to the infrastructure configuration structure, there should be service configuration structures that identify all the components in a particular service (e.g. the retail service).

CIs should be selected by applying a decomposition process to the top-level item using guidance criteria for the selection of CIs. A CI can exist as part of any number of different CIs or CI sets at the same time. For instance, a database product may be used by many applications. Usage links to reusable and common components of the service should be defined – for instance, a configuration structure for a retail service will use infrastructure CIs such as servers, network and software CIs. The ability to have multiple views through different configuration structures improves impact analysis, service reporting, Change Management and Release Management.

The CI level chosen depends on the business and service requirements. Try to decide in advance the lowest CI level that will be required, even if you do not immediately populate the CMDB down to that level. It is worthwhile spending time on this activity and being as forward-looking as possible. It may save costly reorganisations of the CMDB in the future. However, deciding the right level of CIs in advance is not always easy. If possible, obtain a Configuration Management support tool that does not unduly constrain further breakdown of CIs to lower level ones. If this is not possible select a tool that allows the recording of properties of individual CIs, such as build level. Examples of an infrastructure and configuration breakdown are shown in Figures 7.3, 7.4 and 7.5.

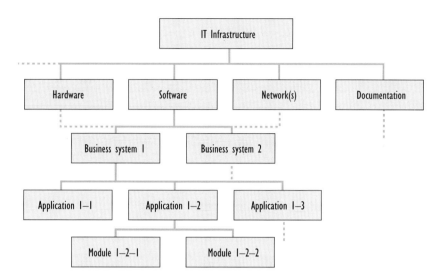

Figure 7.3 - Example configuration breakdown structure

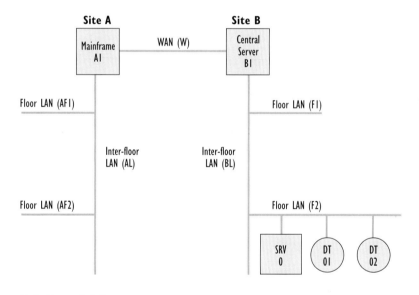

Figure 7.4 - Example infrastructure

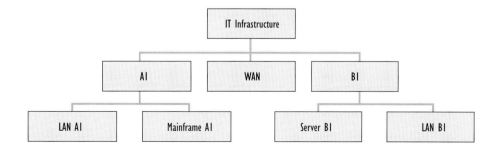

Figure 7.5 - Example configuration breakdown structure (for the infrastructure in Figure 7.4)

Although a 'child' CI should be 'owned' by one 'parent' CI, it can be 'used by' any number of other CIs. If standard software configurations (sets) are used (e.g. all the terminals on a nationwide network have access to identical software sets), then these sets can be defined and 'access' relationships established to the sets. This can considerably reduce the number of relationships that are needed, compared with when individual software CIs relationships are used.

In some cases, a network service may be regarded as part of, or is used by, the IT infrastructure, but cannot be brought under Configuration Management control. For example, an external Wide Area Network (WAN) owned by another organisation can be represented as a single high-level CI with all connections to the network as 'used by' or 'connected to' relationships. Figure 7.6 shows how these relationships might be defined.

Choosing the right CI level is a matter of achieving a balance between information availability, the right level of control, and the resources and effort needed to support it. For example if a Change is to be made to module 1-2-2 in Figure 7.3, it is better to record the Change at module level rather than program level – but it will be more costly to populate and maintain the CMDB down to module level.

On the other hand, actual Changes should be made at the level recorded in the CMDB. Therefore, if it is decided that the CMDB will record software at program level, Changes should be made at this level. For example, if a single module is to be changed, it will be necessary to recompile the whole program to make the Change at program level.

If information at a low CI level would not be valuable – for example, if a keyboard is not usually exchanged independently, or the organisation sees it as a consumable – do not store it. CI information is valuable only if it facilitates the management of Change, the control of Incidents and Problems, or the control of assets that can be independently moved, copied or changed.

The organisation should plan to review the CI level on a regular basis – to confirm (or otherwise) that information down to a low level still valuable and useful, and that the handling of Changes and Problems and the management of assets are not deficient because the CMDB does not go to a sufficiently low level.

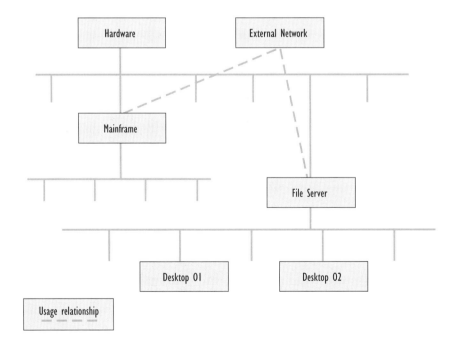

Figure 7.6 - Example of an external network

CI types and life-cycles

Components should be classified into CI types because this helps to identify and document what is in use, the status of the items and where they are located. Typical CI types are: software products, business systems, system software, servers, mainframes, workstations, laptops, routers and hubs.

The life-cycle states for each CI type should also be defined; e.g. an application Release may be registered, accepted, installed, or withdrawn. An example of a life-cycle for a package application Release is shown in Figure 7.7. The role that can promote the CI should be defined, e.g. Configuration Management, Release Management.

Figure 7.7 - Example of an application Release life-cycle on the IT infrastructure

Configuration Management should plan which attributes are to be recorded. As the required attributes may vary for different types of CI, consideration should be given to only current and forecast CI types. Note that some support tools may dictate the decision. Annex 7C gives a suggested list of attributes that should be recorded. It is useful to have an attribute to identify high-risk or critical CIs.

CI relationships

The relationships between CIs should be stored so as to provide dependency information. For example:

- a CI is a part of another CI (e.g. a software module is part of a program, a server is part of a site infrastructure) – this is a 'parent/child' relationship
- a CI is connected to another CI (e.g. a desktop computer is connected to a LAN)
- a CI uses another CI (e.g. a program uses a module from another program, a business service uses an infrastructure server).

There may be many more types of relationships, but all of these relationships are held in the CMDB – this is one of the major differences between what is recorded in a CMDB and what is held in an asset register.

A mechanism is required for associating RFCs, Incident records (IRs), Problem records, Known Errors and Release records with the IT infrastructure CIs to which they refer. All these relationships should be included in the CMDB. RFC, and all Change and Release records should identify the CIs affected. These records should also identify the make-up of the Changes. See Chapter 9, Release Management, for further details.

Identification of software and document libraries

Physical and electronic software libraries should be uniquely identified with the following information:

- contents, location and medium of each library
- conditions for entering an item, including the minimum status compatible with the contents of the library

- how to protect the libraries from malicious and accidental harm and deterioration, together with effective recovery procedures
- conditions and access controls for groups or types of person registering, reading, updating, copying, removing and deleting CIs.

Identification of configuration baselines

A configuration baseline may be created for any or all of the following reasons:

- as a sound basis for future work (e.g. a point in the life of a CI from which you can progress, such as an 'accepted' application)
- as a record of what CIs were affected by an RFC and what CIs were actually changed
- as a point you can fall back to if things go wrong.

Configuration baselines should be unique to their purpose, and the CIs and information to be controlled in the baseline, including all commercial off-the-shelf products and proprietary items with their associated documentation. Configuration baselines should include the associated configuration documentation, including:

- Release records (current, past and planned)
- other Change records (current, past and planned)
- the state of system and its documentation when a Change is approved and when it is applied
- the state of a system and its documentation when a package Release is applied
- hardware and software – standard specifications.

Configuration baselines should be established by formal agreement at specific points in time and used as departure points for the formal control of a configuration. Configuration baselines plus approved Changes to those baselines together constitute the currently approved configuration. Specific examples of baselines that may be identified are thus

- A particular 'standard' CI needed when buying many items of the same type (e.g. desktop computer) over a protracted period. If some servers are to include additional printed circuit boards, this could correspond to 'baseline plus'. If all future desktop computers are to have these boards, a new baseline is created.
- An application Release and its associated documentation
  - to be reverted to (should exist physically and be capable of easy reversion)
  - as the state of software for distribution to remote sites
  - as the state of software to be worked on in the future
  - as the state a system should be in before it can be upgraded to accept new hardware
  - or software.

Several baselines corresponding to different stages in the life of a 'baselined item', can exist at any given time – for example, the baseline for a software Release that is currently live, the one that was last live and has now been archived, the one that will next be installed (subject to Change under Configuration Management control), and one or more under test. Furthermore, if, for instance, new software is being introduced gradually on a regional basis, more than one version of a baseline could be 'live' at the same time. It is therefore best to refer to each by a unique version number, rather than 'live', 'next', 'old'.

Naming conventions

Naming conventions should be established and applied to the identification of CIs, configuration documents and Changes, as well as to baselines, Releases and assemblies. The naming conventions should be unique and take into account the existing corporate or supplier naming/numbering structures. The naming conventions or information management system should permit the management of:

- hierarchical relationships between CIs within a configuration structure
- hierarchical or subordinate relationships in each CI
- relationships between CIs and their associated documents
- relationships between documents and Changes
- relationships between Incidents and Changes.

Configuration Management should arrange for a naming convention to be established for all CIs and control forms, e.g. RFCs. Individual instances of CIs should be uniquely identifiable by means of the CI's name, copy/serial number and version. (The details of copy/serial number and version need to be in the CMDB, but need not be part of the unique identifier.) The version identifies a changed version of what can be regarded as the same CI. More than one version of the same CI can coexist at the same time.

When the naming convention is being planned, it is very important that sufficient account is taken of possible future growth. Identifiers should be relatively short, but meaningful, and should re-use any existing conventions wherever possible. For hardware, if the CI naming conventions are not based on suppliers' device names and serial numbers, a mechanism should be set up to relate Configuration Management and suppliers' identifiers to each other – for example, for the convenience of hardware engineers.

Release records, Change records and other CIs that are 'associated with' the IT infrastructure all need CI identifiers. A simple naming scheme, such as R1, R2, R3, R4,... is recommended, with version numbers used to indicate Changes – for example to Release plans.

Labelling CIs

All CIs should be labelled with the configuration identifier so that they can be easily identified. Plans should be made to label CIs and to maintain the accuracy of their labels.

Physical non-removable labels should be attached to all hardware CIs. All cables/lines should be clearly labelled at each end and at any inspection points. It is advisable to use a standard format and colour for all such labels, because this makes it easier for Users to identify and quote from them, for instance when telephoning the Service Desk to report a fault. Barcode-readable labels improve the efficiency of physical audits.

Definitive copies of software in the DSL should have a software label containing the CI name and version number at the start of the file. All media containing software should be clearly labelled with the CI name, copy number and version number of each of the software items contained on the media (as well as the CI name and serial number of the medium itself).

Definitive copies of documentation should never be issued, but should be retained in a documentation library. If a document will change at some known future date, then a shelf-life date could also be included (e.g. 'the contents of this document are not valid after 30 September 2002').

7.6.3 Control of CIs

The objective of configuration control is to ensure that only authorised and identifiable CIs are recorded in the CMDB upon receipt. The procedures should protect the integrity of the enterprise's data, systems and processes. When a Change is processed, the components being changed move through a number of planned/agreed states. Examples of states are: 'registered', 'fit for use', 'installed', 'in use', 'withdrawn', 'for disposal', 'disposed' and 'under Change'. Procedural and technical controls should be introduced to ensure that unauthorised Change is virtually impossible.

Licences should be managed and the total licence holding updated as CIs are added, updated, withdrawn or decommissioned. Procedures are required to ensure that relevant licence fees have been correctly paid and all irrelevant ones have been stopped, and that the organisation has complied with all legal restrictions relating to bought-in software.

The on-going configuration control processes are:

- register all new CIs and versions
- update CI record with regard to
    - status Changes that occur to CIs (e.g. development to test, test to live, live to archive)
    - updating attributes
    - Changes in ownership or roles
    - relating new versions of documentation arising from Changes, builds and Releases
    - licence control
    - linking CIs to related Incidents, Problem, Change and Release records
- update RFCs with related CIs, status and implementation details (see Chapter 8, Figure 8.3)
- update and archive of CIs and their associated records when CIs are deleted/decommissioned
- protect the integrity of configurations
- update the CMDB after periodic checking of the existence of physical items against the CMDB to ensure accurate information is available.

Registration of new CIs and versions

The process of registration begins with items being ordered or with development being commissioned. Some organisations use their procurement process to ensure that CIs are added when they are ordered. Suppliers may also participate by labelling CIs prior to dispatch. In this way the ordering and delivery of CIs is under Configuration Management control.

All deliveries should be recorded and their contents verified. See paragraph 7.6.4 (Configuration status accounting) for guidance on verification. If the software or hardware does not satisfy the check, rectification action is initiated. Licence holdings and attributes should be updated.

Software developed in house

For software developed in house, the point of 'receipt' is normally the point at which software is ready for operational acceptance. The use of a DSL is recommended, where all software CIs and their documentation are held in their definitive, quality-controlled state. Registration procedures should ensure that details of all authorised software and supporting documentation CIs are entered in the CMDB before the CIs are transferred from the development library into the DSL. The status of the CIs should be altered when they enter the DSL (e.g. from 'planned' to 'present'). Ideally, the utility program or support tool that does the physical library transfer should carry out the CMDB update automatically. Unauthorised or corrupt items should not be allowed in the DSL.

For software CIs that have been configuration-managed during their development stages using the same CMDB, only a status Change, rather than a new entry, may need to be made initially. If a shared database is used for development and live CIs, access controls should be applied to limit access to only the appropriate staff – for example, development staff should only have access to development CIs. If a different tool or database has been used, the CI data should be transferred into the new CMDB. Ideally the CI data should not need rekeying.

Off-the-shelf CIs

Procedures should be planned for off-the-shelf CIs, including hardware, communications equipment, documentation, software packages, operating systems software and utilities. Change Management should ensure that all authorised new CIs are correctly registered in the CMDB before they are delivered and that the status of these CIs is changed as they are delivered, installed, tested and accepted. A check should be made that delivered CIs are authorised. Installation procedures should not commence until this check has been satisfactorily carried out.

New CIs and versions from building and releasing

Good build and Release controls ensure that updated versions of software and hardware are built correctly and distributed to target environments that are compatible with the Release. Configuration Management with Release Management should record and report the versions of software, hardware and documentation that were the result of the build and Release processes. This includes:

- details of the target environment in which the build is to take place
- references to master copies of all components of the build and the build tools
- details of the environment into which the build is to be released
- references and access to prior Releases and configuration records.

When software quality-control checks are successful, the software is authorised for acceptance and copied into the DSL. Care should be taken to ensure that software is not corrupted or changed during the copying or distribution processes.

Updating CIs

The status of CIs changes as they progress from delivery to live use. Ideally, the CMDB should be updated automatically as the status of CIs and Releases changes. Associated documentation, such as test certificates and licences, should be placed in a controlled document library.

Changes to the attributes of CIs in the CMDB should be updated with a related RFC that authorises the Change to the attribute. If corrections need to made to the attributes – for example, after an audit – a Change record should be raised to track the attribute updates.

In many organisations it is difficult to keep up with Changes in ownership and roles, particularly where there is a high staff turnover or contract staff. Procedures to update the CMDB with Changes in ownership are essential in order to ensure that Requests for Change, Incidents and Problems related to CIs are notified to the right parties.

To ensure all IT infrastructure items are as authorised by Change Management, a record of all authorised Changes and enhancements is made on the CMDB. Once a Change is implemented, the CMDB should be amended to show the Change in status of CIs affected by the Change.

Licence control

Configuration Management should verify that secure master copies of software, documentation, data, licences and agreements for supply, warranty and maintenance are lodged within the Configuration Management system or DSL.

The terms and conditions relating to the purchase of software may place legal restrictions on the organisation (e.g. no unauthorised copies to be made). It is particularly important, therefore, regardless of who carries out the implementation, that the CMDB is updated with details of who holds copies of software items. This assists the organisation in discharging its legal obligations, and it assists auditors and the Service Desk to check for the existence of unauthorised copies.

Updating and archiving configuration records of withdrawn/decommissioned CIs

Scheduling and controlling the removal and disposal of CIs is often important for financial and security reasons. There should be procedures in place for decommissioning equipment or software so as to ensure correct disposal of the organisation's assets, and that the relevant records (e.g licence holding, number of desktops supported by a supplier) are updated. The CMDB should be updated and the status of the CIs promoted to the final state, e.g. 'withdrawn' or 'archived'.

Protecting the integrity of configurations

To protect the integrity of the configuration and to provide the basis for the control of Change, it is essential that CIs, their constituent parts and their documentation be held in an environment that:

- is commensurate with the environmental conditions required (e.g for computer hardware, software, data, documents, drawings etc.)
- protects them from unauthorised change or corruption
- provides a means for disaster recovery
- in the case of software, data and documentation, permits the controlled retrieval of a copy of the controlled master
- supports consistency between the as-built state of a configuration and the as-planned state
- is secure and protected by up-to-date anti-virus software.

The processes for procurement, storage, dispatch, receipt and disposal of goods should ensure that equipment, software and documentation is delivered safely to its destination. Storage areas should be secure. Checks on delivery documentation against goods coming into the organisation should be completed and recorded. Installation, environmental and electrical checks should be planned and completed by the appropriate people (not Configuration Management) before connection to the network. Access controls should be defined and enforced so as to provide staff with the correct level of access to the Configuration Management database, physical hardware, software and documentation.

Configuration Management should ensure the integrity of the stored software CIs, irrespective of the medium or library, by:

- selecting a storage medium to minimise regeneration errors or deterioration
- exercising and refreshing archived CIs at a frequency compatible with the storage life of the medium
- storing duplicate copies in controlled locations in order to minimise the risk of loss in the event of a disaster.

Consistent replication of CIs is important in order to ensure that no extraneous items (such as software viruses or test data) are introduced. It is important to use a suitable medium to ensure the software and associated documentation arrives in the condition in which it was replicated. The medium should be selected to preserve the integrity of the contents over the expected life of service delivery.

Configuration Management should ensure that the delivered medium is prepared by approved procedures and should label the medium with the identification of the Release. Software distribution should be designed to ensure that the integrity of software is maintained whilst handling, packaging and delivering software. Automated software distribution to remote locations will save resources and reduce the distribution cycle time. After distributing software over a network it is essential to check that the Release is complete when it reaches its destination.

Updating the CMDB after checking the existence of physical items

All IT staff should be asked to report any instances where they detect unauthorised CIs, or CIs that do not match the information on the CMDB. Depending upon their level of authority, IT staff should:

- report the matter via the Service Desk
- update the CI
- mark the CI as inaccurately recorded
- raise an Incident for investigation
- raise an RFC to correct the CMDB.

Configuration Management should trace the origin of each unregistered item and propose or initiate actions to register, correct, or delete the CIs. The deficiencies that allowed unregistered items to slip through should be corrected and reported to management. Sensitive handling may be required so as to avoid creating a 'black market' in unregistered CIs (e.g. unauthorised compact discs, software from the Internet).

7.6.4   Configuration status accounting

Status reports should be produced on a regular basis, listing, for all CIs under control, their current version and Change history. Status accounting reports on the current, previous and planned states of the CIs should include:

- unique identifiers of constituent CIs and their current status, e.g. 'under development', 'under test', 'live'
- configuration baselines, Releases and their status
- latest software item versions and their status for a system baseline/application
- the person responsible for status change, e.g. from 'under test' to 'live'
- Change history/audit trail
- open Problems/RFCs.

Status accounting reports can be used to establish system baselines and enable Changes between baselines and Releases to be traceable. Status reports may include:

- baseline and Release identifiers
- latest software item versions for a system build/application
- the number of Changes for a system

- the number of baselines and Releases
- the usage and volatility of CIs
- comparisons of baselines and Releases.

7.6.5   Configuration verification and audit

Before a major Release or Change, an audit of a specific configuration may be required to ensure that the Customer's environment matches the CMDB. Before acceptance into the live environment, new Releases, builds, equipment and standards should be verified against the contracted or specified requirements. There should be a test certificate that proves that the functional requirements of a new or updated CI have been verified, or some other relevant document (i.e. RFC).

Physical configuration audits should be carried out to verify that the 'as-built' configuration of a CI conforms to its 'as-planned' configuration and its associated documents. Interrogation facilities are required to check that the CMDB and the physical state of CIs are consistent.

Plans should be made for regular configuration audits to check that the CMDB is consistent with the physical state of all CIs, and vice versa. These audits should verify that correct and authorised versions of CIs exist, and that only such CIs exist, and are in use in the operational environment. From the outset, any ad-hoc tools, test equipment, personal computers and other 'non-registered' items should either be removed or registered through formal Configuration Management. Non-registered and unauthorised items that somehow make an appearance during configuration audits should be investigated, and corrective action should be taken to address possible issues with procedures and the behaviour of personnel. All exceptions should be logged and reported.

The configuration audits should check in addition that Change and Release records have been properly authorised by Change Management and that implemented Changes are as authorised. Configuration audits should be considered at the following times:

- shortly after implementation of a new Configuration Management system
- before and after major Changes to the IT infrastructure
- before a software Release or installation to ensure that the environment is as expected
- following recovery from disasters and after a 'return to normal' (this audit should be included in contingency plans)
- at random intervals
- in response to the detection of any unauthorised CIs
- at regular intervals.

Automated audit tools enable regular checks to be made at regular intervals, e.g. weekly. For example, desktop audit tools compare the build of an individual's desktop to the master build that was installed. If exceptions are found, some organisations return the build to its original state. A rolling programme of configuration audits can help utilise resources more effectively. The Service Desk and support groups should be instructed to check that CIs brought to their attention, e.g the software that a caller is using, are as recorded in the CMDB. Any deviations should be reported to Configuration Management for investigation.

If there is a high incidence of unauthorised CIs detected, the frequency of configuration audits should be increased, certainly for those parts of the IT infrastructure affected by this problem. Note that unauthorised installations are discouraged when the Configuration Management team is seen to be in control and to carry out regular and frequent audits. If an epidemic of unauthorised CIs is detected, selective or general configuration audits should be initiated to determine the scale of the problem, to put matters right, and to discourage a proliferation of unauthorised CIs. Publicity will help to reduce further occurrences.

7.6.6 CMDB back-ups, archives and housekeeping

Back-up copies of the CMDB should be taken regularly and securely stored. It is advisable for one copy to be stored at a remote location for use in the event of a disaster. The frequency of copying and the retention policy will be dependent on the size and volatility of the IT infrastructure and the CMDB. Certain tools may allow selective copying of CI records that are new or have been changed.

The CMDB contains information on back-up copies of CIs. It will also contain historical records of CIs and CI versions that are archived, and possibly also of deleted CIs or CI versions. The amount of historical information to be retained depends on its usefulness to the organisation. The retention policy on historical CI records should be regularly reviewed, and changed if necessary. If the cost to the organisation of retaining CI information is greater than the current or potential value, do not retain it.

Typically, the CMDB should contain records only for items that are physically available or could be easily created using procedures known to, and under the control of Configuration Management. When Configuration Management has been operating for a period of time, regular housekeeping should be carried out to ensure that redundant CI records are systematically deleted.

7.6.7 Providing a Configuration Management service

Configuration Management should add value to the Service Management organisation. Recommended services of the function comprise:

- regular information and an ad-hoc reporting service
- advice on setting up Configuration Management for new groups or technologies
- policy, procedures, roles and responsibilities for Configuration Management
- sample Configuration Management plans
- reports that help to identify how to reduce the number of variant configurations and the complexity of the operational environments
- efficient capture, maintenance and deletion of records
- updated lists and information on standard products, including:
    - making available the public name, location, build and Release information
    - identifying the organisation responsible for providing the product
    - specifying the method and timing for archiving standard products
- a library service to manage controlled copies of documents or software
- licence management
- a configuration audit service.

7.7 Process control

Configuration Management should continually assess the efficiency and effectiveness of the Configuration Management system using regular management reports. A review of the expected growth of demand of Configuration Management activities should be scheduled on a regular basis, for example, every six months, although in more volatile situations more frequent reviews may be appropriate.

7.7.1   Management reporting

Management reports for Configuration Management should cover the following:

- results of configuration audits
- information on any non-registered or inaccurately registered CIs that have been detected and the corrective action
- information on the number of registered CIs and CI versions, broken down by CI category, type and status (and possibly also by location or other CI attributes)
- growth and capacity information
- information on the rate of change of CIs/CMDB and the DSL
- details of any backlogs of Configuration Management work or any delays caused by Configuration Management activities, and proposed remedies
- the Configuration Management staffing position
- the amount of authorised work done out of hours by other IT services staff
- the results of efficiency/effectiveness reviews, growth reviews and audits of the Configuration Management system and proposals for tackling actual or potential Problems
- data and analyses on the number of CIs by type (e.g. services, servers, routers, hubs, software licences, desktop PCs, etc)
- the value of CIs (or assets)
- the location of CIs by business unit, support group or service.

Management reports should be designed to support Service Management activities such as progress monitoring, Problem Management, Change Management, Release Management, Configuration audits and service planning. The reports should be made available for interrogation and trend analysis by IT Service Management and other groups within the IT services structure.

In general, IT Service Management should set the future direction for Configuration Management in the light of these management reports, taking account of the planned Configuration Management workload and growth.

7.7.2   Key performance indicators

Measurable targets for objective metrics should be set for the effectiveness of the Configuration Management process. Consider including the following metrics and set targets to improve them over a realistic timeframe:

- occasions when the 'configuration' is not as authorised
- Incidents and Problems that can be traced back to wrongly made Changes
- RFCs that were not completed successfully because of poor impact assessment, incorrect data in the CMDB, or poor version control
- the cycle time to approve and implement Changes
- licences that have been wasted or not put into use at a particular location
- exceptions reported during configuration audits
- unauthorised IT components detected in use.

Other indicators and targets that may be appropriate are:

- the change in the proportion of Service Desk calls that are received per month that are resolved whilst the User is on the telephone, without the need for further escalation

■ the change in the number and seriousness of Incidents and Problems

■ the change in the average time and cost of diagnosing and resolving Service Desk calls that cannot be resolved immediately

■ the change in the number and seriousness of occasions when a Service Level Agreement has been breached where the Problem can be traced back to errors made in the Change Management, Configuration Management, Release Management, Problem Management or Service Desk functions

■ the number of changes to the CMDB per month because of identified errors in the CMDB.

7.8 Relations to other processes

Configuration Management is heavily dependent upon a number of other disciplines. Effective Change Management, software control, Release Management, operational acceptance testing, and procedures for the installation and acceptance of new/different hardware and network components are all essential. If these are not already in existence, they should be planned alongside Configuration Management.

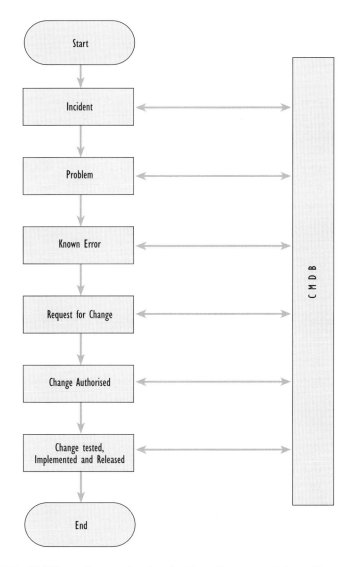

Figure 7.8 - CMDB interfacing to Incident, Problem, Change and Release Management

Effective Problem Management procedures are also highly desirable so as to reap most benefit from Configuration Management. If no Problem Management procedures exist, consideration should be given to planning such procedures as soon as possible. Configuration Management underpins many service support processes such as Incident Management, Problem Management, Change Management and Release Management. Figures 7.8 and 7.9 show the relationships.

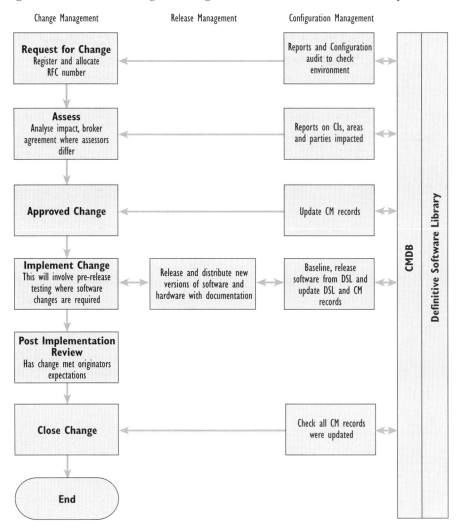

Figure 7.9 - Relationship between Configuration, Change and Release Management

Chapter 8, Change Management, describes procedures for authorising and implementing IT infrastructure Changes. Ideally, Change Management should be regarded as an integral part of a Configuration Management system. However, because many installations have been practising Change Management without adopting full Configuration Management, the subject is treated separately.

Configuration Management contributes to the effective control of Incidents and Problems. Further information on this is available in the Incident Management and Problem Management chapters in this book (Chapters 5 and 6 respectively).

Release Management can be regarded as part of Configuration Management. It covers the building, distribution and implementation of Releases. This chapter covers, in general terms, the procedures required for controlling software, hardware and documentation and the update of the logical model of the IT infrastructure. The logical model is used to control and record the details of the building, Release, distribution, implementation and maintenance of Releases. Further information on Release Management is given in Chapter 9.

It is recommended that a single Configuration Management system be used to control components in both the live and the development environments. If there are multiple platforms, the live Configuration Management system should be designated as the 'master' and links defined to the development control and build tools in order to control the movement of components into and out of independent testing environments.

There should be strong ties between Configuration Management and the Finance, Administration and Purchasing functions of the organisation. CIs are the organisation's property, whether they are hardware, software, documents, or anything else. Configuration Management is responsible for making Finance aware of any Changes in the location and condition of this property. Approval to pay for IT infrastructure components should involve verification by Configuration Management that those CIs have actually been received, have been installed, and are working correctly.

7.9 Tools specific to the Configuration Management process

7.9.1 Configuration Management system

Many organisations have some form of Configuration Management in operation, but it is often paper-based. For large and complex infrastructures, Configuration Management will operate more effectively when supported by a *software* tool that is capable of maintaining a CMDB. The CMDB contains details about the attributes and the history of each CI and details of the important relationships between CIs. Ideally, the CMDB should be linked to the DSL and other software libraries. Often, several tools need to be integrated to provide the fully automated solution across platforms.

The Configuration Management system should prevent Changes from being made to an IT infrastructure without valid authorisation via Change Management. The authorisation record should automatically 'drive' the Change. As far as possible, all Changes should be recorded on the CMDB at least by the time that the Change is implemented. The status (e.g. 'live', 'archive', etc) of each CI affected by a Change should be updated automatically if possible. Example ways in which this automatic recording of Changes could be implemented include automatic updating of the CMDB when software is moved between libraries (e.g. from 'acceptance test' to 'live', or from 'live' to an 'archive' library), when the service catalogue is changed, and when a Release is distributed.

The Configuration Management system should, in addition, provide:

- sufficient security controls to limit access on a need-to-know basis
- support for CIs of varying complexity e.g. entire systems, Releases, single hardware items, software modules, or hierarchic and networked relationships between CIs; by holding information on the relationships between CIs, Configuration Management tools facilitate the impact assessment of RFCs
- easy addition of new CIs and deletion of old CIs
- automatic validation of input data (e.g. are all CI names unique)
- automatic establishment of all relationships that can be automatically established, when new CIs are added
- support for CIs with different model numbers, version numbers, and copy numbers
- automatic identification of other affected CIs when any CI is the subject of an Incident report/record, Problem record, Known Error Record or RFC

- integration of Problem Management data within the CMDB, or at least an interface from the Configuration Management system to any separate Problem Management databases that may exist

- automatic updating and recording of the version number of a CI if the version number of any component CI is changed

- maintenance of a history of all CIs (both a historical record of the current version – such as installation date, records of Changes, previous locations, etc – and of previous versions)

- support for the management and use of configuration baselines (corresponding to definitive copies, versions etc), including support for reversion to trusted versions

- ease of interrogation of the CMDB and good reporting facilities, including trend analysis (e.g. the ability to identify the number of RFCs affecting particular CIs)

- ease of reporting of the CI inventory so as to facilitate configuration audits

- flexible reporting tools to facilitate impact analyses

- the ability to show graphically the configuration or network maps of interconnected CIs, and to input information about new CIs via such maps

- the ability to show the hierarchy of relationships between 'parent' CIs and 'child' CIs.

7.9.2   Software Configuration Management

Support tools should allow control to be maintained, for applications software, from the outset of systems analysis and design right through to live running. Ideally, organisations should use the same tool to control all stages of the life-cycle, although this may not be possible if all the platforms cannot be supported by one software tool. If this is not possible, then the IT infrastructure Configuration Management tool should at least allow Configuration Management information to be transferred from a software development Configuration Management system into the CMDB without the need for rekeying.

7.9.3   Change Management and Release Management support

To support Change Management and Release Management, the Configuration Management tools should provide automated support for the following:

- identification of related CIs affected by a proposed Change to assist with impact assessment

- recording of CIs that are affected by authorised Changes

- implementation of Changes including package Releases in accordance with authorisation records

- registering of CI status Changes when authorised Changes and Releases are implemented

- recording of baselines of CIs and CI packages, to which to revert with known consequences – for example, if an implemented Change fails.

7.9.4   Configuration auditing

Automating configuration audits significantly increases the efficiency and effectiveness of the audits. Audit tools can determine exactly what software is installed and identify most critical aspects of hardware configuration. This means a greater coverage of audited CIs with the resources available, and staff can focus on handling the exceptions rather than doing the audits.

If the DSL is not integrated with the CMDB it may be worth automating the comparison of the DSL contents with the CMDB.

154

7.9.5   Enterprise system and tools

The following systems will provide automated support for some elements of Change Management, Configuration Management and Release Management that are required to support the IT infrastructure:

- IT Service Management systems
- enterprise frameworks that provide integration capabilities to link in the CMDB or tools
- system, network and application management tools that provide software distribution, discovery and audit functions
- the Configuration Management system used by development, integration or test teams.

Existing or planned systems within the organisation should be analysed during the requirements definition and considered during architectural design. This may be to provide a core Configuration Management process or a solution for a specific aspect. These examples can be quoted:

- Service Management tools are good at linking CIs to a service and integrating Incident Management, Problem Management and Change Management with the CIs
- system and network management tools may provide discovery tools to help with the population of the CMDB and subsequent audits
- Configuration Management systems that currently control software may be used to control hardware and documentation.

7.9.6   Other tools

There are many support tools that can assist Change Management, Configuration Management and Release Management. These may come in a variety of combinations and include:

- document-management systems
- requirements analysis and design tools, systems architecture and CASE tools, which can facilitate impact analysis from a business perspective
- database management audit tools to track physical databases
- distribution and installation tools
- comparison tools (software files, directories, databases)
- build and Release tools (that provide listings of input and output CIs)
- installation and de-installation tools (that provide listings of CIs installed)
- compression tools (to save storage space)
- listing and configuration baseline tools (e.g. full directory listings with date–time stamps and check sums)
- audit tools (also called 'discovery' or 'inventory' tools)
- detection and recovery tools (where the build is returned to a known state)
- reporting tools.

These individual tools and solutions may be integrated with the main service or the Configuration Management system where the effort of integration is beneficial. Otherwise, the integration may be undertaken at the procedural or data level.

7.10   Impact of new technology

Internet technology may change the way that software and documents are controlled and accessed. For example, organisations may have a policy of looking for the latest version of a software package or document on the Internet.

Examples of new technology's impact on Configuration Management include:

- growth in Service Management, network, enterprise and System Management tools
- interfaces to system and network management tools
- software Configuration Management coming into the scope of Service Management tools
- graphical representations with drill down
- reporting tools that access objects from several databases, providing integrated reports across systems – e.g. the CMDB, DSL and Service Management tools
- links to discovery, collection and audit tools.

7.11   Guidance on Configuration Management

There are three aspects of Configuration Management where special guidance can perhaps be given.

7.11.1   Level of control

Many organisations start by defining very high-level CIs. Identifying *critical* services and their components is, however, a useful place to start with Configuration Management. Some items may be more critical at particular times of the day or year. Examples of critical or high-risk CIs are:

- critical power supplies, server and machine rooms
- routers and communications for main sites
- executives' connections, computers and software applications
- items that could affect regulatory compliance for the organisation
- connections to secure areas and systems
- security items
- EDI and database feeds, e.g. payroll feeds
- external interfaces to trading partners, suppliers, Customers and business partners
- interfaces to branches with Customer systems
- new technology items that need to be tracked initially.

Some organisations drown in too much detail. They assume that, just because they have low-level details in one part of the structure, this is required throughout all the other configurations. Although this may help consistency and understanding, it will result in poor control data because there could well be insufficient resources to maintain all the data. A replanning exercise may be required to return to an appropriate level of control, using input from the CMDB. Another idea is to have a configuration clean-up or decommissioning activity to remove old kit or redundant items – it also removes the need to maintain the control details.

So the target is **maximum control with minimum records**.

7.11.2 Versions or Variants?

Although the same CI cannot be used in more than one location on an IT infrastructure, it is quite possible to use a slightly different version of what could otherwise be regarded as the same CI. This slightly different version would have a different version number, and such CIs are called 'variants'.

To appreciate how variants can be useful, consider a computer with two disc drives labelled A and B, both initially using version 1.1. If B is modified to increase the capacity and data-transfer rate, it becomes version 1.1.1. Drive A could be left unmodified to retain backwards compatibility. If a design fault is subsequently found in A and is corrected (taking A to version 1.2), this Change should be propagated to B (taking it to version 1.2.1). A and B could be regarded as different, unrelated CIs; however, it can be advantageous, because they share a large number of common components, to regard one as a variant of the other. Another and very common example of the use of variants is where a 'standard' system is 'customised' for particular applications.

There is normally a trade-off involved. The use of variants can result in fewer CIs to manage and may make it easier to identify items for commonality of treatment, be this in error handling or for the implementation of Changes. The use of variants will, however, introduce extra complexity to the Configuration Management system, and/or other systems such as Problem Management that rely on it.

General guidance is thus: if a CI can be regarded as slightly different from another related CI, and Problems affecting one are likely to affect the other, or Changes made to the one will probably have to be made to the other, then use of a variant should be considered; otherwise, a different CI should be used.

7.11.3 Selection of Configuration Management tools

Many software suppliers include some Asset Management or Configuration Management functions in their product offerings. It is important to understand the functionality in the existing and proposed service and system management tools to avoid any overlap or gaps. For example, some tools support only two levels of CI and this can be very restrictive.

As organisations depend increasingly on software, the ability to manage and control all types of software is becoming more important. Care should be taken when selecting software Configuration Management tools to make sure that a range of the organisation's platforms can be supported or your organisation may end up with a tool for every platform. The ability to control software files automatically can save time and reduce errors. The length of the identifier is crucial with software, because there are often duplicate filenames in different parts of a structure.

Annex 7A: The central function for Change, Configuration and Release Management

A central Change, Configuration, and Release Management function will enable some organisations to implement control more efficiently and effectively. A central function may be responsible for managing Changes to hardware, software, and all items of documentation that are relevant to the running, support and maintenance of live systems.

The primary responsibilities of a central Change, Configuration, and Release Management function are to:

■ produce and maintain the Change and Configuration Management plan, Configuration Management design and Release policy for the organisation

■ implement consistent Change Management, Configuration Management and Release Management practices across the organisation

■ identify CIs that need to be managed and controlled

■ integrate the central function with interfaces to other service managers, projects, suppliers and customers

■ ensure that the CMDB and DSL reflect the authorised state of the IT infrastructure and services

■ maintain and control hardware standards, technical standards and master copies of documents

■ provide supporting services, including registration and checking of Releases delivered from third parties

■ distribute reports and management information on CIs (e.g. the extent to which Problems and errors are affecting which CIs; and on life-expiry dates, licence fee renewal dates and costs)

■ ensure the Configuration Management system is aware and capable of coping with future workloads and growth (e.g. that adequate staff and resources are provided for Configuration Management)

■ ensure that all staff are familiar with and operate the Configuration Management, Change Management and software distribution policies, processes and systems for their work

■ define status accounting requirements to support other Service Management processes

■ organise regular checks of the status of the CMDB and DSL against the installed systems; arrange configuration audits and process audits; monitor exceptions and implement corrective action

■ make recommendations on strategy, policy and system design, including how to drive down the variant configurations and infrastructure complexity

■ investigate major Problems caused by poor control, and identify remedial actions

■ provide advice and guidance on infrastructure standards

■ provide advice on where Release components should be located on the infrastructure

■ communicate and advise projects on what to include in their Configuration Management and Release plans to ensure a successful transfer to the final service.

Setting up a Change, Configuration and Release Management function

The planning process for setting up an appropriate function could take anything from three to six months, from inception to the first phase of implementation. This period could be considerably longer if finance is not readily available or there are long lead times.

Experience has shown that it takes at least one month for staff in each area to complete training to the point where they can be effective. The support processes should not be implemented until staff are adequately trained. If staff try to take on control activities too soon, they may lose the cooperation of the other parts of the organisation by being perceived as a 'bottleneck'.

The planning and implementation of the central function involves several aspects:

Initial assessment

These control processes underpin a number of other processes, such as Problem Management, and the Service Desk. Plan to do an initial assessment of Service Management and support before and after introducing a process, in order to assess the benefits.

Planning a central function

Commitment from senior management is required to initiate a central function. A recommended approach is to integrate Change Management and Configuration Management and certain aspects of Release Management as a single function. The central function may also include handover and acceptance procedures for accepting CIs into Configuration Management.

Medium and large organisations will require dedicated resources to provide an adequate level of control. Large organisations may have local Configuration Managers with indirect reporting lines to the central configuration manager e.g. site Configuration Manager, or the software Configuration Manager for a major infrastructure programme.

Producing a Change and Configuration Management plan for a central function

The Configuration Management methodology should be defined in a Change and Configuration Management plan (C&CM plan) that includes:

- Configuration Management organisational roles and responsibilities
- architecture and design of the CMDB, DSL, Configuration Management tools and libraries
- Change Management, Configuration Management and Release Management policies and procedures.

The control processes between the interfaces should also be included, e.g. among projects, suppliers, and application teams and support teams. Projects and external suppliers should have a Configuration Management plan that defines the scope, configurations, procedures and interfaces to the IT services organisation.

A C&CM plan describes the scope of the infrastructure to be controlled and how the processes should be implemented to achieve the agreed objectives. The plan should be regularly updated. It should reflect the current scope, objectives and processes and should include the objectives for the next six to twelve months. It should include:

- the scope and objectives of Configuration Management including the services and platforms that are to be controlled and to what level, as well as a list or diagram of the high-level CIs and their relationships, and the schedule for bringing assets and CIs under control.

- overall Configuration Management, Change Management and Release Management policy
- related policies, standards and processes
- the organisations responsible for Configuration Management and their interfaces to the central function (e.g. in-house teams, systems integrators, subcontractors and suppliers)
- relevant Configuration Management systems, their scope and key interfaces between them – systems that may comprise a mixture of repositories and libraries and should include the locations of
  - CMDB
  - DSL
  - software and document controlled libraries
- controlled environments within which CIs are manipulated
- links and interfaces to other Service Management systems
- tools to be used on each platform
- the schedule and procedures for performing Configuration Management activities:
  - configuration identification
  - control
  - status accounting
  - configuration audit
  - verification
- licence management
- targets to improve the control processes (efficiency and effectiveness)
- the retention period for CIs (where, depending on the CI type, there may be a predefined number of versions, or one version for a predetermined period of time retained).

Roles

The roles within the function should include Configuration Manager, Asset Manager, Change Manager, Change administrator, Release Manager and relevant Change Advisory Board(s). The terms of reference, structure and escalation mechanisms for the Change Advisory Board(s) should be agreed. The Configuration Manager should attend the main Change Advisory Board(s).

Plan support tools

The central function should evaluate available support tools and instigate procurement of the selected tool and hardware on which to run the tools. This is a very important activity because the nature of the support tool(s) could heavily influence the operation of the central function.

Plan staffing and training

The disciplines require staff who will adopt a painstaking approach and pay due attention to detail. Central support staff are required, other than in very small installations. Consider the following factors when planning staff numbers:

- whether Configuration Management is to be responsible for projects as well as the IT infrastructure
- whether the group is also to be responsible for Change Management, Configuration Management and/or Release Management

- whether hardware/network installation and acceptance responsibilities are allocated to the group

- the size of the IT infrastructure, the level at which control is to be maintained, and hence the number of CIs to be controlled

- the number of staff performing control activities in other groups and projects

- the extent to which support tools are available

- the size, frequency and complexity of software Changes and Releases

- the number of Change Advisory Boards, attendance and frequency of meetings.

Change Management, Configuration Management and Release Management are usually on the critical path between projects, applications development and live operations. The central function may be involved in all Changes to live hardware, software and networks. Plan for enough trained staff to cover for annual leave and other absences. The minimum practical staffing level is two people – including the Configuration Manager – although, where appropriate, such as in very small organisations, one of these two could be a 'reserve'.

If Change Management, Configuration Management and Release Management activities are already being carried out within other groups, try to recruit staff from these groups into the central function, even if only on a temporary basis until new staff are trained. Where staff are not readily available, consider the use of consultants and contract staff to perform basic control activities until staff can be recruited and trained.

All staff who hand over (to IT Services), accept, install or Change any CIs should do so only if Change Management/Configuration Management authorisation has been given and the CMDB and DSL have been updated with details of the new CI(s) or Changes.

Consider the need for overtime or shift working. When urgent Releases or emergency fixes are required, Changes should always be subject to configuration control and should always be recorded in the CMDB. There are three options:

- provide staff at all hours

- make staff available on call

- delegate authority to someone who is available (e.g. Problem Management, or computer operations staff) – where adequate procedures and training will be required for the target staff – but not under any circumstances vendor or user staff.

Staff should be given a programme consisting of on-the-job training and formal training courses. There should be formal training in the Configuration Management discipline, and training should be given in the use of all support tools to be used. Staff should also be given a general understanding of the hardware, the software, the network and the telecommunications configuration over which they are to have control. Training should be given in other responsibilities as appropriate. It is, furthermore, useful to give staff an appreciation of the workings of the Problem Management and Service Desk systems and how Configuration Management assists these operations.

As soon as the support tools have been installed and are available for use, training staff in their use should be carried out. It may be possible to combine this training with the testing of the tools. Staff training in new procedures should be planned.

Annex 7B: Specific responsibilities of the Configuration Management team

Configuration Manager responsibilities

A Configuration Manager:

1. Works to the overall objectives agreed with the IT Services Manager; implements the organisation's Configuration Management policy and standards.

2. Evaluates existing Configuration Management systems and the design, implementation and management of new/improved systems for efficiency and effectiveness – including estimating and planning the work and resources involved, and monitoring and reporting on progress against plan.

3. Proposes and agrees scope of the Configuration Management processes, function, the items that are to be controlled, and the information that is to be recorded. Develops Configuration Management standards, Configuration Management plans and procedures.

4. Mounts an awareness campaign to win support for new Configuration Management procedures. Ensures that changes to the Configuration Management methods and processes are properly approved and communicated to staff before being implemented. Plans, publicises and oversees implementation of new Configuration Management systems.

5. Arranges recruitment and training of staff. Trains Configuration Management specialists and other staff in Configuration Management principles, processes and procedures.

6. Evaluates proprietary Configuration Management tools and recommends those that best meet the organisation's budget, resource, timescale and technical requirements. Directly or indirectly customises proprietary tools to produce effective Configuration Management environments in terms of databases and software libraries, workflows and report generation.

7. Creates and manages the Configuration Management plan, principles and processes and their implementation. This includes CI registration procedures; access controls and privileges. Ensures that the correct roles and responsibilities are defined in the Configuration Management plans and procedures.

8. Proposes and agrees CIs to be uniquely identified with naming conventions. Ensures that staff comply with identification standards for object types, environments, processes, life-cycles, documentation, versions, formats, baselines, Releases and templates.

9. Proposes and/or agrees interfaces with Change Management, Problem Management, Network Management, Release Management, computer operations, logistics, finance and administration functions.

10. Plans and executes population of the CMDB. Manages and maintains CMDB, central libraries, tools, common codes and data. Ensures regular housekeeping of the CMDB.

11. Provides reports, including management reports (indicating suggested action to deal with current or foreseen shortcomings), impact analysis reports and configuration status reports.

12. Uses or provides the CMDB to facilitate impact assessment for RFCs and to ensure that implemented Changes are as authorised. Creates Change records, configuration baselines, and package Release records in order to specify the effect on CIs of an

authorised Change. Ensures any changes to Change authorisation records are themselves subject to Change Management procedures. Ensures that the CMDB is updated when a Change is implemented.

13. Provides the CMDB to help identify other CIs affected by a fault that is affecting a CI.

14. Performs configuration audits to check that the physical IT inventory is consistent with the CMDB and initiates any necessary corrective action.

15. Initiates actions needed to secure funds to enhance the infrastructure and staffing levels in order to cope with growth and change.

16. Assists auditors to audit the activities of the Configuration Management team for compliance with laid-down procedures. Ensures corrective action is carried out.

Configuration Librarian responsibilities

The Configuration Librarian is the custodian and guardian of all master copies of software and documentation CIs registered with Configuration Management. The major tasks of this role are:

- to control the receipt, identification, storage, and withdrawal of all supported CIs
- to provide information on the status of CIs
- to number, record, store and distribute Configuration Management issues.

Specific responsibilities are to:

- assist Configuration Management to prepare the Configuration Management Plan
- create an identification scheme for Configuration Management libraries and the DSL
- create libraries or other storage areas to hold CIs
- assist in the identification of products and CIs
- maintain current status information on CIs
- accept and record the receipt of new or revised configurations into the appropriate library
- archive superseded CI copies
- hold the master copies
- issue copies of products for review, change, correction or information when authorised to do so
- maintain a record of all copies issued
- notify holders of any changes to their copies
- collect and retain information that will assist in the assessment of what CIs are impacted by a Change to a product
- produce configuration status accounting reports
- assist in conducting configuration audits
- liaise with other Configuration Libraries where CIs are common to other systems.

Annex 7C: Suggested CI attributes

The following attributes are examples that could be used in the CMDB. Note that hardware CI types will have different attributes from software CI types.

Attribute	Description
CI Name	The unique name by which this type of CI is known.
Copy or Serial Number	The number that uniquely identifies the particular instances of this CI – for example, for software the copy number, for hardware the serial number.
Category	Classification of a CI (e.g. hardware, software, documentation etc).
Type	Description of CI type, amplifying 'category' information (e.g. hardware configuration, software package, hardware device or program module).
Model Number (hardware)	Model of CI (corresponding, for example, to supplier's model number e.g. Dell model xxx, PC/aa model yyy).
Warranty expiry date	Date when the supplier's warranty expires for the CI.
Version Number	The version number of the CI.
Location	The location of the CI, e.g. the library or media where the software CIs reside, the site/room where a service is located.
Owner Responsible	The name and/or designation of the owner responsible for the CI.
Responsibility Date	Date the above owner became responsible for the CI.
Source/supplier	The source of the CI, e.g. developed in-house, bought in from company xxxxx etc.
Licence	Licence number or reference to licence agreement.
Supply Date	Date when the CI was supplied to the organisation.
Accepted Date	Date when the CI was accepted by the organisation as satisfactorily tested.
Status (current)	The current status of the CI; e.g. under 'test', 'live', 'archived'.
Status (scheduled)	The next scheduled status of the CI (with the date or indication of the event that will trigger the status change).
Parent CI(s) relationships	The unique CI identifier(s) – name/copy/number/model/number/ of the 'parent(s)' of this CI.
Child CI(s) relationships	The unique CI identifier(s) of all 'children' of this CI.
Relationships	The relationship of the CI with all CIs other than 'parent' and 'child' (e.g. this CI 'uses' another CI, this CI 'is connected to' another CI, this CI is 'resident on' another CI, this CI 'can access' another CI).
RFC Numbers	The identification number of all RFCs affecting this CI.
Change Numbers	The identification number of all Change records affecting this CI.
Problem Numbers	The identification number of all Problem records affecting this CI.
Incident Numbers	The identification number of all Incident records affecting this CI.
Comment	A comment field to be used for textual narrative; for example, to provide a description of how this version of the CI is different from the previous version.

For RFCs, Change records, package Release records, etc, the names, copy numbers, model numbers and version numbers of CIs affected by the Change, and how they are affected, should be recorded in the CMDB. A reversion path, and the consequences of reversion, should also be recorded.

8 CHANGE MANAGEMENT

8.1 Goal of Change Management

Changes arise as a result of Problems, but many Changes can come from proactively seeking business benefits such as reducing costs or improving services. The goal of the Change Management process is to ensure that standardised methods and procedures are used for efficient and prompt handling of all Changes, in order to minimise the impact of Change-related Incidents upon service quality, and consequently to improve the day-to-day operations of the organisation.

To make an appropriate response to a Change request entails a considered approach to assessment of risk and business continuity, Change impact, resource requirements and Change approval. This considered approach is essential to maintain a proper balance between the need for Change against the impact of the Change.

It is particularly important that Change Management processes have high visibility and open channels of communication in order to promote smooth transitions when Changes take place.

8.1.1 Purpose

The purpose of this chapter is to provide information on how to establish a Change Management process, including the procedures, tools and dependencies that will be necessary to plan for, implement and run Change Management. The chapter also describes the benefits that organisations can expect to receive.

8.1.2 Best practice

The definition of best practice in the area of Change Management is inevitably controversial; it is, however, generally accepted that Change Management and Configuration Management are best planned and implemented concurrently. Implementing Change and Configuration Management concurrently allows the organisation to weigh the risks of not implementing either process properly at the planning stages.

8.1.3 Program/project management and Change Management

In order to be able to define clear boundaries, dependencies and rules, Change Management should be integrated with processes used to control very large organisational programs or projects. An example of how the processes could be integrated is shown in Figure 8.1.

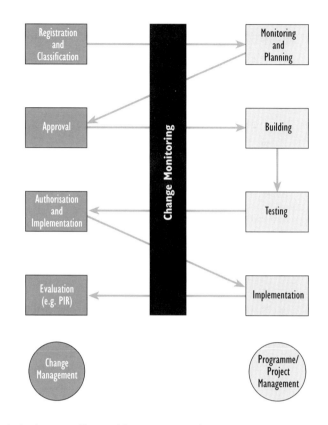

Figure 8.1 - Boundaries between Change Management and program management

8.2   Scope of Change Management

Change Management is responsible for managing Change processes involving:

■   hardware

■   communications equipment and software

■   system software

■   'live' applications software

■   all documentation and procedures associated with the running, support and maintenance of live systems.

This means that changes to any components that are under the control of an applications development project – for example, applications software, documentation or procedures – do not come under Change Management but would be subject to *project* Change Management procedures. The Change Management team will, however, be expected to liaise closely with Application Management project managers to ensure smooth implementation and consistency within the changing management environments.

It is the Change Management process that produces approval (or otherwise), for any proposed Change. While Change Management makes the process happen, the decision authority is the Change Advisory Board (CAB), which is made up for the most part of people from other functions within the organisation. Note also that it is Configuration Management who is responsible for ensuring that information regarding the possible implications of a proposed Change is made available, and that these possible impacts are detected and presented appropriately.

There will be occasions when a proposed infrastructure Change will potentially have a wider impact upon other parts of the organisation (e.g. applications development projects or business operations), or vice versa. To mitigate possible negative impacts from either direction, it is imperative that the infrastructure and other Change Management systems are appropriately interfaced (see Figure 8.1).

Inputs to the Change Management process will comprise:

- RFCs
- CMDB
- Forward Schedule of Changes (FSC).

Activities undertaken will involve:

- filtering Changes
- managing Changes and the Change process
- chairing the CAB and the CAB/Emergency Committee (see Paragraph 8.3.2)
- reviewing and closing RFCs
- management reporting.

Outputs from the process will be:

- FSC
- RFCs
- CAB minutes and actions
- Change Management reports.

Change Management is not responsible for identifying components affected by Change or updating Change records (the domain of Configuration Management), nor is it responsible for the Release of new of changed components (the domain of Release Management). The relationships between Capacity Management, Change Management, Configuration Management, and Release Management are illustrated in Figure 8.2.

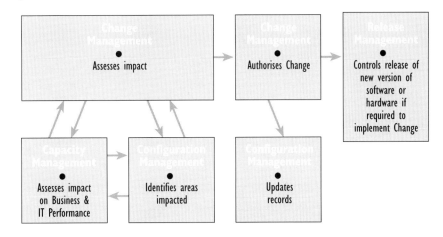

Figure 8.2 - Relationship between Capacity Management, Change Management, Configuration Management and Release Management.

As an example of scoping, the following is extracted from *A Code of Practice for IT Service Management* – PD0005 – from BSI:

Change Management comprises:

- raising and recording Changes
- assessing the impact, cost, benefits and risk of Changes
- developing the business justification and obtaining approval
- management and co-ordination of Change implementation
- monitoring and reporting on the implementation
- closing and reviewing the Change requests.

Emergency Changes are sometimes required and enterprises should plan for these carefully. They usually follow the Change process but some details may be documented retrospectively. Change records should be reviewed regularly to identify trends and assist the organisation to improve the service by identifying high-risk components.

8.2.1   Why Change is important

'Change' has many erudite definitions but possibly the most apt is the simplest:

Change is the process of moving from one defined state to another.

Everything changes and, in business, where life is sufficiently complex already, the reliance on information systems and technology causes management to spend an astonishing amount of time

- assessing the impact of business change on IT
- analysing the impact of IT Change on the business
- identifying the Problems that continually arise that require more Change
- introducing the new ideas and gadgets that cause even more Change.

Managing Change has become a full time occupation.

If Changes can be managed to optimise risk exposure, severity of impact and disruption, and of course to be successful at the first attempt, the bottom line for the business is the early realisation of benefits (or removal of risk), with a saving of money and time.

Although focused at the mid-range mark in the scale of things, the guidance in this chapter is adaptable – after all, planning, controlling, managing risk, minimising disruption, communicating, implementing and measuring are hardly exclusive to any one kind or size of organisation or infrastructure.

This chapter provides guidance on managing Changes that is scaleable for:

- small and large Changes
- Changes with major or minor impact
- Changes in a required timeframe
- cost
- different kinds and sizes of organisations.

8.2.2　Boundaries between Incident resolution and Change Management

Chapter 5 of this book discusses the Incident life-cycle and in conjunction with Chapter 6, Problem Management, sets the scene for the inclusion of Change Management in these processes. Nevertheless, it is worthwhile considering the boundaries between Incident resolution and Change. **An Incident is not a Change and a Problem may not lead to a Change**. A Change in infrastructure management terms is the result of Problem fixing where there is *a state different from a previously defined condition*. This may be manifested in a number of ways, both visible and invisible to the naked eye.

Here is an example: A PC breaks down and so is taken away and replaced with a new one. Infrastructure management demands that, following the service call and Incident logging, resolution and fixing, Configuration Management records have been properly updated. Service Desk procedures will ensure that the person who reported the Incident in the first place knows that the new PC, and any training and ancillary items that may need to go with it, have been ordered, and when they can be expected.

It is important to know the distinction between a Change request and a service request. Many organisations mis-classify service requests, such as the desire to change a password or perhaps to extend service hours, as Change requests; this results in a swamped Change Management process. The examples given are Changes, but Changes that can be filtered and managed more efficiently than using all of the processes described in this book.

One area that until relatively recently even infrastructure management neglected was regression or back-out strategy. The original guides certainly mentioned the issue of backing out from 'problem' Changes, but it is more and more important to think about back-out *well* before implementation. Very often, back-out is the last thing to be considered; risks may be assessed, mitigation plans cast in stone, but how to get back to the original start point is often ignored or considered only when regression is the last remaining option. The Change Management process should ensure that any Change plans include plans for back-out in the event of serious unforeseen problems.

8.2.3　Application development and Change Management

If you merely inform applications developers and systems analysts that all Change is now under the control of a single Change Management process, you are unlikely to receive enthusiastic support. There are many good reasons for such a single Change Management process. However, the dynamics of Change to systems designs and to programs makes it well nigh impossible to take control of the Changes to the software at any time until systems-tested versions of unique programs, and sometimes suites of programs, are in the Customer acceptance testing phase.

In terms of progress of program development, it makes sense for Change Management to know what is going on, but day-to-day version control and so on is more sensibly left to the applications development team, with emphasis on good and rapid communications. The funding of Change Management and Configuration Management in applications software development may arise from program/project budgets (indeed, it is considered best practice in many organisations). Release of products to the operational environment is also better funded this way, in order to extend the scope of the processes without ballooning the budget of Service Management. For more information, see Chapter 9, Release Management.

Consider the implications for Configuration Management. Very few infrastructure management software tools are designed for controlling applications software development. In any medium-sized to large organisation, there could be a significant number of people writing new applications. At what level do you want to start with Configuration Management? Some options might include:

- the line of program code that is (regularly) changed
- the software module
- common modules
- complete programs
- linked programs
- suites of programs.

Hard-and-fast recommendations are not appropriate. **You should decide for yourself** in the light of knowledge of your business drivers, systems and resources. An organisation needs to make sensible decisions based on business drivers, risk, manpower, tools capability, organisational competence and the cost-benefit equation at the micro-level of Change Management and Configuration Management. If the decision is taken to control *all* Changes centrally, there will need to be a major investment in appropriate software tools and training. Please refer to Section 8.8 for more information.

The scale of the Configuration Management problem is clear; the scale of the Change Management problem is perhaps even worse, since the impact of business change should also be taken into account where it will eventually filter down to operational Change Management.

8.2.4   Business change and Change Management.

The Change Management process manages Changes to the day to day operation of the business. It is no substitute for the organisation-wide use of methods such as PRINCE2 to manage and control projects.

In later sections of this Chapter, you will read about CABs and their occasional role in assessing the need for Change, and the timescale and importance of Changes. Where appropriate, the CAB should be involved with program and project management teams to ensure that Change issues, aims, impacts and developments are cascaded throughout the organisation. One way in which Change Management can help Change planners is by building models of Changes and liaising with capacity planners to assess the impact of the models.

8.3   Basic concepts

The basic concepts of Change Management are principally process-related and managerial, rather than technical (whereas Incident Management is primarily technical, with a strong emphasis on the mechanical nature of some of the processes). This section therefore focuses on providing the information you will need to identify the most important components for your organisation.

Figures 8.3a and 8.3b represent a flowchart of *basic* Change Management procedures. Figure 8.4 illustrates the use of *standard* Change Management procedures (Change models) within the Change life-cycle.

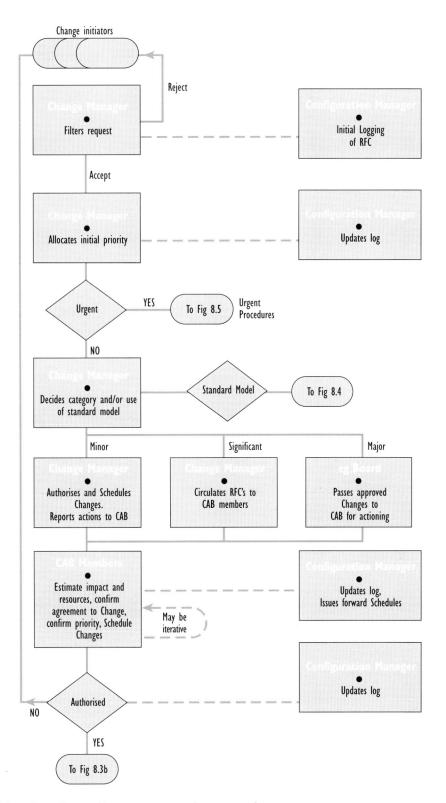

Figure 8.3a – Basic Change Management procedures – part 1.

NB These processes (or very similar) will apply to standard changes, as defined by your organisation

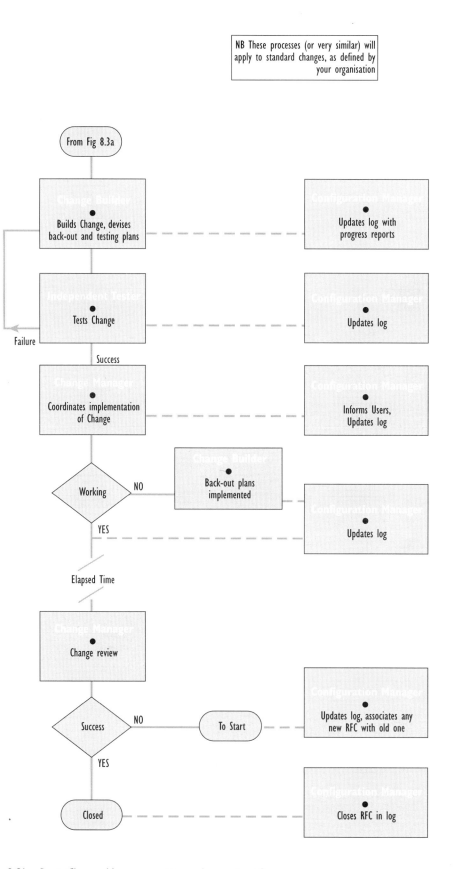

Figure 8.3b – Basic Change Management procedures – part 2.

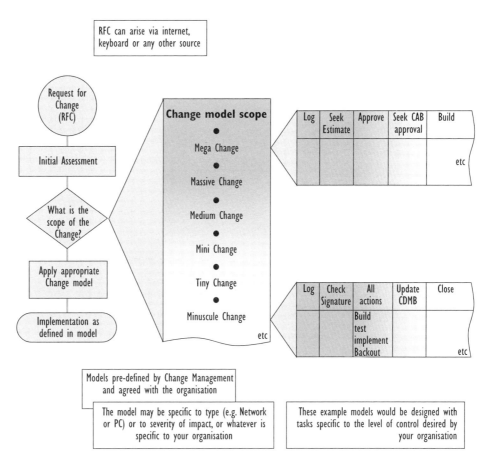

Figure 8.4 – An approach for standard Change Management procedures.

A standard Change is a change to the infrastructure that follows an established path, is relatively common, and is the accepted solution to a specific requirement or set of requirements. Examples might include an upgrade of a PC in order to make use of specific software, new starters within an organisation, and PC, software and network connections for temporary or seasonal changes to requirements. The crucial elements of a standard Change are that:

- the tasks are well-known and proven
- authority is effectively given in advance
- the train of events can usually be initiated by the Service Desk
- budgetary approval will typically be preordained or within the control of the Change requester.

Once the approach has been established and documented, a standard Change process should be developed and promulgated to ensure that such Changes are efficiently processed to support the organisation's business needs.

8.3.1 Requests for Change

Requests for Change (RFCs) are triggered for a wide variety of reasons, from a wide variety of sources. The reasons include:

- required resolution of an Incident or Problem report
- User or Customer dissatisfaction expressed via Customer liaison or Service Level Management

- the proposed introduction or removal of a new CI
- a proposed upgrade to some component of the infrastructure
- changed business requirements or direction
- new or changed legislation
- location change
- product or service changes from vendors or contractors.

RFCs can be concerned with any part of the infrastructure or with any service or activity. Here are some examples:

- hardware
- software
- documentation
- telecommunications facilities
- engineering cover
- training courses
- IT infrastructure management procedures
- tactical plans
- environmental infrastructure.

RFCs can, of course, be in paper form, or – as is increasingly the case – be held electronically, perhaps on the company intranet.

The following items should be included in an RFC form, whether paper or electronic:

- RFC number (plus cross reference to Problem report number, where necessary)
- description and identity of item(s) to be changed (including CI identification(s) if Configuration Management system is in use)
- reason for Change
- effect of not implementing the Change
- version of item to be changed
- name, location and telephone number of person proposing the Change
- date that the Change was proposed
- Change priority
- impact and resource assessment (which may be on separate forms where convenient)
- CAB recommendations where appropriate (which may be held separately, with impact and resource assessments, where convenient)
- authorisation signature (could be electronic)
- authorisation date and time
- scheduled implementation (Release identification and/or date and time)
- location of Release/implementation plan
- details of Change builder/implementer
- back-out plan
- actual implementation date and time
- review date

- review results (including cross-reference to new RFC where necessary)
- risk assessment and management
- impact on business continuity and contingency plans
- status of RFC – i.e. 'logged', 'assessed', 'rejected', 'accepted', 'sleeping'.

A Release or implementation plan should be provided for all but the simplest of Changes and it should document how to back out from the Change should it fail. On completion of the Change, the results should be reported for assessment to those responsible for managing Changes, and then presented as a completed Change for Customer agreement (including the closing of related Incidents, Problems or Known Errors). Clearly, for major Changes there will be more Customer input throughout the entire process, but the main point is that, no matter how small the Change, the Customer should be consulted before any Change is implemented.

As the Change proceeds through its life-cycle, the Change request and the CMDB should be updated, so that the person who initiated the Change is aware of its status. Actual resources used and the costs incurred should be recorded as part of the record. A Post-Implementation Review (PIR) should be carried out to confirm that the Change has met its objectives, that Customers are happy with the results; and that there have been no unexpected side-effects. Lessons learned should be fed back into future Changes. Small organisations may opt to use spot checking of Changes rather than large-scale PIR; in larger organisations, spot-checking will have a value when there are many similar Changes taking place.

8.3.2   Change Advisory Board

The Change Advisory Board (CAB) is a body that exists to approve Changes and to assist Change Management in the assessment and prioritisation of changes. As and when a CAB is convened, its members should be chosen who are capable of ensuring that all Changes are adequately assessed from both a business and a technical viewpoint. To achieve this mix, the CAB needs to include people with a clear understanding of the Customer business needs and the User community, as well as the technical development and support functions. See also Paragraph 8.5.5.

It is suggested that CAB membership, when needed, should comprise:

- Change Manager
- Customer(s)
- User manager(s)
- User group representative(s)
- applications developers/maintainers (where appropriate)
- experts/technical consultants
- services staff (as required)
- office services staff (where Changes may affect accommodation and vice versa)
- contractor's or third parties' representatives (as required – for instance in outsourcing situations).

It is important to emphasise that the CAB:

- will be composed according to the Changes being considered
- may vary considerably in make-up even across the range of a single meeting
- should involve suppliers when that would be useful
- should reflect both user and Customer views
- is likely to include the Problem Manager and Service Level Manager and Customer Relations staff for at least part of the time.

When major Problems arise, there may not be time to convene the full CAB, and it is therefore necessary to identify a smaller organisation with authority to make emergency decisions. Such a body is known as the CAB emergency Committee (CAB/EC). Change procedures should specify how the composition of the CAB and CAB/EC will be determined in each instance, based on the criteria listed above and any other criteria that may be appropriate to the business. This is intended to ensure that the composition of the CAB will be flexible, in order to represent business interests properly when major Changes are proposed. It will also ensure that the composition of the CAB/EC will provide the ability, both from a business perspective and from a technical standpoint, to make appropriate decisions in any conceivable eventuality.

A practical tip worth bearing in mind is that the CAB should have stated and agreed assessment criteria. This will assist in the Change assessment process, acting as a template or framework by which members can assess each Change.

8.3.3   Change metrics

Change Management (ideally in consultation with business managers) needs to think about measures that have *specific* meaning. While it is relatively easy to count the number of Incidents that become Problems that become Changes, it is infinitely more valuable to look at the underlying cause of such Changes, and to identify trends. Better still to be able to measure the impact of Changes and to demonstrate reduced disruption over time because of the introduction of Change Management, and also to measure the speed and effectiveness with which the IT infrastructure responds to identified business needs.

Measures taken should be linked to business goals wherever practical – and to cost, service availability, and reliability. Any predictions should be compared with actual measurements. Section 8.7, Metrics and management reporting, provides more information.

8.3.4   The Forward Schedule of Change, and Change models

One area of Change Management that has moved on more rapidly than any other is the concept of building Change models prior to implementation. These are mostly applied to smaller standard Changes such as new or upgraded desktop equipment. Capacity Management can help also, to build large models of complex Changes in order to assess the likely impact prior to the real thing. In general, capacity model-building takes place for Changes that are out of the ordinary, either in terms of complexity or scale – or both. See also Chapter 9 (Release Management).

The issue of responsibility for the assessment of the impact of major Change should be defined. It is not a best-practice issue in that organisations are so diverse in size, structure and complexity that there is not a 'one size fits all' solution. It is, however, recommended that major Change is discussed at the outset with all parties – program/project management and Change Management – in order to arrive at sensible boundaries of responsibility and to improve communications. Although Change Management is responsible for ensuring that Changes are assessed and, if approved, subsequently developed, tested, implemented and reviewed, clearly final responsibility for the IT service – including Changes to it – will rest with the IT director, the IT Services Manager and the Customers who control the funding available. The CAB will recommend the adoption (or not) of more significant Changes, but their impact should be discussed on a sufficiently wide stage and this may well take the final responsibility beyond that of the Service Management, or indeed the IT, Change process. 'Responsibility' here covers the whole scope of the Change process and associated risk and budgetary considerations.

A concept at the other end of the scale of Change Management and Configuration Management is that of small-scale Change that can be satisfied by use of 'standard' Change models – for example, a PC exchange or a regular software update. So long as a predefined schedule has been fulfilled, together with all criteria (perhaps criteria relating to build or test processes, for example), Change Management can authorise such Changes without reference to the full Change Management processes. Figure 8.4 illustrates how a process of using standard models of Change, predefined by Change Management with the agreement of the other service support managers, can be integrated within the usual Change processes. Note that the definition of the scope or severity of the Changes that relate to use of the model are organisation specific.

The concept of scheduling Changes for implementation remains constant, however it is recommended very strongly that Change Management install Changes to meet business schedules rather than IT schedules. It was not uncommon for IT management to schedule major Changes over the weekend to minimise disruption to services, but those same managers were also likely to schedule downtime during working hours for essential maintenance. Nowadays, most managers actively avoid any scheduled downtime within service hours and ensure that the majority of Changes are scheduled in the same way, with allowance made either for major Problems that may arise through delayed implementation or for very urgent Changes.

In order to facilitate this process, Change Management should coordinate the production and distribution of a 'Forward Schedule of Changes' (FSC) and a 'Projected Service Availability' (PSA). The latest versions of these documents should be available to everyone within the organisation, preferably contained within a commonly available Internet or intranet server. The FSC contains details of all the Changes approved for implementation and their proposed implementation dates. The PSA contains details of Changes to agreed SLAs and service availability because of the currently planned FSC. These documents should be agreed with the relevant Customers within the business, with Service Level Management, with the Service Desk and with Availability Management. Once agreed, the Service Desk should communicate any planned additional downtime to the User community at large, using the most effective methods available.

If your organisation has drawn up process models of the Change Management process and integrated those models within an overall Service Support model, it is a simple task to evaluate the effect of a Change without the risk and expense of changing the process in real life. Similarly, if you can build a model of a major Change, you can elicit the help of the Capacity Management, Business Continuity Management, Availability Management and Service Level Management to evaluate the impact of the Change on services, service levels and business continuity plans. With the aid of such a model, you can evaluate the Change for completeness and construct a schedule, perhaps of Changes to be phased in if necessary, or simply to ensure that everything that should be in place to make the Change successful *is* in place.

Be aware that there is a considerable difference between flowcharts and process models. Flowcharts (some useful examples of which are provided in this guide), allow Change Management to view simple information flows but do not abstract 'real life'. A process model, however, provides a picture that is capable of detailed evaluation and engenders confidence. A case study at Appendix B (based on anonymised data from a major outsourcing organisation that encountered Problems in a Europe-wide implementation of IT infrastructure library processes) will help you to evaluate the use of flowcharts and process models.

By planning a Change using models and schedules to support project plans, it is possible to predict the impact of the Change. You can also look at the implementation of the plans to compare predictions with reality, both to improve future planning and to ensure that the Change proceeds smoothly. See Paragraph 8.5.9 for information about building Changes.

8.3.5 Outsourcing and Change Management

In the case of outsourcing of service provision, bear in mind that those providing outsourced services often make economies of scale by using giant mainframes and large operational/networking organisations, or perhaps they have massive purchasing power because of the scale of their buying. In this case, the adoption of ITIL guidance is clearly going to have a major impact in terms of reducing the cost of providing services, making service provision more reliable, and improving efficiency.

When outsourcing is under consideration, the receiver of services needs to take into account the following issues concerning the Change Management process:

- who is responsible for managing day-to-day Changes arising from RFCs, from whatever sources (see Paragraph 8.3.1)?
- what control do I have over the service provider so that I am not being made to pay for unreasonable Changes?
- how do I know that Changes are not approved piecemeal, with a consequent impact on service and service cost?
- who is responsible for ensuring that major business changes are properly costed, approved, planned, controlled and implemented?
- who is responsible for the integrity of systems and services following Changes?
- has security of systems been properly considered?
- who should sit on the CAB?

It is not practical to provide general advice because outsourcing contracts vary so much in terms of:

- cost
- ownership of hardware and software
- the degree to which the business enters into a partnership with the provider (rather than a simple provider–consumer relationship)
- the nature of the services provided
- the scope of those services (infrastructure, service/help desks, applications software development, etc).

It is thus up to you to ensure that service providers (outsourced or in house) provide the Change Management function and processes that match the needs of your organisation. Some organisations in outsourcing situations refer RFCs to their suppliers for estimates prior to approval of Changes.

Perhaps the most sensible piece of advice is the most obvious: ensure that you coordinate the Change Management, Incident Management, Release Management and Configuration Management processes across all of the organisations involved in service support, delivery and management. It may be necessary to model the processes in order to make meaningful comparisons.

Change Management should consider:

- what should be in the plan
- ownership
- circulation
- what key businesses should be supported
- how those businesses are supported by IT
- links to business continuity and IT contingency plans
- the critical components
- timescales
- risks
- regression strategy
- invocation.

8.3.6   Critical outage plan

Although planning for the recovery of critical business systems is not a task that is the direct responsibility of Change Management, their involvement is not merely sensible but essential. This is because any plans to recover IT systems and services that are fundamental to the business will be subject to Change and should be controlled to ensure smooth operation.

It is, of course, also necessary to consider what should be done in the event of the plans going awry – or even if you need to back out from Changes resulting from use of the plans. In these instances, the earlier advice about planning for back-outs very early in the planning phase becomes particularly germane. Clearly, there should be a link to Change scheduling processes.

8.4.   Benefits, costs and possible problems

8.4.1   Benefits

Efficient service management requires an ability to change things in an orderly way, without making errors and taking wrong decisions. *Effective* Change Management is indispensable to the satisfactory provision of services, and requires an ability to absorb a high level of Change.

Specific benefits of an *effective* Change Management system include:

- better alignment of IT services to business requirements
- increased visibility and communication of Changes to both business and service-support staff
- improved risk assessment
- a reduced adverse impact of Changes on the quality of services and on SLAs
- better assessment of the cost of proposed Changes before they are incurred
- fewer Changes that have to be backed-out, along with an increased ability to do this more easily when necessary
- improved Problem and Availability Management through the use of valuable management information relating to changes accumulated through the Change Management process
- increased productivity of Users – through less disruption and, higher-quality services

- increased productivity of key personnel through less need for diversion from planned duties to implement urgent Changes or back-out erroneous Changes
- greater ability to absorb a large volume of Changes
- an enhanced business perception of IT through an improved quality of service and a professional approach.

8.4.2   Costs

The two principal costs of Change Management are for staff and software tools support.

Staff costs

Staff costs include costs for the Change Management role and team, CAB members, and Change builders, including Configuration and Release Management. These costs should of course be outweighed by the benefits that are, or will be, gained. In practice, most organisations already have a number of people who are spending time on handling Changes.

Although adherence to the guidance in this chapter may appear to increase the amount of management time spent on Changes, in practice you will find that management will spend less time on Changes as the need to handle issues arising from ineffective Change Management is eliminated.

Support tools

The cost of support tools, together with any hardware requirements, needs to be considered. Although tools that integrate support for Change Management, Configuration Management, Problem Management and Service Desks are likely to be more expensive than 'simple' Change Management tools, the additional cost is often justifiable. For larger organisations, management processes can be virtually impossible to implement effectively without adequate support tools.

8.4.3   Possible problems

The Change Management process that you implement should be appropriate to the size of your organisation; an over-bureaucratic process can diminish your effectiveness. Paper-based systems (often found in very small organisations or organisations establishing Change Management for the first time) are difficult to administer and often result in bottlenecks; they are really only practical for **very** small organisations.

There may be cultural difficulties in getting staff, Customers and Users to accept that a single Change Management system should be used for all aspects of an infrastructure. It may require education to convince everyone that all components of an infrastructure can, and very often do, impact heavily upon each other, and that Changes to individual CIs require coordination. Attempts may be made to implement Changes without reference to the Change Management process. Measures should be introduced to prevent and detect such illicit changes, including:

- conducting regular independent audits to check that Change Management staff, other Service Management staff and Users are adhering to the Change Management procedures
- instituting management controls over the activities of in-house and contractors' support staff, and engineers
- implementing Configuration Management control of all CIs and versions
- detecting User access to equipment or software that is unknown to the Configuration Management system via the Service Desk
- training new and existing staff in IT Service Management.

It may be difficult to ensure that contractors' representatives, such as hardware engineers, adhere to the organisation's Change Management procedures. It is recommended that contracts with suppliers should, where possible, include the need for such compliance. Condition 12 of the standard CCTA CC88 Contract, part 2-C reads:

> *If the CONTRACTOR proposes to modify any part of the Contractually Maintained Hardware (CMH) the CONTRACTOR shall notify the AUTHORITY and request the AUTHORITY's agreement to the proposed modification, such an agreement not to be unreasonably withheld. If such an agreement is given, then the modification shall be carried out at a mutually convenient time.*

The BSI publication *A Code of Practice for IT Service Management* – PD0005 – also lists points to consider as possible problems. Clearly addressing these points will transform the problems into benefits.

From PD0005: Possible problems with Change Management.

- *the scope of a Change is too wide for the resources available, over-stretching the staff and causing delays*
- *ownership of the impacted systems is unclear, resulting in delays and incomplete assessments*
- *if Change Management is implemented without Configuration Management, the solution will be much less effective*
- *the process is too bureaucratic giving excuses for not following it*
- *inaccurate configuration data may result in poor impact assessments leading to the wrong people being consulted about the Change*
- *poor synchronisation of upgrades between platforms and across locations makes Changes difficult or impossible to schedule*
- *back-out procedures are missing or untested*
- *progressing Change requests is manually intensive; it is advisable to start with a simple database or an automated system*
- *lack of backing from senior and middle managers will lengthen implementation times, staff will resist the controls that they would prefer to avoid unless they can see the commitment from manager*
- *the process frequently fails when emergency Changes should be done.*

8.5 Activities

As well as managing the Change processes and procedures, Change Management has a responsibility for managing the interfaces between itself and the other business and IT functions. A sample process model of best practice in Change Management is encapsulated in this guidance. However, it should be apparent that certain processes are mandatory for best practice – for example, Change logging, Configuration Management updating, and impact analysis.

The way in which an organisation decides to implement the Change Management process is however, to a large extent driven by the resources available (time, priorities, people and, above all, money).

8.5.1 Planning the implementation of operational processes

Change Management should plan the implementation of operational procedures for the activities described in this section, or amend any existing procedures to best conform to these guidelines. Figure 8.3 provides a flowchart of these procedures.

As mentioned in Paragraph 8.3.4, process models provide a richer picture than a flowchart but require greater understanding and are therefore discussed later in this guide in a case study.

8.5.2 Change logging and filtering

Procedures for documenting RFCs, using standard forms, email forms or intranet screens, should be decided. Where a computer-based support tool is used, the tool may dictate the format. Where no standard is imposed by a support tool, or if a paper-based system has to be used, it is recommended that the items shown in Paragraph 8.3.1 be included on the RFC form.

It is further recommended that all members of the organisation be authorised to request Changes. Otherwise, innovation might be stifled or important concerns may go unreported. Even so, where there are large numbers of Users, it is suggested that User requests should require signature by a senior User manager prior to submission. This will filter out any requests that do not have the support of the wider User community, or are impractical, and help collate similar or identical requests, thus reducing request volumes. However, User managers should also be careful not to stifle innovation or discourage staff from proposing Changes.

All RFCs received should be logged and allocated an identification number (in chronological sequence). Where Change requests are submitted as a resolution to a Problem record (PR), it is important that the original PR number is retained so that the link between the Problem and its resolution is readily apparent.

It is recommended that the logging of RFCs is done by means of an integrated Service Management tool, capable of storing both the data on all CIs and also, importantly, the relationships between them. This will greatly assist when assessing the likely impact of a Change to one component of the system on all other components. All actions should be recorded, as they are carried out, within the Change Management log. If this is not possible for any reason, then they should be manually recorded for inclusion at the next possible opportunity.

Procedures need to specify who has access to the logging system and what the levels of access will be. Normally, the system is open to any authorised personnel to create, or add reports of progress to an RFC (though the support tool should keep Change Management aware of such actions). However, only Change Management staff, or Configuration Management support staff if Change Management is an integral part of a Configuration Management system, should be allowed to close an RFC.

The procedures should stipulate that, as Changes are logged, Change Management should briefly consider each request and filter out any that are totally impractical. These should be returned to the initiator, together with brief details of the reason for the rejection, and the log should record this fact. A right of appeal against rejection should exist, via normal management channels, and should be incorporated within the procedures.

8.5.3   Allocation of priorities

Every RFC should be allocated a *priority* that is based on the impact of the Problem and the urgency for the remedy. This priority rating is used to decide which Changes should be discussed and assessed first, either by Change Management or by the CAB if necessary. Change Management should be responsible for assigning this priority. The priority of RFCs ideally should be decided in collaboration with the initiator and, if necessary, with the CAB; but it should not be left to the initiator alone, as a higher priority than is really justified may result. **Risk assessment is of crucial importance at this stage.** The CAB will need information on business consequences in order to assess effectively the risk of implementing or denying the change.

The following priority ratings are provided as *examples only*. Many software tools allow a wide range of priority ratings to be set.

- **Immediate.** Causing loss of service or severe usability problems to a larger number of Users, a mission-critical system, or some equally serious problem. Immediate action required. Urgent CAB or CAB/EC meetings may need to be convened. Resources may need to be allocated immediately to build such authorised Changes.

- **High.** Severely affecting some Users, or impacting upon a large number of Users. To be given highest priority for Change building, testing and implementation resources.

- **Medium.** No severe impact, but rectification cannot be defered until the next scheduled Release or upgrade. To be allocated medium priority for resources.

- **Low.** A Change is justified and necessary, but can wait until the next scheduled Release or upgrade. To be allocated resources accordingly.

RFCs will have already been annotated with the priority defined and agreed within the organisation, which is a function of the impact and urgency of the Problem, to indicate the order in which they should be 'fixed'. This 'severity code' should be reviewed and (unless there is a good reason why not) should be used as a basis for the Change priority. Timeframes for each priority level should be predetermined and escalation processes defined.

8.5.4   Change categorisation

The issue of risk to the business of any Change should also be considered prior to the *approval* of any Change. Change Management should examine each RFC and decide how to proceed based on the (predefined) *category* into which the RFC falls. The categorisation process examines the impact of the approved Change on the organisation in terms of the resources needed to effect the Change. Note that the structure and complexity of these categories will very much depend on the needs of the business, including the range of priority ratings identified (see Paragraph 8.5.3).

The prioritisation process above is used to establish the order in which Changes put forward should be considered. Any of the example priorities given might apply to a Change that falls into any of the example impact-assessment categories below. Where minor Changes are involved, Change Management can delegate the authority to approved specific parties, such as Service Desk personnel. However, adequate reporting structures should be put in place; while authority can be delegated, accountability cannot.

Example categories are set out below. It is expected that the majority of RFCs will fall into the first two example categories.

Minor impact only, and few 'build' or additional 'runtime' resources required.

Change Management should have delegated authority to authorise and schedule such Changes, but these should be logged so that:

- records and work patterns can be identified
- accurate and complete costs for each service, Customer area etc, are available
- repetitive Changes, follow-on Changes, and associated Problem/Incident areas can be identified.

Recording every Change in summary helps to deliver an effective and efficient service to the Customer by allowing wastefully repetitive tasks to be spotted and eliminated. If Change Management has any doubts about authorising any such Change, the Change can be referred informally to members of the CAB for a wider assessment.

Significant impact, and/or significant build or runtime resources required.

Depending on the urgency of the Change to be made, Change Management should decide whether to talk to members of the CAB or to convene a CAB/EC. Prior to any meeting all documentation should be circulated for impact and resource assessment.

Major impact, and/or very large amount of build or runtime resources required, or impact likely upon other parts of the organisation.

Where a major Change pertains directly to IT, the RFC should be referred to the organisation's top Management Board or other appropriate body for discussion and a policy decision. Such Changes, once approved should be passed back, perhaps via the CAB, for scheduling and implementation.

8.5.5   CAB meetings

It should not be necessary to insist on face-to-face meetings; much of the assessment referral process can be handled electronically via support tools or email. Only in very complex, high-risk or high-impact cases will a formal CAB meeting be necessary. It is, however, a good idea to schedule a regular meeting – say every six months, or when major projects are due to deliver products. The meetings can then be used to provide a formal review and sign-off of approved Changes, a review of outstanding Changes, and, of course, to discuss any impending major Changes. Where meetings *are* appropriate, they should have a standard agenda.

A standard CAB agenda should include a review of:

- failed Changes, backed-out Changes, or Changes applied without reference to the CAB by Incident Management, Problem Management or Change Management
- RFCs to be assessed by CAB members
- RFCs that have been assessed by CAB members
- Change reviews
- the Change Management process, including any amendments made to it during the period under discussion, as well as proposed Changes
- Change Management wins/accomplishments for the period under discussion, i.e. a review of the business benefits accrued by way of the Change Management process.

CAB meetings represent a potentially large overhead on the time of members. Therefore all RFCs, together with the FSC and the PSA, should be circulated in advance, and flexibility allowed to CAB members on whether to attend in person, to send a deputy, or to send any comments via Change Management. Relevant papers should be circulated in advance to allow CAB members (and others who are required by Change Management or CAB members) to conduct impact and resource assessments.

In some circumstances it will be desirable to table RFCs at one CAB meeting for more detailed explanation or clarification before CAB members take the papers away for consideration, in time for the next meeting.

Change reviews are discussed further in Paragraph 8.5.12.

8.5.6 Impact and resource assessment

When conducting the impact and resource assessment for RFCs referred to them, Change Management, CAB, CAB/EC or any others (nominated by Change Management or CAB members) who are involved in this process, should consider the following items:

- the impact that the Change will make upon the Customer's business operation
- the effect upon the infrastructure and Customer service, as defined in the SLA, and upon the capacity and performance, reliability and resilience, contingency plans, and security
- the impact on other services that run on the same infrastructure (or on software development projects)
- the impact on non-IT infrastructures within the organisation – for example, security, office services, transport, business – Customer Help Desks
- the effect of not implementing the Change
- the IT, business and other resources required to implement the Change, covering the likely costs, the number and availability of people required, the elapsed time, and any new infrastructure elements required
- the current FSC and PSA
- additional ongoing resources required if the Change is implemented.

Certain Changes that do not affect the specification of CIs – for example, a hardware repair – may not need to be assessed for impact in advance. However, it is recommended that Changes intended to correct software errors should be subject to formal RFCs and impact assessment.

Based upon these assessments, and the potential benefits of the Change, each of the assessors should indicate whether they support approval of the Change. CAB members should also decide whether they are content with the priority allocated by Change Management and be prepared to argue for any alterations that they see as necessary.

CAB recommendations

CAB members should come to meetings prepared to make decisions on which Changes should go ahead, based on the priority assessment of the Changes. The CAB should be informed of any Changes that have been implemented as a Work-around to Incidents and should be given the opportunity to recommend follow-up action to these.

Note that the CAB is an advisory body only. If the CAB cannot agree to a recommendation, the final decision on whether to authorise Changes, and commit to the expense involved, is the responsibility of management (normally the Director of IT or the Service Manager, or the Change Manager as their delegated representative). The Change Management procedures should specifically name the person(s) authorised to sign off RFCs. Depending on the nature of the Change, references to Service Level Agreements may be required. In any event, Customer sign-off will be required at some point

8.5.7 Change approval

The culture of the organisation in which you work will, to a large extent, dictate the manner in which Changes are approved. Hierarchical structures may well impose many levels of Change approval, while flatter structures may allow a more streamlined approach.

Obtaining approval

Formal approval should be obtained for each Change from the Change authority. The Change authority may be Change Management, the Service Manager, or some other nominated person or group. For low risk Changes, the Change authority may choose to be informed of Changes authorised, rather than be involved in authorising each Change individually. The levels of approval for a Change should be judged by the size or risk of the Change. For example, Changes in a large enterprise that affect several distributed groups may need to be approved by a higher-level Change authority.

There are three principal approval processes that should be in place in the Change Management process: financial approval, technical approval, and business approval. Financial approval indicates that the cost of a Change has been assessed and that it is either within approved budgetary limits or meets cost – benefit criteria that may have been set for Change approval. The technical approval stage is an assurance that the Change is feasible, sensible and can be performed without inappropriate detriment to the services provided to the business. If the technical experts are required to provide cost estimates (as is the case in many organisations), then this phase needs to precede financial approval. Customer approval is necessary to ensure that the business managers are content with the Change proposals and the impact on their business requirements.

8.5.8 Change scheduling

Although it may be better (or advisable) to implement one Change at a time – for example, in order to simplify diagnosis should an error occur – this is not usually practical. For instance, a hardware Change may require an operating system Change to support it; applications software may need to be changed so rapidly that a policy of 'one Change at a time' is impracticably slow; or a simple software Change may require simultaneous introduction of new documentation, procedures *and* training.

Consider also, as a further example, the number of concurrent Changes inherent in the introduction of a new standard desktop configuration. Where concurrent Changes occur, they should still be packaged into a Release so that the whole thing can be backed out from if problems occur. A packaged Release should be considered as a single Change from this point of view, even though it may contain many individual Changes, because it will either be implemented or backed-out as a single Change unit.

Wherever possible, Change Management should schedule approved Changes into target Releases and recommend the allocation of resources accordingly. There is clear continuity between the Change Management and Release Management processes. Release Management processes impact upon the Change Management process and, in particular, have a role in developing and maintaining standard Changes that introduce new or revised software and hardware into the infrastructure. As Releases are the manifestation of Changes, the Change process initiates the Releases under the agreed, documented and maintained Release process.

Wherever possible, software Changes should be implemented in the form of packaged Releases. It is very important to have a clearly defined software product Release strategy that interfaces to the Change Management system. For further information on this, see Chapter 9, Release Management.

It is also important to limit the size of a Release to manageable proportions, especially as it is unlikely that any Release will be completely fault-free. It follows that the larger the Release, the more effort will be required to identify and address any new errors. It also follows that there will be a correspondingly larger effort required in support activities, such as Service Desk calls, following a new Release.

It is recommended that Change Management issue FSCs. FSCs should include details of all Changes that have been authorised for implementation over a previously agreed (with the business) period, and the Release(s) that they have been allocated to. Note that some organisations will have clear plans for the short term and less detailed plans in the longer term, all of which need to be included in the FSC. Brief details of (probably major) Changes planned for the next two years should also be included. The FSC should be distributed to all Customers and Users or their representatives, application developers, service staff including the Service Desk, and any other interested parties. Distribution of FSCs outside Service Management should be done via the Service Desk or Customer liaison process.

Change schedules should be widely distributed since the proposed Changes and their timing will affect planning and practices in many areas, both within and outside Service Management. Promulgation outside Service Management will usually be through the Service Desk and the Service Level Management and Customer Relationship Management. Within Service Management, access to the schedule should be provided to all processes. Change Management should reinforce this information with a proactive awareness programme where specific impact can be detected; such as anticipated impacts upon Capacity Management, Availability Management or other processes.

It is most important to take into consideration the business needs of the organisation in the construction of any schedule, bearing in mind both the needs of the Customer and the needs of the end User.

8.5.9   Change building, testing and implementation

Authorised RFCs should be passed to the relevant technical groups for building of the Changes. This might involve:

- building a new production module
- creating a new version of one or more software modules
- purchasing equipment or services externally
- preparing a hardware modification
- producing new or amended documentation
- preparing amendments to User training.

Change Management has a coordination role, supported by Release Management and normal line management controls, to ensure that these activities are both resourced and also completed to schedule. Release Management has a more important role in smaller Changes, such as when applications software development teams provide Configuration Management installation and back-out instructions/files.

It is important to ensure that the same standards and methods that were used for an original component are again used for the Change. Back-out procedures should be prepared and documented in advance, for each authorised Change, so that if errors occur after implementation, these procedures can be quickly activated with minimum impact on service quality.

To prevent Changes from adversely impacting on service quality, it is strongly recommended that Changes be thoroughly tested in advance (including back-out procedures where possible). Testing should include aspects of the change such as:

- performance
- security
- maintainability
- supportability
- reliability/availability
- functionality.

This advice is particularly relevant to the desktop environment, where constant technology updates take place. In many cases, this will require a separate 'test environment'. It is recognised that it is not always possible or justifiable to fully test all Changes in advance; it may be possible in some instances, though, to use modelling techniques to assess the likely impact of a Change instead of, or in addition to, ordinary testing.

Change Management has an overseeing role to ensure that all Changes that can be, are thoroughly tested. In all cases involving Changes that have not been fully tested, special care needs to be taken during implementation. Change Management should assess the risk to the business of any Change that is to be installed without complete testing having taken place. Testing should also include adequate regression testing to ensure that other areas of the infrastructure are not adversely affected by the Change.

Remember that testing does not have to stop merely because a Change or product has gone live. Normal operation and service use will be tested first and invoked in live use first. It is therefore still relevant to test performance and behaviour of Changes in unusual, unexpected or future situations so that further correcting action can be taken before any detected errors become manifest in live operation.

The implementation of such Changes should be scheduled when the least impact on live services is likely. Support staff should be on hand to deal quickly with any Incidents that might arise. Where it is possible to introduce such Changes into a limited environment – for instance for a pilot group of Users – this approach should be considered.

Change Management has responsibility for ensuring that Changes are implemented as scheduled, though this will be largely a coordination role as the actual implementation will be the responsibility of others (e.g. engineers will implement hardware Changes).

8.5.10   Urgent Changes

The number of urgent proposed Changes should be kept to an absolute minimum, because they are generally more disruptive and prone to failure. All Changes likely to be required should, in general, be foreseen and planned, bearing in mind the availability of resources to build and test the Changes.

Nevertheless, occasions will occur when urgent Changes are essential and so procedures should be devised to deal with them quickly, without sacrificing normal management controls. Such procedures are shown in Figure 8.5, and described in the following paragraphs.

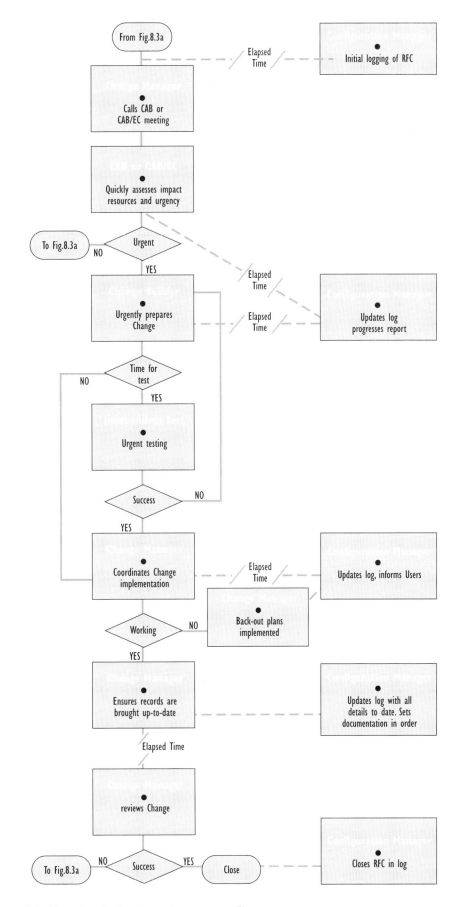

Figure 8.5 – Procedure for implementing an urgent Change.

Incident control staff, computer operations and network management staff may have delegated authority to circumvent certain types of Incident (e.g. hardware failure) without prior authorisation by Change Management. Such circumventions should be limited to actions that do not Change the specification of CIs and that do not attempt to correct software errors. The preferred route for circumventing Incidents caused by software errors should be to revert to the previous trusted state or version, as relevant, rather than attempting an unplanned and potentially dangerous Change. Change approval is still a prerequisite!

8.5.11 Urgent Change building, testing and implementation

Approved Changes should be allocated to the relevant technical group for building. Where timescales demand it, Change Management, in collaboration with the appropriate technical manager, should ensure that sufficient staff and resources (machine time etc) are available to do this work, even if this means calling staff in from home. Procedures and agreements – approved and supported by management – should be in place so as to allow for this. The cost of emergency call-outs should be covered somewhere in the approved running costs of Service Management. Back-out plans should still be devised despite the urgency of the Change.

As much testing of the urgent Change as is possible should be carried out. Completely untested Changes should not be implemented if at all avoidable. Experience has shown that when Changes go wrong, the cost is usually greater than that of adequate testing. Again, remember that there is still merit in testing even after a Change has gone live.

Change Management should give as much advance warning as possible to Customers and Users about any imminent Change. This should be done via the Service Desk or other help desk, as available. When any urgent Changes are implemented, particularly those that have not been adequately tested, Change Management should ensure that an adequate technical presence is available, to tackle any Incidents that may occur.

If a Change, once implemented, fails to rectify the urgent outstanding Problem, there may need to be iterative attempts at fixes. Change Management should take responsibility at this point to ensure that business needs remain the primary concern. It is important that each iteration is controlled in the manner described in this section. Change Management should ensure abortive Changes are swiftly backed out from.

If too many attempts at an urgent Change are abortive, there are three questions that need addressing:

1. Has the Problem been correctly analysed?
2. Has the proposed remedy been adequately tested?
3. Has the solution been correctly implemented?

In such circumstances, it may be better to provide a partial service, with some User facilities withdrawn, in order to allow the Change to be thoroughly tested, to suspend the service temporarily and then implement the Change.

It may not be possible to update all Change Management records at the time that urgent actions are being completed (e.g. during overnight or weekend working). It is, however, essential that manual records are made during such periods, and it is the responsibility of Change Management to ensure that all records are completed retrospectively, at the earliest possible opportunity. This is vital to ensure valuable management information is not lost. An example could be the updating of an attribute defining 'success', 'failure' or perhaps 'partial failure' of a Change. The updating should be carried out by the person responsible for applying the Change, and should happen no later than the

Post Implementation Review – and perhaps with the cooperation of the project team, Release or applications software development manager.

8.5.12 Change review

Change Management must review all implemented Changes after a predefined period has elapsed. This process may still involve CAB members; Change Management may look to them for assistance in the review process.

Change reviews may be tabled at CAB meetings, for CAB members' information and to agree any follow-up action that may be needed. The purpose of such reviews is to establish that:

- the Change has had the desired effect and met its objectives
- Users and Customers are content with the results, or to identify any shortcomings
- there have been no unexpected or undesirable side-effects to functionality, availability, capacity/performance, security, maintainability etc.
- the resources used to implement the Change were as planned
- the implementation plan worked correctly (so include comments from the implementers)
- the Change was implemented on time and to cost
- the backout-plan functioned correctly, if needed.

Any problems and discrepancies should be fed back to CAB members (where they have been consulted or where a committee was convened), impact assessors, product authorities and Release authorities, so as to improve the estimating processes for the future.

Where a Change has not achieved its objectives, Change Management (or the CAB) should decide what follow-up action is required, which could involve raising a revised RFC. If the review is satisfactory or the original Change is abandoned, the RFC should be formally closed in the logging system.

8.5.13 Reviewing the Change Management process for efficiency and effectiveness

Change Management should instigate follow-up actions to correct any problems or inefficiencies arising in the Change Management system itself as a result of ineffective Changes. For example, a large Change backlog may indicate that Change Management is under-resourced; a high incidence of unsuccessful Changes indicates that Change assessment or Change building is not working satisfactorily. Change record reviews may also show up problems in other processes, such as Problem Management, in the reliability of system components, or in staff's or Users' procedures and/or training. These problems should be reported to the managers concerned and highlighted in the Change Management reports to management.

It is also recommended that Service Management review the Change Management process periodically for efficiency and effectiveness. Such a review should be carried out shortly after the Change Management process is implemented, to ensure that the plans were carried out correctly and that the process is functioning as intended. Any problems should be traced back to source and corrected as soon as possible. Thereafter, regular formal reviews of the Change Management process should take place – at least every six months. The Change Manager should also continually assess the efficiency and effectiveness of the Change Management process.

It should be noted, with respect to any review, that a high number of RFCs does not necessarily indicate a problem with the Change Management process – it may just reflect volatile systems. Any attempt to reduce the number of RFCs may stifle innovation. The prime indicator of an effective Change Management process is that the right 'mix' of RFCs is maintained, not that the number of RFCs has been reduced over time.

Other indicators of an effective Change Management process include:

- a reduction of adverse impacts on service quality resulting from poor Change Management
- a reduction in the number of Incidents traced back to Changes implemented
- a decrease in the number of Changes backed out
- a low number of urgent (and therefore unplanned) Changes – this should include emergency, out-of-hours Changes referred back for clarification
- no evidence of Changes having been made without reference to the Change Management and Configuration Management system(s)
- close correlation between FSCs and the actual implementation of Changes
- no high-priority RFCs in backlogs, and the size of backlogs not increasing
- evidence of accurate resource estimating, when resource estimates are retrospectively compared with actual resources used
- regular reviewing of RFCs and implemented Changes, and the clearing of any review backlogs
- successful implementation of changes that clearly benefit the business and satisfy Customers
- a low incidence of unjustifiably rejected RFCs.

These items can be used as metrics for measuring the effectiveness and, to an extent, the efficiency of the Change Management process. In measuring that efficiency, it is necessary to consider, the amount of Change successfully implemented per unit of staff costs, including, for example, the costs of assessors, builders, and testers. This may be difficult to assess in absolute terms, but it should generally be possible to observe an increase in efficiency over time, especially in the early days of the Change Management process when the learning curve is steepest.

8.5.14   Roles and responsibilities

Clearly, the Change Management role should be filled, with defined responsibilities, for the Change Management process to work effectively. A suggested list of responsibilities for the Change Management roles is outlined below:

Change Manager

The main duties of the Change Manager, some of which may be delegated, are listed below.

■ Receive, log and allocate a priority, in collaboration with the initiator, to all RFCs. Reject any RFCs that are totally impractical.

■ Table all RFCs for a CAB meeting, issue an agenda and circulate all RFCs to CAB members in advance of meetings to allow prior consideration.

■ Decide which people will come to which meetings, who gets specific RFCs depending on the nature of the RFC, what is to be changed, and people's areas of expertise.

■ Convene urgent CAB or CAB/EC meetings for all urgent RFCs.

■ Chair all CAB and CAB/EC meetings.

■ After consideration of the advice given by the CAB or CAB/EC, authorise acceptable Changes.

■ Issue FSCs, via the Service Desk.

■ Liaise with all necessary parties to coordinate Change building, testing and implementation, in accordance with schedules.

■ Update the Change log with all progress that occurs, including any actions to correct problems and/or to take opportunities to improve service quality.

■ Review all implemented Changes to ensure that they have met their objectives. Refer back any that have been backed out or have failed.

■ Review all outstanding RFCs awaiting consideration or awaiting action.

■ Analyse Change records to determine any trends or apparent problems that occur. Seek rectification with relevant parties.

■ Close RFCs.

■ Produce regular and accurate management reports.

Establishing a Change Advisory Board

If a CAB is established, it needs to have appropriate terms of reference (e.g. meeting regularity, scope of influence, links to program management). To ensure proper representation, members of this Board should include representatives from the following areas:

■ Customers affected by the Change
■ representatives of all major areas within the Service Management process
■ the application development teams
■ senior Users, or their representatives.

The Change Manager should act as Chair of this Board. Change Management, or Configuration Management, support staff, can act as secretary.

Change Advisory Board (CAB)

The main duties of a CAB member are listed below:

■ Review all submitted RFCs. As appropriate, determine and provide details of their likely impact, the implementation resources, and the ongoing costs of all Changes.

■ Attend all relevant CAB or CAB/EC meetings. Consider all Changes on the agenda and give an opinion on which Changes should be authorised. Participate in the scheduling of all Changes.

■ (CAB/EC only). Be available for consultation should an urgent Change be required.

■ Provide advice to Change Management on aspects of proposed urgent Changes.

8.6 Planning and implementation

Bear in mind once more the advice that Change Management processes should be appropriate to the size of your organisation and that making processes over-bureaucratic will diminish the effectiveness of your actions.

8.6.1 Designating the Change Manager role

Where there is no existing Change Management or Configuration Management system, the first step should be to allocate responsibility for the Change Management role. A list of responsibilities is given in Paragraph 8.5.14. Support staff may be required. Where Change Management is implemented as part of a wider Configuration Management process, the roles of Change Manager and Configuration Manager may be combined if scale allows.

The Change Manager's first task is to agree with Service Management on a goal of the Change Management process, and a way of measuring its efficiency and effectiveness. The Change Manager's personal objectives and targets should be based on the mission statement and the efficiency and effectiveness of the Change Management process.

The Change Manager's next task, in conjunction with management, is to agree the scope of the Change Management and Configuration Management process. Plans should be made to ensure that the infrastructure and other Change Management systems are effectively interfaced to each other. The Change Management authorities in other parts of the organisation should be involved in setting up these interfaces, and management commitment will be needed to ensure they work.

8.6.2 Deciding on a Change Management system

It is necessary to decide early on whether the Change Management and Configuration Management system is to be a paper-based or a tool-based system. Paper-based systems are inadequate for all except the very smallest systems, and therefore it is strongly recommended that some form of software support tool is used, if available. Note, however, that back-up computer or clerical procedures will be required should the primary tool-based system be unavailable owing to hardware failure etc.

It is recommended that the logging and implementation of Changes is done under the control of an integrated Configuration Management system, or an integrated IT Service Management system. It is therefore desirable to select a tool that integrates Change Management and Configuration Management, or can be enhanced or customised to do so.

Procurement of support tools, setting up the data (i.e. configuration inventory data, Change authorities etc), and staff training and familiarisation with the support tools should be completed prior to implementation.

8.6.3 Planning system reviews

Plans should be made for the Change Management and Configuration Management reviews, metrics, management reports and audits described in Paragraphs 8.5.12 and 8.5.13 and in Section 8.7.

8.6.4 Implementation planning

Planning to implement Change Management should be undertaken concurrently with Configuration Management and Release Management planning. (Ideally, all of the service support processes should be considered holistically at the outset, even though phased implementation may in fact take place.)

Plans should be made to bring the Change Management and Configuration Management combined system into service. These plans should include installation and test plans for any software tools, as well as training plans for Change Management staff, other staff, and Users. Publicity material and any seminars should be prepared in readiness for a Change Management launch. Emphasis should be placed on selling the benefits of Change Management to both staff and Users.

8.6.5 Guidance

Dependencies

As stated in Paragraph 8.6.2, paper-based Change Management systems are inadequate for most systems, and so support tools are normally required. Section 8.8 describes the requirements for Change Management tools and gives some information on tools currently available.

A number of supporting processes are also required for Change Management to be **fully** effective. These include the Problem Management, Configuration Management, Service Desk and Release Management processes, as described in the other chapters of this book.

Management commitment is required to ensure that adequate resources are made available, and also to ensure that an adequate level of discipline is engendered among all Service Management staff so as to prevent circumvention of Change Management procedures.

Staff training will be required in the new Change Management procedures and in the use of support tools. CAB members will also need training in the roles expected of them.

Audit trails need to be built into the Change Management tools and procedures to simplify the process of auditing the Change Management process for compliance with its specified procedures.

Procedures

It is unlikely to be practical to parallel-run Change Management systems, and so, when implementing a Change Management system based on ITIL guides, a direct cutover from any previous system is recommended. In some cases, it may be possible to run down an existing system whilst introducing and extending a new method.

Any Changes that were initiated through an existing non-ITIL-compliant Change Management system, or without being subjected to Change Management, should be transferred into the new system at implementation time.

Any initial difficulties with the new Change Management system should be identified as quickly as possible after implementation and resolved. Any support tools should be thoroughly tested before 'go live', but if there are any problems with them after implementation, it may be necessary temporarily to revert to manual methods, even though these are likely to be slow and inefficient.

People

IT Management support is needed to resource the CAB and give the appropriate level of authority, to promote the Change Management system, and to overcome any resistance to formalised Change Management.

Users' and staff awareness of the Change Management procedures is essential. It is important to make it clear that these procedures are mandatory, and to make it difficult or impossible for Changes to be implemented outside the Change Management system.

A proper assignment of responsibility is needed to ensure service quality. The Service Manager is the head of the Service team, and has overall responsibility for service quality. The Change Manager is directly responsible to, and will require the support of, the Service Manager in order to ensure that the correct level of importance is given to Change Management procedures.

Tracking is necessary to ensure compliance. It is recommended that an independent audit be carried out regularly (at least annually) by the organisation's computer audit group to ensure compliance with Change Management procedures.

Contractors' participation is required to ensure adherence. It is essential to ensure that contractors' representatives (e.g. hardware engineers, environmental or accommodation maintenance staff) are aware of, and adhere to, the organisation's Change Management procedures.

Timing

Implementation should not begin until the system is ready, the CAB is set up, and everyone involved is aware of and trained in the new procedures. Change Management, in collaboration with Service Level Management, should then liaise with other managers and User managers to set an implementation date and time that will have the least potential adverse effect on service quality (e.g. during periods of low work throughput).

Implementation of a new Change Management system will be easier if it can be timed to allow Change activity to be 'frozen' immediately prior to and during the implementation. This may not be possible, however, if the new system is being introduced to counteract problems arising from an existing but inadequate Change Management system.

The regular scheduling of Changes can be very important. Serious consideration should be given to the introduction of regular 'Change slots' – times when Changes can be implemented with minimal impact upon User service (for instance between 1800hrs and 2000hrs on Tuesdays and

Thursdays). Such slots should, of course, be agreed with the Customers and the User. If testing of Changes has to be carried out in a non-dedicated environment, consideration might also be given to the provision of 'test slots'.

Service Management should review the efficiency and effectiveness of the Change Management process shortly after the Change Management system has been brought into use (say one to three months after). Regular reviews should take place every two to four months until confidence is established that the system is functioning satisfactorily. Subsequently, Service Management should review the Change Management process regularly, and at least every six months. In between these more formal and scheduled reviews, the Change Manager should continually monitor the effectiveness and efficiency of Change Management.

The suggested frequency of management reporting on the status of Change Management is as follows:

- to the Change Manager: weekly or more frequently, depending on the quality and stability of services
- to the Director of IT and senior User managers: monthly
- to the senior Customer committees: quarterly.

8.7 Metrics and management reporting

Regular summaries of Changes should be provided to service, Customer and User management. Different management levels are likely to require different levels of information, ranging from the Service Manager, who may require a detailed weekly report, to the senior management committees that are likely only to require a quarterly management summary.

Consider including the following facts and statistics in management reports:

- the number of Changes implemented in the period, in total and by CI, configuration type, service, etc
- a breakdown of the reasons for Change (User requests, enhancements, business requirements, service call/Incident/Problem fixes, procedures/training improvement, etc)
- the number of Changes successful
- the number of Changes backed-out, together with the reasons (e.g. incorrect assessment, bad build)
- the number of Incidents traced to Changes (broken down into problem-severity levels) and the reasons (e.g. incorrect assessment, bad build)
- the number of RFCs (and any trends in origination)
- the number of implemented Changes reviewed, and the size of review backlogs (broken down over time)
- high incidences of RFCs/PRs relating to one CI (these are worthy of special attention), giving the reasons (e.g. volatile User requirement, fragile component, bad build)
- figures from previous periods (last period, last year) for comparison
- the number of RFCs rejected
- the proportion of implemented Changes that are not successful (in total and broken down by CI)
- Change backlogs, broken down by CI and by stage in the Change Management process.

Consideration needs to be given, in consultation with the Customer, to the manner in which the management information is presented. In many cases, percentages, and graphical or pictorial representations, are more meaningful than bare numerical data.

The information can be used as a basis for assessing the efficiency and effectiveness of the Change Management process. For this, it is necessary to filter out effects that are outside the direct control of Change Management. For example, frequent Changes affecting a particular CI may be a result of fragility of that item, and should not reflect badly on Change Management as might at first be inferred. Similarly, frequent Changes in User facilities may reflect a rapidly changing User requirement.

Once again, it is worthwhile cross-referencing the BSI publication *A Code of Practice for IT Service Management* (PD0005), where the following is stated:

Change Management reports can include all or some of the following:

- number of Change requests
- number and % of Changes
- rejected
- emergency Changes
- in Change status
- number of Changes awaiting implementation, by:
  - category
  - time outstanding
- number of implemented Changes, by:
  - configuration component
  - service
- change backlogs and bottle-necks
- costs per Change and cost summaries
- business impact of Changes
- Changes by business area
- frequency of Change to CIs.

8.7.1 Auditing for compliance

This paragraph is a checklist for organisations that wish to audit their Change Management process (using the organisations' computer audit group, which is independent of the Service Team), for compliance to the procedures and advice in this chapter. It is recommended that such an audit is completed at least annually, and may be required more often, initially or where particular problems are evident.

The audit should include an examination of the following items:

- randomly selected RFCs – normal, urgent and standard Changes
- Change records
- CAB minutes
- FSC
- review records for random RFCs and implemented Changes.

Checks must be made to ensure that:

- all RFCs have been correctly logged, assessed and actioned
- FSC have been adhered to, or there is a good reason why not
- all items raised at CAB meetings have been followed up and resolved
- all Change reviews have been carried out on time
- all documentation is accurate, up-to-date and complete.

8.8 Software tools

For all but the smallest of organisations, a Configuration Management-based tool, capable of storing all relevant configuration items (CIs), and the important relationships between them, should be used. Such a tool should have the following facilities:

- RFCs and PRs stored upon the same database, in an easily accessible format
- the ability to identify the relationship between RFCs, PRs and CIs
- the capability to link RFCs to projects
- the means to identify easily the other CIs that will be impacted whenever a Change to any specific CI is proposed
- automatic production of requests for impact and resources assessment to the 'owners' of the impacted CIs
- the ability for all authorised personnel to submit RFCs from their own terminal or location
- the ability to 'progress' requests through the appropriate stages of authorisation and implementation and to maintain clear records of this progress
- the ability to allow Change Management staff, Change builders, testers, etc to add text to Change records
- clear definition of back-out procedures should a Change cause problems
- automatic warnings of any RFCs that exceed pre-specified time periods during any stage
- automatic prompting to carry out reviews of implemented Changes
- automatic generation of management and trend information relating to Changes
- the ability to build Changes
- automatic production of FSCs
- a process/workflow feature.

A range of tools is available that to varying degrees integrate all five Service Support processes. An integrated toolset is the recommended option but free standing PC-based database and spreadsheet packages can also be used to log Changes in many environments.

8.9   Impact of new technology

8.9.1   The business domain

Rather than focusing immediately on technology, it is better to consider the role of Change Management in protecting and enhancing critical business processes. Figure 8.6, from the 'Business Perspective' series, illustrates a major dilemma for businesses dependent on IT. Change Management has in the past been associated with the bottom left quadrant of the grid, where business and IT are broadly aligned. Increasingly, IT can cause Change (new technology) or enable Change, all the while increasing business dependence on IT.

As managing Change across the organisation becomes more difficult and as methods to manage programmes and projects emerge and are refined, so must the Change Management processes espoused by BSI, CCTA and others help ameliorate these management issues.

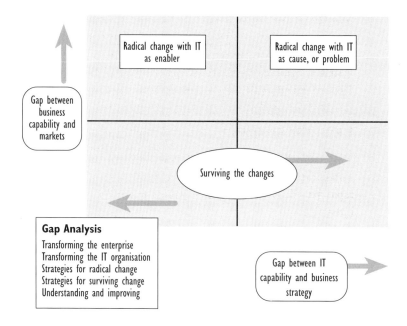

Figure 8.6 - The business perspective on Change

Figure 8.7 represents the four principal components over which we wish to exercise Configuration Management control. John Zachman (an American Configuration Management guru) proposed some years ago that, if IT wished to follow the example of Configuration Management experts such as the aviation and engineering domains, then business and IT processes would have to be defined to an excruciating and hitherto unprecedented level of detail in order to be controlled.

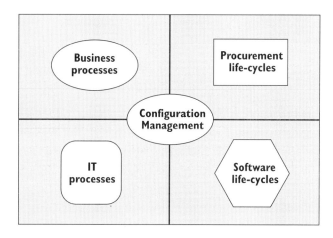

Figure 8.7 - The scope for extending Change Management and Configuration Management control

The influence of Configuration Management (and therefore Change Management) would extend throughout the business and IT domains, providing enormous benefit but also requiring a strategic investment of not inconsiderable dimensions from the business. As a result, it will become increasingly important for Change Management to be fully integrated and influential in the management of major Change. Already we can see investment in methods to manage business Change programmes and projects (PRINCE2 for example).

8.9.2   Technology

When the IT Infrastructure Library was first published, the focus for Change Management was to gain control of the increasingly large numbers of IT related Changes, to an extent caused by the rapid growth of technology. Within a few years, business had become dependent on IT to an hitherto unprecedented degree such that the rapid growth of technology was causing major problems for both the business and IT sides of the organisation. Growth of the Internet is a prime example of this. The good news, however, is that principles of Change Management remain unchanged. What has changed is in the need to make processes much more effective and sensitive to the rapid pace of business and technology change).

The Internet

Software tools support has evolved rapidly to accommodate some of the issues of sensitivity and effectiveness. A number of vendors provide tools that operate in an Internet environment, with remote updating of central databases. As the World Wide Web and the Internet have improved access to information and enabled both business and IT to expand their sphere of influence, security of data has become much more of a problem. This has lead to an increase of responsibility of Change Managers for assessing the impact of Changes on security and finding themselves in need of guidance (see ITIL Security Management - ISBN 0-11-330014-X).

Applications software development

Another area in which Change Management is beginning to influence is applications software development and requirement specification. The impact of new applications running in a live environment has been an issue for ITIL-trained personnel for many years. However, their role in the development life-cycle was largely unknown – although the ITIL book Software Lifecycle Support (ISBN 0-11-330559-1) was published to cover the problem, the issue was not high enough on the agenda of the service providers and therefore was largely ignored until recently.

The major activities of Release Management are defined in the Change life-cycle; as with software maintenance, the technical concepts of an often ignored process (or perhaps a process that is difficult to describe in terms of importance to the business) can be seen to be of particular importance to those in the front line of Service Management. This is illustrated in Figure 9.1 in the Release Management chapter of this guide.

As proper Configuration Management controls are extended to applications software development, so the influence of Change Management has spread to the requirements specification. Requirements specifications now (should!) take into account infrastructure management issues at the design stage. By so doing, infrastructure management not only improves the chances of smooth live operations of new applications, but also reduces the problem of maintenance (and maintenance of software has been proven to cost many many times more than the cost of development).

9 RELEASE MANAGEMENT

9.1 Goal of Release Management

Many service providers and suppliers may be involved in the Release of hardware and software in a distributed environment. Good resource planning and management are essential to package and distribute a Release successfully to the Customer. Release Management takes a holistic view of a Change to an IT service and should ensure that all aspects of a Release, both technical and non-technical, are considered together.

The goals of Release Management are:

- to plan and oversee the successful rollout of software and related hardware

- to design and implement efficient procedures for the distribution and installation of Changes to IT systems

- to ensure that hardware and software being changed is traceable, secure and that only correct, authorised and tested versions are installed

- to communicate and manage expectations of the Customer during the planning and rollout of new Releases

- to agree the exact content and rollout plan for the Release, through liaison with Change Management

- to implement new software Releases or hardware into the operational environment using the controlling processes of Configuration Management and Change Management - a Release should be under Change Management and may consist of any combination of hardware, software, firmware and document CIs

- to ensure that master copies of all software are secured in the Definitive Software Library (DSL) and that the Configuration Management Database (CMDB) is updated

- to ensure that all hardware being rolled out or changed is secure and traceable, using the services of Configuration Management.

The focus of Release Management is the protection of the live environment and its services through the use of formal procedures and checks.

Release Management works closely with the Change Management and Configuration Management processes to ensure that the shared CMDB is kept up-to-date following Changes implemented by new Releases, and that the content of those Releases is stored in the DSL. Hardware specifications, assembly instructions and network configurations are also stored in the DSL/CMDB.

Release Management is often funded from major projects rather than being included in the cost of the normal service to Customers. Although there are costs associated with implementing Release Management, these are far less than the potential costs of not adequately planning, managing and controlling software and hardware Releases.

9.2 Scope of Release Management

Release Management undertakes the planning, design, build, configuration and testing of hardware and software to create a set of Release components for a live environment. Activities also cover the planning, preparation and scheduling of a Release to many Customers and locations.

Release Management activities include:

- Release policy and planning
- Release design, build and configuration
- Release acceptance
- rollout planning
- extensive testing to predefined acceptance criteria
- sign-off of the Release for implementation
- communication, preparation and training
- audits of hardware and software prior to and following the implementation of Changes
- installation of new or upgraded hardware
- storage of controlled software in both centralised and distributed systems
- Release, distribution and the installation of software.

The main components to be controlled are:

- application programs developed in-house
- externally developed software (including standard off-the-shelf software as well as customer-written software)
- utility software
- supplier-provided systems software
- hardware, and hardware specifications
- assembly instructions and documentation, including User manuals.

All deliverables need to be managed effectively, from development or purchasing, through customisation and configuration, through testing and implementation, to operation in the live environment.

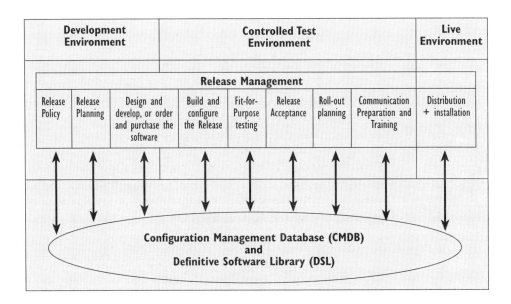

Figure 9.1 – Major activities in Release Management

Release Management should be used for:

- large or critical hardware rollouts, especially when there is a dependency on a related software Change in the business systems, i.e. not every single PC that needs to be installed

- major software rollouts, especially initial instances of new applications along with accompanying software distribution and support procedures for subsequent use if required

- bundling or batching related sets of Changes into manageable-sized units.

Figure 9.1 outlines the major activities in Release Management and their position in the life-cycle of a Change. Configuration Management records should be updated during build and Release to ensure that there are trusted Releases that can be reverted to in case of problems. A Release should be under Change Management and the content and timing of a Release should be authorised in advance via the Change Management process.

9.3 Basic concepts

9.3.1 Release

The term 'Release' is used to describe a collection of authorised Changes to an IT service. A Release is defined by the RFCs that it implements. The Release will typically consist of a number of Problem fixes and enhancements to the service. A Release consists of the new or changed software required and any new or changed hardware needed to implement the approved Changes. Releases are often divided into:

- *Major software Releases and hardware upgrades,* normally containing large areas of new functionality, some of which may make intervening fixes to Problems redundant. A major upgrade or Release usually supersedes all preceding minor upgrades, Releases and emergency fixes.

- *Minor software Releases and hardware upgrades,* normally containing small enhancements and fixes, some of which may have already been issued as emergency fixes. A minor upgrade or Release usually supersedes all preceding emergency fixes.

- *Emergency software and hardware fixes,* normally containing the corrections to a small number of known Problems.

There are normally dependencies between a particular version of software and the hardware required for it to operate. This will drive the packaging of software and hardware together to form a new Release of the service, along with other functional requirements. For example a new version of an application software system may require an upgrade to the operating system and one or other of these two Changes could require a hardware change, e.g. a faster processor or more memory.

Release Management is concerned with changes to defined IT services. These can be implemented by rolling out a combination of new applications software together with upgraded or new hardware, or simply changes to the service hours or support arrangements.

9.3.2 Release policy and planning

The main roles and responsibilities in Release Management should be defined to ensure that everyone understands their role and level of authority and those of others involved in the process.

The Release policy covers Release numbering, frequency and the level in the IT infrastructure that will be controlled by definable Releases. The organization should decide the most appropriate approach, depending on the size and nature of the systems, the number and frequency of Releases required, and any special needs of the Users – for example, if a phased rollout is required over an extended period of time. All Releases should have a unique identifier that can be used by Configuration Management.

A Release policy may say, for example, that only strict 'emergency fixes' will be issued in between formally planned Releases of enhancements and non-urgent corrections.

9.3.3 Release unit

'Release unit' describes the portion of the IT infrastructure that is normally released together. The unit may vary, depending on the type(s) or item(s) of software and hardware.

Figure 9.2 gives a simplified example showing an IT infrastructure made up of systems, which are in turn made up of suites, comprising programs, which are made up of modules.

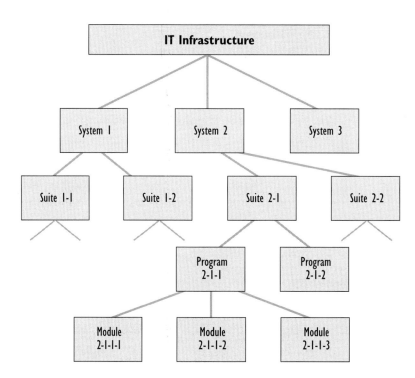

Figure 9.2 - Simplified example of an IT software infrastructure

The general aim is to decide the most appropriate Release-unit level for each software item or type of software. An organisation may, for example, decide that the normal Release unit for its Transaction Processing (TP) services should be at system level. Such a policy means that each time a Configuration Item (CI) forming part of the TP service is changed, a full Release of the whole of that system is normally issued. The same organisation may decide that a more appropriate Release unit for PC software should be at suite level, whilst the Release unit of a batch application should be at program level.

The following factors should be taken into account when deciding the appropriate level for Release units:

- the amount of Change necessary at each possible level
- the amount of resources and time needed to build, test, distribute and implement Releases at each possible level
- ease of implementation
- the complexity of interfaces between the proposed unit and the rest of the IT infrastructure
- the disk space available in the build, test, distribution and live environments.

9.3.4 Release identification

Releases should be uniquely identified according to a scheme defined in the Release policy. The Release identification should include a reference to the CI that it represents and a version number that will often have 2 or 3 parts. Example Release names are as follows:

- major Releases: Payroll_System v.1, v2, v3 etc…
- minor Releases: Payroll_System v.1.1, v.1.2, v.1.3 etc…
- emergency fix Releases: Payroll_System v.1.1.1, v.1.1.2, v.1.1.3 etc…

9.3.5 Types of Release

Full Release

The major advantage of full Releases is that all components of the Release unit are built, tested, distributed and implemented together. There is no danger that obsolete versions of CIs that are incorrectly assumed to be unchanged will be used within the Release. There is less temptation to short-circuit testing of supposedly unchanged CIs and of the interfaces from changed CIs to unchanged ones.

Any problems are therefore more likely to be detected and rectified before entry into the live environment. The disadvantage is that the amount of time, effort and computing resources needed to build, test, distribute and implement the Release will increase. Although in some circumstances the testing of a delta Release (see below) may need to be as extensive as that for an equivalent full Release, the amount of building effort required to test a delta Release is normally less than for a full Release.

Regression testing as part of the process of implementing a full Release allows a large number of components to be retested to ensure that there is no degradation in system function or behaviour.

An example of a Full Release could consist of the complete Release of a new version of client desktop software, or client desktop hardware, or both.

Delta Release

A delta, or partial, Release is one that includes only those CIs within the Release unit that have actually changed or are new since the last full or delta Release. For example, if the Release unit is the program, a delta Release contains only those modules that have changed, or are new, since the last full Release of the program or the last delta Release of the modules.

There may be occasions when Release of a full unit cannot be justified. In such cases, a delta Release may be more appropriate. A decision should be made on whether delta Releases are allowed, and under what circumstances. There is no single 'correct' choice. It is recommended that delta Releases be allowed, with the decision being taken case by case.

In each case the Change Advisory Board (CAB) should make a recommendation, based upon all the relevant facts, on whether the Release unit stipulated in the Release policy is appropriate or whether a delta Release is preferable. In making its recommendation, the CAB should take into account:

- the size of a delta Release in comparison with a full Release, and hence the resources and effort required

- the urgency of the need for the facilities to be provided by the Release to the Users

- the number of CIs (below the Release unit level) that have changed since the last full Release – a very large number may enforce a full Release

- the possible risk to the business if compatibility errors are found in the Release (e.g. would it be preferable to wait for a full Release than to risk interface problems arising with a delta Release?)

- the resources available for building, testing, distributing and implementing the delta Release (e.g. if implementation is to be via non-technical staff, is it easier to implement a complete new Release than a delta Release?)

- the completeness of impact analysis information to make an informed and objective decision.

Package Release

To provide longer periods of stability for the live environment by reducing the frequency of Releases, it is recommended that, where appropriate and where the resulting larger amount of Change can be confidently handled without problems, individual Releases (full units, delta Releases or both) are grouped together to form 'package Releases'. For example, Changes to one system or suite will often require Changes to be made to others. If all these Changes have to be made at the same time, they should be included in the same package Release.

A package can, for example, contain an initial version of a new TP service, several new versions of batch programs, a number of new and initial versions of individual modules, together with the Release of a complete new desktop system (both hardware and software). Both full and delta Releases may be included.

The use of package Releases can reduce the likelihood of old or incompatible software being wrongly kept in use. It can encourage organisations to ensure that all Changes that should be made concurrently, in different suites and systems, *are actually made* concurrently. It can also encourage organisations to test the interworking of these suites and systems fully.

Care should be taken, however, not to exceed, in any particular package Release, the amount of Change that can be handled comfortably. When making a decision on what to include in the package, care should be taken to ensure that the full impact of all individual parts on each other part is understood and has been properly assessed.

9.3.6   Definitive Software Library

The 'Definitive Software Library' (DSL) is the term used to describe a secure compound in which the definitive authorised versions of all software CIs are stored and protected. This one storage area may in reality consist of one or more software libraries or file-storage areas that should be separate from development, test or live file-store areas. It contains the master copies of all controlled software in an organisation. The DSL should include definitive copies of purchased software (along with licence documents or information), as well as software developed on site. Master copies of controlled documentation for a system will also be stored in the DSL in electronic form.

The exact configuration of the DSL that is required for Release Management should be defined before development commences. The DSL forms part of the Release policy or Change and Configuration Management plan for the organisation. The definition should include:

- medium, physical location, hardware and software to be used, if kept online (a DSL can simply be a secure tape library, if properly controlled and catalogued) – some Configuration Management support tools incorporate software libraries, which can be regarded as a logical part of a DSL

- naming conventions for filestore areas and physical media

- environments supported, e.g. test and live environments

- security arrangements for submitting Changes and issuing software, plus backup and recovery procedures

- the scope of the DSL: e.g. source code, object code from controlled builds and associated documentation

- retention period for old Releases of software

- capacity plans for the DSL and procedures for monitoring growth in size

- audit procedures

- procedures to ensure that the DSL is protected from erroneous or unauthorised Change (e.g. entry and exit criteria for items).

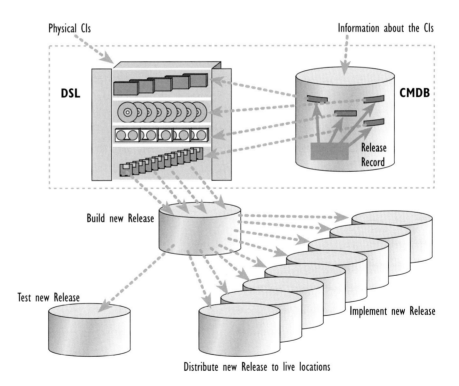

Figure 9.3 - DSL and CMDB relationship

Figure 9.3 shows the tight relationship between the DSL and the CMDB. It also shows how the CMDB holds a secure record or index of the exact contents of each given Release.

9.3.7   Definitive Hardware Store (DHS)

An area should be set aside for the secure storage of definitive hardware spares. These are spare components and assemblies that are maintained at the same level as the comparative systems within the live environment. Details of these components and their respective builds and contents should be comprehensively recorded in the CMDB. These can then be used in a controlled manner when needed for additional systems or in the recovery from major Incidents. Once their (temporary) use has ended, they should be returned to the DHS or replacements obtained.

9.3.8   Configuration Management Database (CMDB)

The CMDB is updated and referred to throughout the Release Management process concurrently with updates to the DSL. It should contain the following information in support of the Release Management process:

- definitions of planned Releases, including the constituent hardware and software CIs together with a reference to the original Change requests
- records of the CIs impacted by planned and past Releases, covering both hardware and software
- information about the target destination for the Released components (e.g. the physical location for hardware and the servers that will receive the software changes).

9.3.9   Build management

The software and/or hardware components that comprise a new Release of an IT service should be assembled in a controlled manner to ensure a reproducible process. For software, the standard approach is to receive new source code from developers and then to generate the executables using controlled procedures on dedicated build hardware. This process is called 'build management' and is the responsibility of Release Management. It is quite common to automate the build procedures to reduce the reliance on human intervention and so make it more reliable. Build procedures and automation should be controlled as additional CIs themselves. These may be generic or specific to the Release.

Hardware components may also need assembling and configuring. This should be performed in a controlled and documented way. It is quite common to write scripts to automate the installation of systems and application software onto servers and workstations. Depending on the implementation plan, this may be able to be performed in advance (for example, if equipment is being replaced) or it may have to occur in situ in the live environment.

Build management becomes the responsibility of Release Management from the controlled test environment onwards.

9.3.10   Testing

Before a Release can be rolled out to the live environment, it should undergo stringent testing and User acceptance. This should include functional testing, operational testing, performance testing and integration testing. Change Management should ensure that there is a formal User acceptance and sign-off before Release Management can continue to roll out the Release. Insufficient testing is the most common single cause of failure of all Changes and Releases.

9.3.11   Back-Out plans

A back-out plan should be produced to document the actions to be taken to restore the service should the rollout of a Release fail, either partially or totally. The production of back-out plans for each Change is the responsibility of Change Management, but Release Management has a role in ensuring that the back-out plans for each Change within a Release operate together to create a Release back-out plan.

There are two approaches and a combination of both can be used:

- A failed roll-out may be completely reversed to allow the complete restoration of the IT service to its previously known state. This is critical for a full Release and preferable for a delta Release.

- Contingency measures may need to be taken to restore as much as possible of the IT service, if it is not possible to restore it fully. This may be considered for a delta Release in the event that a backout and recovery is not practical.

Examples:

- A Release may have only partially been rolled out because the disk space on the target server is too small and so only some of the software changes have been implemented. In this case, it is necessary to document the procedure for backing out the failed rollout and restoring the application to the state prior to that failure. This would require the rollout plan to include a step to take a back-up of the application files being changed (or possibly the whole system) prior to the rollout of the new Release.

- A rollout plan may include replacing some critical hardware or software component (such as a mainframe computer or its operating system) and there may not be time to reinstate the old components, should something go wrong. The back-out plan may document how a spare hardware component, or mobile recovery, can be used to provide the service required.

- A back-out plan may also have to be invoked if the implementation of the Change is taking longer than expected and will impact normal services to Customers. In this instance, the back-out plan should contain timing details specifying the latest point at which implementation can continue before the back-out plan has to be invoked. In this instance, it is important to try to determine the length of the back-out, so that it can be completed before the Customer is impacted.

A back-out plan should be verified as part of the risk assessment of the overall rollout plans, and it should be agreed with the end Users as sufficient. For example, a service might not be critical, in which case it might be agreed that manual procedures can be used whilst the rollout is completed successfully.

Back-out plans should be tested as part of the process of verifying the rollout process.

9.4   Benefits and possible problems

9.4.1   Benefits

As organisations become more dependent on IT, the effective control and security of their computer systems assumes greater importance. Organisations should be able to cope with a high frequency of software and hardware Releases across the organisation without sacrificing IT service quality. The controls and mechanisms within Release Management help support this requirement in an efficient and economic manner.

The principal benefits of Release Management, when combined with effective Configuration Management, Change Management and operational testing functions are:

- a greater success rate in the Release of hardware and software and therefore an improved quality of service delivered to the business

- consistency in the Release processes of the hardware platforms or software environments

- minimisation of the disruption of the service to the business through synchronisation of Releases within packages involving hardware and software components from different platforms and environments

- assurance that the hardware and software in live use is of good (or known) quality, because the Releases are built properly, from hardware and software components that have been subject to quality control and effective testing, and have been constructed under Change Management

- stable test and live environments, because Changes are normally combined into Releases and so there should be fewer individual implementations

- better use of User resources because of combined efforts when testing new Releases – this also means that it will be easier to justify the cost of system-wide regression testing

- minimisation of regression-testing requirements, offering greater coverage than is possible with small Changes that occur frequently or too close together

- better expectation setting within the organisation on publication of a Release schedule in advance

- error reduction through the controlled Release of hardware and software to the live environment, e.g. avoiding incorporating an incorrect version into the Release

- a complete record (or audit trail) of Changes to the live environment is maintained, both of software distributions and of hardware Changes

- proper control and safeguarding of hardware and software assets, upon which an organisation may be heavily dependent

- an ability to absorb high rates of Change to the live systems, effectively and without adversely affecting IT service quality – this is achieved by releasing a large number of Changes together as a single, controlled and well-understood Release

- the ability to build and control the software used at remote sites from a central location

- savings in support costs through the ability to maintain consistent software over a large number of locations

- reduced likelihood of there being illegal copies of software in use at any location

- easier detection of wrong versions and unauthorised copies of software

- reduced risk of unnoticed introduction of viruses or other malicious software
- reduced time to Release and fewer delays
- fewer Releases to be rolled out to Customers
- smoother transitions of Releases from the development activities (projects) to the Customer's business environment.

As the efficiency and effectiveness of Release Management grows, the productivity of IT services staff is likely to increase. More importantly, productivity benefits are likely to be realised amongst end Users, as Releases should be fewer and better planned, with appropriate training and documentation of higher quality.

9.4.2 Possible problems

The potential problems in implementing Release Management are:

- There may be some initial resistance from staff who are familiar with the old procedures and who may not welcome change. To overcome this, the benefits of the new procedures should be carefully explained during an awareness campaign, and there should be a close working relationship with the team implementing the Changes.

- Experience has shown that those teams that are in most need of help with Release Management often have the least time to adopt it. One way round this is to look for minimal-impact ways to gain a foothold and to provide them with some hands-on assistance at the beginning.

- Circumvention of the Release Management procedures may be attempted. This needs to be dealt with firmly, particularly if it involves the installation of unauthorised software, as this is the most likely cause of viruses or untested software that make support very difficult and costly.

- Staff may also be tempted to bypass the standard procedures to install an emergency fix. This should be banned, and disallowed by software security rules as far as possible.

- There may be some reluctance to carry out a controlled build in the test environment, relying instead on copying over software from the development environment.

- In a distributed system, difficulties may arise if new versions of software or hardware are not installed and activated on time at remote locations. The use of software distribution tools, backed up by regular audits, can help avoid this problem.

- Some people (including IT management) may view the Release Management procedures as cumbersome and expensive. Nevertheless, they are almost invariably necessary to cope efficiently and effectively with software Changes.

- Unclear ownership and responsibilities between operational groups and development teams (project teams) may exist – for instance, there may be a lack of understanding about who is responsible for managing components of a Release at different points in the Release cycle.

- Insufficient resources available for adequate testing will reduce the effectiveness of these procedures, or a high number of variants in the live environment may limit complete testing.

- If sufficient machine and network resources are not available, then it may be impossible to build and test new Releases and equipment adequately, or in a timely fashion. Time needs to be allowed in testing for a Release to fail the first time and be reworked. Similarly, back-out procedures should be proven in a controlled test environment.

- A lack of understanding of the Release contents, build and installation components, can lead to mistakes.

- Testing in one area may be acceptable but may fail in another area – e.g. different infrastructure or parameters not set to the same values.

- Staff may be reluctant to back out from a Release, and there may be pressure to transfer inadequately tested software and hardware into the live environment.

- Poor, restricted or non-representative testing environments and procedures may exist.

In all cases, the Release Management plan and the principles and policies on which it is based may be subject to a publicity campaign at the outset and periodically thereafter in order to set expectations and goals.

9.5 Planning and implementation

9.5.1 Planning

To be effective, Release Management is heavily dependent upon Configuration Management, Change Management and operational acceptance testing. If these functions do not already exist, they should be planned in conjunction with Release Management.

Planning Release Management should include:

- Release policies and procedures
- Release roles and responsibilities of all staff
- responsibilities of central Release Management staff
- tools to support the Release of hardware and software into the live environment, e.g. software distribution
- staff to support Release Management
- training
- guidelines for the scheduling of events within an organisation and the production of outline Release schedules for predictable events (where, for example, an organisation might mandate that all events be recorded in a certain way or use a particular event database)
- template documents to assist with the planning of specific Releases
- the management and use of appropriate and effective build and test environments
- ensuring that correct Release mechanisms are in place
- ensuring that there is sufficient space in the build, test, distribution and live environments for a successful Release.

Procedures should be documented for:

- designing, building and rolling out a Release to the organisation
- software Release and distribution, including control and maintenance of the DSL
- purchasing, installing, moving and controlling software and hardware that are relevant to Release Management
- the management and use of any supporting tools and facilities
- Release Management tracking, review, risk management and Problem escalation.

Representatives of the IT staff affected should review the procedures. Amendments required to documentation to reflect changes in procedures or policy should be subject to normal Change Management control and properly authorised. Superseded versions of documentation should be withdrawn from use.

Release policy

A Release policy document for an organisation should be produced to clarify the roles and responsibilities for Release Management. There may be one document per organisation, or an umbrella set of guidelines and specific details for each supported system or IT service. The Release policy normally forms part of an organisation's overall Change Management plan.

A Release policy is revised or extended when an organisation adopts a new technical infrastructure. Piloting of new Release Management procedures should form part of a project to implement a new infrastructure. For example, a new approach to releasing software may need to be developed when an organisation decides to adopt a new hardware or software platform. This may be something as small as a new programming language or as major as a completely new hardware platform with its own operating system, or a network management system.

A Release policy should include:

- guidance on the level in the IT infrastructure to be controlled by definable Releases (e.g. whole application systems or individual program files)
- Release naming and numbering conventions
- a definition of major and minor Releases, plus a policy on issuing emergency fixes
- direction on the frequency of major and minor Releases (e.g. the norm for an organisation might be to have a schedule planned a year in advance to contain a major Release every three months)
- identification of business-critical times to avoid for implementations, and how these should be managed (e.g. an organisation may decide to avoid changing its payroll system in the last two weeks of each month, thus giving a predictable window into which new Releases can be planned)
- expected deliverables for each type of Release (e.g. installation instructions and Release note)
- guidance as to how and where Releases should be documented (e.g. which tool to use and how)
- the policy on the production and degree of testing of back-out plans
- the agreed role: responsibility of the central Release Management function in technical reviews of the application architecture and design
- a description of the Release Management control process (e.g. review meetings, progress assessments (checkpoints), escalation, impact analysis and checking of co-requisites)
- documentation of the exact configuration of the DSL and the definition of acceptance criteria for new software additions (see below for some sample rules).

Sample rules for adding software to the DSL:

- all items are bona fide, and have genuinely been ordered or commissioned
- all software is as expected and no malicious additions are included (this is a particular problem with PC software packages, which could contain viruses)

- all developed software has successfully passed a documented quality review

- all amendments to previous versions have been authorised by Change Management and no other amendments have been included – this may require file comparison facilities to check

- all items to be added to the DSL have been correctly logged in the CMDB; the CMDB should be updated when the items are added (if this does not happen automatically as part of the file transfer into the DSL).

Release and rollout planning procedures

Procedures, templates and guidance should be planned to enable the central Release Management staff to take products from application groups and projects, and then to release the software and hardware efficiently and effectively. Documentation should be developed to assist with:

- understanding the organisation's infrastructure standards and Release Management requirements

- understanding the Service Management and operational requirements, including instructions on how to deal with failures, dependencies and other 'operational' requirements

- guidance on how to design, build and configure a Release for each platform

- understanding the Release acceptance procedure; including the definition of entry and exit criteria

- learning how to use the rollout planning template to assist projects and application groups incorporate all required activities and resources

- understanding communication, preparation and training requirements

- understanding distribution and installation procedures (see below).

Procedures and documents for purchasing, installing, moving and controlling software and hardware that are relevant to Release Management include:

- purchase requests and ordering
- leasing agreements
- licence agreements
- support agreements
- Service Level Agreements (e.g. for ordering new equipment or software)
- procedures for installation and moving equipment
- procedures for disposing equipment and software media
- health and safety guidelines
- security policies and procedures
- the Change Management and Configuration Management plans
- acceptance and authorisation procedures.

A project can cover development and Release of the end product. In that case, communications between Release Management and Project Management needs to be clearly defined. For products developed under the control of PRINCE2, Release authorisation requires Operations Acceptance and User Acceptance letters. As a project is a temporary thing, the acceptance documentation should be formally handed over to Release Management for future reference and maintenance.

Hardware Release and distribution procedures

The distribution of hardware and the creation of the necessary environment for a Release should be carefully planned. The detailed issues relating to these activities are included in the ICT Infrastructure Management book.

Software Release and distribution procedures

Standard procedures should be documented for distributing software Releases from test-build environments into the live environment(s), and for bringing them into use in these environments. Where the build environment is not resident on the same computer as the appropriate test or live environment(s), it is necessary to use a communications link or some form of portable magnetic medium (removable disk or tape).

All reasonable steps should be taken to obviate the possibility of software corruption during distribution to the target environment. Any technical aids available (e.g. checksums on the data transmission), should be used to detect errors so that corrective action can be taken.

As well as transmitting the content of the build to its target environment, it is often necessary to execute some additional processes on the target machine so as to enable operation of the new software to commence. This may involve such actions as the archiving of superseded software versions and the loading of existing live data into a new database structure; and it almost always involves some 'switch-on' action such as a library switch or unit reload.

If a software Release is to be distributed to a large number of locations, it may be essential for all Users to start using the new Release at the same time – for example, if a legal change is to be introduced nationwide at start of business on a specific day, or if a distributed corporate database is involved. If the Release is to be implemented in many locations concurrently, special steps may be necessary. Scale may determine that distribution of the Release to all locations has to be spread over a period of time. The dormant Release can then be installed at each location in readiness for live implementation, with some form of 'switch' triggered to bring all Releases into use at the appropriate time. The switch may involve issuing a command at either a central control site or at a number of distributed sites; alternatively, some form of software switch may be embedded in the Release itself, to be activated upon some predefined event. A Release such as this is a major activity with a potentially significant impact on the business. Therefore it should be the subject of careful and extensive testing, planning and management.

All necessary scripts and parameters for use at implementation should be controlled in essentially the same way as those for build time. The objective is to make the implementation process as simple, foolproof and secure as possible. Ideally, the Release Management team should only need to issue a single command from a terminal or console to initiate the implementation process, once distribution of the Release has been successfully completed. It should also be possible to check from the distribution centre that the implementation has been successful. If transmission is via magnetic media, then some 'local' actions are unavoidable, although ideally this should be limited to physically mounting the tapes or disks, updating local procedures and manuals, etc.

Unless the distribution and implementation process can be controlled automatically, or from the centre using software tools, human procedures should ensure that distributed software arrives when expected and is checked in whatever way is practical for authenticity; and that the software is brought into use when required. These procedures should include the following activities:

- central Release staff inform remote staff when to expect distributed software to arrive
- remote staff report to the central Release staff when the distributed software has arrived successfully

- central Release staff check that all software is received as expected at remote locations
- central Release staff issue clear instructions about when the software is to be implemented
- remote staff report to the centre when the software has been implemented.

The Release record on the CMDB states which installations are to receive the Release. The CMDB should be updated to reflect the receipt and implementation of the Release at each remote site.

Change Management procedures require that back-out plans be made in advance for all Changes that are to be implemented. In the case of new software Releases, this will normally involve withdrawal of the new Release and reversion to the previous, trusted, Release. This may not, however, be possible (e.g. the new Release implements a mandatory legislative change, and so it is obviously not possible to use the old program versions). In such cases, alternative back-out plans need to be made. In all cases the back-out plans should, where possible, be tested and proved to be workable.

Software Releases often involve the use of a hierarchy of distribution or staging servers. It is essential before a Release is attempted that all software and hardware environments used within the distribution are checked to ensure that there is sufficient spare space to contain the intended Release. Once the Release has either been accepted as successful or been rolled back, all environments involved within the process should be reviewed again, to ensure that redundant hardware or software components are removed.

Release roles and responsibilities

Releases that consist of many different types of software and hardware may involve many people in the Release and control processes. The typical responsibilities for accepting components of a Release should be defined centrally, and then this can be modified as required for specific Releases. Typical roles are the Change Manager (see Chapter 8), the Release Manager and the Test Manager.

Where there are standard build and installation procedures that are predefined and approved, it is feasible to allow further activities without specific reference to Change Management each time – for example, standard installation of a desktop application to a new workstation. The CMDB should be updated, preferably automatically, each time to reflect the Changes. This method can only be allowed where each installation satisfies any documented prerequisites and conforms to agreed operational constraints, such as a limit on the number of additional workstations at a given location.

If there are no common roles, responsibility for the acceptance and handover should be documented within a specific responsibility table for the organisation. An example of a responsibility matrix for an organisation that supports client-server applications is shown in Table 9.1. Such a matrix will help to identify gaps and overlaps and typical roles can be planned for the future.

Release Responsibilities Class of Object	Development Released from	Controlled test Environment		Live	
		Accepted by	Authority to Release to Live	Accepted and Supported by	Control Records
Bought-in package	Development Manager	Test Manager	Change Manager	Operations Manager	CMDB DSL
Customised modules	Development Manager	Test Manager	Change Manager	Operations Manager	CMDB DSL
Physical database changes	Development Manager	Database Administrator	Change Manager	Database Administrator	CMDB DB script in DSL
Server	Server Builder	Server Manager	Change Manager	Server Manager	CMDB
Desktop build (e.g. a new application)	Desktop Development Manager	Test Manager	Change Manager	Desktop Support Manager	CMDB DSL
Desktop Application (already built and within operational constraints)	Desktop Development Manager	Desktop Support Manager	Desktop Support Manager Change Manager	Desktop Support Manager	CMDB DSL
Desktop computers	Logistics	Desktop Support	Desktop Support Manager Change Manager	Desktop Support Manager	CMDB
Release Authorisation/ Change Record	Development Manager	Test Manager	Release Manager Change Manager Test Manager Operations Manager Desktop Support Service Desk User at each site	Service Desk Users	CMDB

Table 9.1 - Example responsibility matrix

Figure 9.4 shows the involvement of Release Management and Change Management in a request for something new or outside agreed operational constraints. It also shows that the Service Desk team can build additional workstations to the same specification without referring to Change Management explicitly for each and every request – so long as it conforms to the predefined operational limits and the CMDB is updated. The same can apply for installing an application on an existing workstation using authorised instructions. Table 9.1 helps to explain some of these roles by example. Desktop build (e.g. a new application) is released from the 'Desktop Development Manager' – who is *NOT* part of Release Management or Computer Operations. Release Management is about overseeing the process and Operations Management is concerned with running the current live systems, but 'Desktop Development' is concerned with designing and building the next Release of a system – which in this case is a desktop build (i.e. a particular configuration of system and application software).

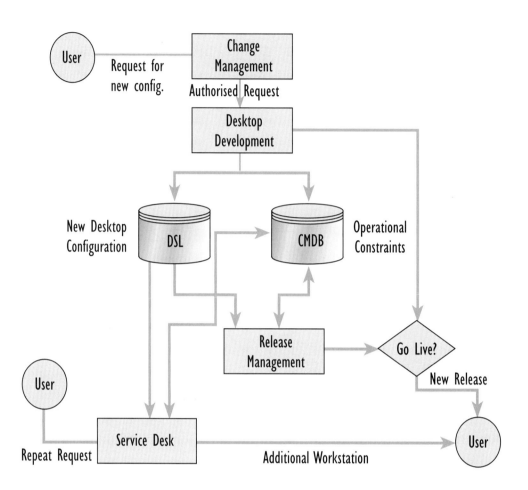

Figure 9.4 - Release Management and Change Management

Staffing

The number of Release Management staff needed depends on the scale of operations. Because Release Management is on the critical path between applications development and live operations, and is involved in all important Changes to live systems, there should be enough trained staff to cover for annual leave and absences.

Larger projects should consider the resource loading on central staff and provide additional resources (preferably using secondment from other areas, such as the Service Desk) or funding to perform Release Management, Change Management and Configuration Management activities.

Release Managers require a sound technical background, with a good understanding (or an ability to get it) of the IT infrastructure and the services it provides. A good working knowledge of support tools and utilities, and a good grasp of the principles and practices of IT Infrastructure Management – especially Change Management and Configuration Management – are essential. An awareness of the organisation's business strategy and its priorities is also needed. Staff management and project management skills are highly desirable.

In a small company the Release Management function can well be combined with several other Service Management disciplines, in particular Change Management and Configuration Management. In a larger organisation there may be dedicated Release Management staff for particular systems, assuming that there is not too much need to coordinate Releases. In these cases, there may also be a central software distribution function to support all of that work, i.e. a team dedicated to this specialised task.

Training

Release Management staff should be given technical training in the principles and practices of Change Management and Configuration Management and of software maintenance and development, and in the use of support tools and utilities. A more general awareness of the IT infrastructure and the services it provides should also be imparted, together with an appreciation of the organisation's business issues.

Application development managers and project managers should be trained in the Release policy, procedures and tools. Procedures and guidance should be published and made available to all staff involved in Release and rollout management.

Training may also be required for the operational Users who release the service to the business, and for business Users who need the 'new service' to meet business needs.

9.5.2 Implementation

Software Release and distribution

When the necessary staff, procedures, hardware and support tools are in place and all necessary training has been completed, the DSL and build environment(s) should be physically created and the necessary security permissions established so as to limit access to authorised Release Management staff. The DSL and test/build environments should be tested in accordance with criteria defined at the planning stage.

In particular, applications development staff should be told when to start delivering Release material for inclusion in the DSL, and arrangements should be made for all bought-in software to be delivered directly to Release Management for lodging in the DSL and passed to Configuration Management for recording in the CMDB.

Build management and software distribution procedures should be tested before they are brought into use. If a gradual approach has been adopted, as recommended, the first Release build will be when the deliverables from the selected development project or from the chosen supplier are to be subject to operational acceptance testing. By the time Releases to the live environment are needed, the build and Release control procedures will have been used for putting software into the operational acceptance testing environment, thereby providing another chance for many classes of potential problems with procedures and tools to be found and corrected.

Plans should be made in case the new procedures or tools fail. If software Releases are urgently required, it may be necessary to revert temporarily to previous procedures until the new procedures are corrected. Where possible, it is recommended that the procedures or tools for *distributing* software to remote sites be tested separately from those for *implementing* the software at the remote sites, thereby allowing problems with each of these phases to be isolated and corrected separately.

Although the procedures should be thoroughly tested before being brought into live use, time should nevertheless be allowed to resolve any teething problems in the early stages of live use.

Release Management and roll out procedures

To ensure that the procedures are fully adopted, the central Release Manager should:

- champion the new processes and encourage project managers and application teams to use them
- monitor the take-on and benefits of the new Release and rollout processes
- monitor the level of help and support provided to application groups and projects
- report exceptions to the organisation's Release policy
- function within, or report to, the programme or project office where one exists
- automate Release procedures wherever possible
- ensure that all Customer, support staff and Service Desk staff are trained and provided with the appropriate documentation and information.

9.5.3   Costs

The costs associated with Release Management include:

- development of best practices, and procedures for Release and rollout management
- education and training in Release Management policy, procedures and tools
- staff costs to develop and run the procedures and tools
- file storage costs to accommodate the DSL
- costs associated with build, test, distribution and archive environments for all supported hardware and software
- accommodation for secure equipment stores (to hold controlled inventories of hardware ready for roll out)
- the cost of spare equipment e.g. to provide hot-swaps for failures in the live environment
- the cost of computer and network resources for moving software into and out of the DSL, and for building, distributing and implementing software Releases
- the cost of software support tools (and the cost of any additional hardware or software needed to run these tools)
- the cost of the effort required to automate procedures (e.g. build, storage and distribution)
- initial operating costs, which may be slightly greater than normal while the Release Management staff are learning the procedures
- costs associated with the installation and management of distribution and staging servers
- software distribution costs.

In almost all cases, the costs associated with implementing Release Management will be outweighed by the benefits it brings. For example, many organisations cannot function satisfactorily unless they can handle a high volume of software and hardware changes without sacrificing quality. Release Management gives them that ability.

Without adequate control, organisations are at risk from such things as computer fraud, inadvertent software corruption, software viruses and other malicious software. The damage caused by these can require an enormous sum to rectify.

It is good practice to record existing costs as soon as possible, so that improvements through good practices can be tracked.

It is possible to fund Release Management centrally or on a project-by-project basis. A common approach is for projects to pay for the initial costs of implementing Release Management in a new area and then to pass the ongoing support work onto a centrally funded group.

9.6 Activities

9.6.1 Release planning

Planning a Release involves:

- gaining consensus on the Release contents
- agreeing to the phasing over time and by geographical location, business unit and Customers
- producing a high-level Release schedule
- conducting site surveys to assess existing hardware and software in use
- planning resource levels (including staff overtime)
- agreeing on roles and responsibilities
- obtaining detailed quotes and negotiating with suppliers for new hardware, software or installation services
- producing back-out plans
- developing a quality plan for the Release
- planning acceptance of support groups and the Customer.

Release planning inputs include:

- project life-cycle
- service-related deliverables
- authorised RFCs
- Release policy
- an overview of business needs
- constraints and dependencies
- CAB output
- templates.

Release planning outputs include the plan for a particular Release, and high-level test plans and acceptance criteria for the Release. The outputs of Release planning are normally documented in the Change Management plan for a particular project.

Release Management should work with Change Management to agree the exact content of each Release.

9.6.2 Designing, building and configuring a Release

Procedures should be planned and documented for building software Releases, reusing standard procedures where possible. A configuration of a particular Release of software and hardware may be based upon a set of available components, some of which may be developed in-house and others bought in. The instructions to assemble a Release in this manner should be considered part of the definition of the Release and treated as a controlled CI.

Conducting the actual build involves, at a minimum, compiling and linking application modules produced in-house and any bought-in software that is held in source form, in each case from the DSL. It may also involve incorporation into the Release of any bought-in software, in object form, that is to be included. It may include generating databases and populating them with test data or, for live builds, static reference data (e.g. the Post Office Address File). Where necessary, it includes the generation (or, minimally, transcription from the DSL) of the operating system, the DBMS run-time components, etc.

It is quite common to write automated installation routines to ensure accurate rollout of a Release. These may include one-off routines to convert data or initialise databases. Any automation or one-off jobs should have equivalent back-out routines to enable the Release to be reversed in the event of problems.

Software licences and training in the use of support tools will be required for central Release Management staff. New health and safety requirements need to be considered when releasing new or changed equipment. New or changed data feeds (e.g. Electronic Data Interchange links) may need to be ordered and tested as part of this activity. Changes to hardware or software support contracts may need to be negotiated.

All software, parameters, test data, run-time software and any other software that is required for the Release should be under Configuration Management control. Quality control checks should be performed on this software before the application is built. A complete record of the build results should be logged in the CMDB. This ensures that a build can be repeated should it be necessary.

The high-level test plans for the Release need to be expanded to include specific tests to verify the successful rollout of the Release, by satisfying critical success factors and exit criteria. For example, an automated installation routine may be developed for a new Release of software component, and this needs to be tested separately from the software application itself.

Design, build and configure inputs:

- Release definition
- Release plans

Design, build and configure outputs:

- detailed Release assembly and build instructions, including the exact sequence of operations
- purchase orders, licences and warranties for third-party software and hardware
- automated installation scripts and associated test plans
- master copies of the installation media and installation instructions, to be stored in the DSL
- back-out procedures.

9.6.3   Release acceptance

The testing of the Release should be performed by independent business staff and involve IT staff to verify any changed support procedures. Any back-out procedures should be tested as part of this activity, which should prove that the built Release can be installed and run as required. This includes testing both the installation procedures and the function of the final system.

Testing should cover the installation procedures and the functional integrity of the resultant system. There should be a sign-off for each stage of testing. The final acceptance and sign-off for the Release to go into the live environment should be an agreed stage of the Change Management process. All levels of support should be involved in the testing of major Releases.

Release acceptance should be performed in a controlled test environment that can be reinstated to known configurations of both software and hardware. These configurations should be described in the Release definitions and stored in the CMDB, along with any other related CIs.

If a Release is rejected, it should be rescheduled through Change Management. Rejected Releases should be tracked and reported through Change Management as failed Changes. Failed Releases and their impact on operations and support staff resources should be monitored.

Release acceptance inputs comprise:

- a controlled test environment(s) configured to replicate the current live versions of the application with documentation of the test configuration
- Release definition and plans
- Release test plans and acceptance criteria
- copies of the installation media and installation instructions
- test plans for the installation scripts
- documented back-out procedures.

The end result of the acceptance activity should be a sign-off on the completeness and accuracy of the whole Release. The outputs should include:

- tested installation procedures
- tested Release components
- tested back-out procedures
- known defects to be carried forward into the live environment
- test results
- support documentation including the system overview; updated support procedures; diagnostic aids
- operating and administration instructions
- contingency and back-out plans
- a training schedule for Service Management, support staff and Customers
- acceptance test documentation signed by all relevant parties
- authorisation to implement the Release (done through Change Management).

9.6.4 Rollout planning

Rollout planning extends the Release plan produced so far to add details of the exact installation process developed and the agreed implementation plan. Rollout planning involves:

- producing an exact, detailed timetable of events, as well as who will do what (i.e. a resource plan)
- listing the CIs to install and decommission, with details on the method of disposal for any redundant equipment and software
- documenting an action plan by site, noting any implications of different time zones on the overall plans (e.g. an international organisation may well not have a single common Release window when none of its systems is being used throughout the world)
- producing Release notes and communications to end Users
- planning communication

- developing purchasing plans

- acquiring hardware and software where, because this often involves the acquisition and deployment of numerous high-value assets, the rollout plan should include the procedures to be followed for their secure storage prior to rollout and the mechanisms to trace their deployment during the implementation (which could involve the use of asset tags or other electronically readable labels)

- scheduling meetings for managing staff and groups involved in the Release.

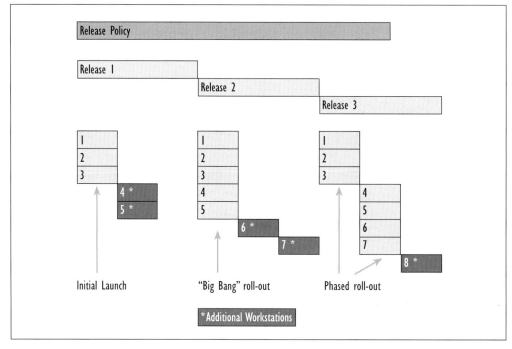

Figure 9.5 - Rollout options

Figure 9.5 illustrates a typical sequence of events over time. The Release policy endures across all Releases of the system and defines the overall approach. The sequence of events is as follows:

1. There is an initial launch of 'Release 1' of the system to three workstations (1–3).

2. Two further workstations (4+5) are then added.

3. Release 2 of the system is then rolled-out in a 'big bang' approach to all workstations (1–5) at once.

4. Two further workstations (6+7) are then added, in two steps.

5. There is a phased implementation of the upgrade to 'Release 3' of the system, initially upgrading only three workstations (1–3) and then the remaining four (4–7).

6. A further workstation (8) is then added to the system.

This scenario illustrates a number of important points:

- Releases can be rolled out into the live environment wholesale (the 'big bang' approach), or piecemeal (also known as a 'phased' implementation). There are many types of 'phased' implementation, namely:

    - when portions of the function are delivered to the live environment in phases, but all end Users are affected simultaneously (e.g. incremental changes to a centralised mainframe application)

  - where each Release is implemented gradually across the total population of end Users (e.g. one geographical location at a time)
  - hardware Changes could be phased in first, followed subsequently by software changes
  - a combination of all of these approaches.

■ The phased implementation that is illustrated in the Figure 9.5 is the second type in the list above. Note that it is only possible to employ this approach if the system has been designed to allow both new and old versions of the application to coexist. If this is not allowed, then the only alternative is to upgrade all affected parts (both hardware and software) together in a 'big bang' implementation.

■ In general, it is best to avoid the high degree of risk inherent in the 'big-bang' approach, because all Users of the IT service in question can be affected if the implementation fails. Examples of where there might be no choice are the replacement of a significant piece of computer hardware and, upgrading the operating system on a critical server.

■ Small Changes can be made to the live environment without needing to create a whole new Release of the system (e.g. adding further workstations). This is only the case when the additions are just further examples of what has already been defined for that Release. However, there will almost certainly be operational constraints (e.g. a maximum number of Users) that may not be exceeded in the corporate definition of 'small Change'. Note that, in any event, no Change can take place without an RFC being raised.

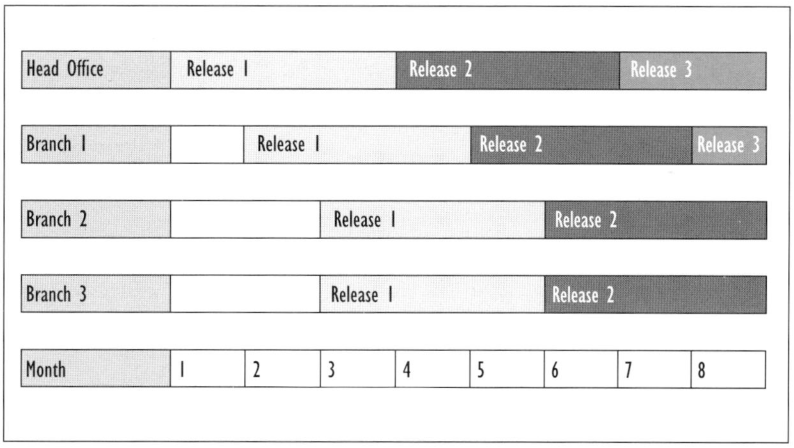

Head Office	Release 1		Release 2		Release 3	
Branch 1		Release 1		Release 2		Release 3
Branch 2			Release 1		Release 2	
Branch 3			Release 1		Release 2	
Month	1	2	3	4	5	6	7	8

Figure 9.6 - A phased roll out across several geographical locations

Figure 9.6 shows an example of a phased rollout of a system to a number of different geographical locations. It assumes that new versions of the system will work with at least the previous one. The example used assumes that new functionality is implemented first in the head office of the organisation, then in a pilot branch, and finally in the remaining branches.

If there are a very large number of locations to deal with, it may still take a long time to implement the initial system or later upgrades in all branches, thus increasing the likelihood of needing to support even more versions of the system in the live environment concurrently.

9.6.5   Communication, preparation and training

Customer liaison staff, Customers and support staff need to know what is planned and how it might affect them. This is normally accomplished through training sessions, periods of parallel working, and involvement in the Release acceptance stage. Problems and Changes that need to be made during rollout should be communicated to all parties to keep them informed and to set their expectations. This activity normally includes running a series of rollout planning meetings with all of the interested parties to ensure that the plans are properly reviewed, checkpoints are established and all parties agree their responsibilities.

It is important to publicise the Release mechanism. It is also important to publicise any constraints to end Users (for example that it may not be possible to effect an update to all PCs overnight in a large organisation).

Health and safety requirements need to be considered when installing new or changed equipment and handing it over to Users. Checks should be made for any hardware, software, networking, cabling or capacity issues that are outstanding. New or changed data feeds (e.g. Electronic Data Interchange (EDI) links) need to be ordered and tested as part of this activity.

Changes to hardware or software support contracts may also need to be communicated to the relevant staff. The responsibility for this communication clearly rests with the Service Desk, but Release Management may be better placed to undertake the detailed communication.

Inputs to this activity are:

- the detailed Release definition and rollout plan
- copies of the installation media and installation instructions
- current versions of support, training and User documentation
- acceptance forms.

Outputs should comprise the:

- final versions of User and support training materials and documentation
- updated Release plans and documentation.

9.6.6   Distribution and installation

Distribution of the software Releases from the build environment into the controlled test environment and then into the live environment should be accomplished with any associated hardware or co-requisite changes.

The processes for procurement, storage, dispatch, receipt and disposal of goods should ensure that equipment is delivered safely to its destination in its expected state. Storage areas should be secure. Checks on the receipt of goods against supporting delivery documentation are required for Configuration Management. Installation, environmental and electrical checks should be planned and completed before connection to the network.

Software distribution should be designed so that the integrity of software is maintained during handling, packaging and delivery. Automated software distribution to remote locations will save resources and reduce the distribution cycle time. After distributing software over a network, it is essential to check that the Release is complete when it reaches its destination.

Bringing application software Releases into active use in these environments is the final step in effecting the Change. It is quite common to distribute a new version of an application to a target installation, but to do so in a way that it remains dormant until activated. This should be accomplished by following the tested installation procedures. These may require running automated installation routines or other one-off utilities to effect the Change. To ensure a smooth rollout, an automated check of the target platform is required so as to ensure that it satisfies hardware and software prerequisites. This would call upon the audit services of Configuration Management, but Release Management drives the process.

The CMDB should be updated following installation or disposal of hardware or software, to ensure that it reflects the final position. It may be necessary to retrieve old versions of software that have been superseded, to prevent software licence rules from being violated.

For some types of Release (e.g. for desktop upgrades) it may be appropriate for the end Users to perform a final acceptance test of the installed software. For substantial Changes, the Customers should develop or be given a checklist of tests to perform. An installation Customer satisfaction survey can be used to provide formal feedback.

After a successful installation, the Configuration Management records should be updated with the location and the owner of the hardware and software. This will assist support staff to locate equipment and resolve subsequent Incidents and Problems more efficiently.

Distribution and installation inputs are:

- detailed rollout plans
- tested installation procedures
- tested Release components
- tested back-out procedures.

Distribution and installation outputs should comprise:

- an updated IT service, with updated User and support documentation
- updated CMDB records to reflect new live components
- decommissioned CIs (such as redundant software and hardware)
- any Known Errors in the live system introduced as part of the new Release.

9.7 Process control

9.7.1 Key performance indicators

A number of key performance indicators (KPIs) should be monitored to assess the effectiveness of the Release Management process. Consider choosing some measures that show a clear indication of at least some of the following:

- Releases built and implemented on schedule, and within budgeted resources (but care should be taken to isolate any problems that are outside the control or responsibility of Release Management, such as application development delays)

- very low (ideally no) incidence of Releases having to be backed out due to unacceptable errors (note however that software Releases need not be entirely error-free; a decision can be made to go ahead with a Release despite the presence of errors, provided that they are of a minor nature, and within the permitted fault tolerances – see Chapter 6, Problem Management)

- low incidence of build failures

- secure and accurate management of the DSL

- no evidence of software in the DSL that has not passed quality checks and no evidence of reworks on any software that was extracted from the DSL

- DSL sizing matching the demand for space, and timely and accurate housekeeping of the DSL

- compliance with all legal restrictions relating to bought-in software

- accurate distribution of Releases to all remote sites

- implementation of Releases at all sites, including remote ones, on time

- no evidence of unauthorised reversion to previous versions at any site

- no evidence of use of unauthorised software at any site

- no evidence of payment of licence fees or wasted maintenance effort, for software that is not actually being used at any particular location

- no evidence of wasteful duplication in Release building (e.g. multiple builds of remote sites, when copies of a single build would suffice)

- accurate and timely recording of all build, distribution and implementation activities within the CMDB

- a post-mortem carried out on all Release activities, and all necessary corrective or follow-up action taken, together with any process improvements

- the planned composition of Releases matching the actual composition (which demonstrates good Release planning)

- IT and human resources required by Release Management being subject to good ongoing forward planning.

9.7.2   Management reporting

Other metrics that may be monitored include:

- the number of major and minor Releases per reporting period
- the number of problems in the live environment that can be attributed to new Releases, which need only be measured during the first few months of a new Release's life, classified by root cause, (e.g. 'wrong version of file' or 'missing files')
- the number of new, changed and deleted objects introduced by the new Release – e.g. how many modules and programs
- the number of Releases completed in the agreed timescales; this requires the central Release Management function to publish predefined targets (service levels or SLAs) for software distributions and other common tasks.

9.8 Relations to other processes

Release Management should use the controlling processes of Configuration Management and Change Management.

9.8.1 Configuration Management

Whenever new versions of software are added to the DSL, its details should be simultaneously included in the CMDB. Similarly, whenever new or changed hardware is rolled out, the CMDB should be updated. The CMDB should always contain the current status information on all authorised software and hardware and is used to ensure that only the correct components are included in a Release.

Release Management may use various services of Configuration Management during the implementation of a Release (e.g. configuration audit to ensure that the target environment is as expected). It is possible to combine these two functions with or without Change Management to form one organisational unit.

9.8.2 Change Management

The CAB, as defined in the Change Management process, with advice from Release Management, is responsible for recommending the content and scheduling of Releases. Release Management is then responsible for implementing the agreed Releases. Release Management is normally represented on the CAB and is involved in establishing the organisation's Release policy.

Although Release Management oversees the details of the roll out of a Change, it is under the control and authority of Change Management.

9.8.3 Software from Developers and suppliers

When software is accepted from developers or suppliers, it is placed into the DSL and registered in the CMDB. Release Management is responsible for building Releases from the DSL into the controlled test environment. When testing has successfully concluded, Release Management should distribute the Release into the live environment.

9.8.4 Problem Management and the Service Desk

At the end of the successful distribution and installation of a new Release, various records in the Problem Management system need updating as follows:

- any related Problems or enhancement requests should be closed
- any known Problems introduced by the new Release should be added to the database to allow Service Desk staff to support the new Release
- Problem Management and Service Desk staff should be informed of the new Release so that they can support its use in the live environment. Such staff should receive training in any new or revised support procedures.

Problem Management staff are also often involved in identifying faults that will lead to Requests for Change (RFCs) and so eventually lead to new Releases.

9.8.5   Project Management and PRINCE2

For software developed under the control of a PRINCE2 project, Release authorisation requires Operations Acceptance and User Acceptance letters.

Release Management should assist project management in planning and implementing a Release, but it does not take control.

9.9   Tools specific to the Release Management process

9.9.1   Change Management tools

Release Management should make use of any tools used by the Change Management process to record information about planned Changes. Release Management requires these tools to be extended to hold information about Releases and links to the Changes that they, either singly or grouped, each implement.

A good system will allow the tracking of the status of both individual Changes and the Releases that implement them, as well as providing facilities for staff to authorise, electronically, various phases in the life-cycle of a Release. Ideally, the final steps should automatically trigger the software distribution into the test and live environments using interfaces to those tools.

9.9.2   Configuration Management tools

Hardware and software CIs should be recorded in the CMDB and, ideally, their status should be amended as the Release progresses. This requires the ability to store proposed Changes to the CMDB and to trigger updates to those records from the Change Management system.

9.9.3   Software Configuration Management (SCM) tools

There are many tools available to help manage the different versions of software source code during its development. Of particular value is the ability of the SCM tool to manage relationships. This enables a Change to any one CI to be assessed for impact upon other parts of the system, and thereby to identify what actions are required to ring-fence the Change as complete, and to plan appropriate testing.

Release Management benefits greatly from those SCM tools that can handle packages of Changes linked to an original Change request. This also implies the use of an SCM tool that can integrate with the Problem and Change request information typically held in a Service Desk tool.

9.9.4   Build management tools

A sound Release Management process requires the automated build of new Releases of software applications. This relies on being able to drive program compilations and links, in the correct sequence, under program control using the correct versions of the source code as stored in the SCM tool.

This process (see Figure 9.7) also requires making use of the cross-reference information stored in the software Configuration Management tool to determine which 'parent' objects need to be rebuilt when lower-level units are changed. For example, if a header or 'include' file is changed, then it is necessary to identify all source modules that need to be recompiled. Similarly, the names of the programs to be relinked should be determined, based on the list of modules that were recompiled.

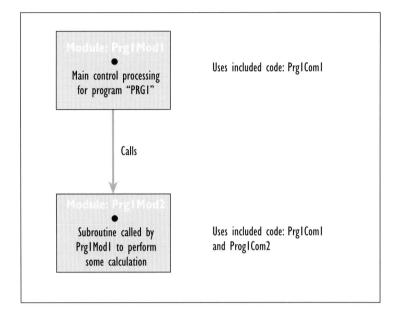

Figure 9.7 - Example module hierarchy diagram for Program PRG1

Some more mature software Configuration Management tools also include build components to help with this process and eliminate the need to record manually dependency information. Where no proprietary tools are available, it is often feasible to script simple build procedures using command languages. However this is not straightforward without any specialised help, because an accurate build requires an understanding of the dependencies between the Changed CIs and so you may be limited to regenerating entire systems. Dedicated tools optimise the build process so that only those components affected are rebuilt. They also ensure that the correct version of the source code is used.

To complete the task (see Figure 9.8), the automated build process should save the generated executables in the DSL and update the CMDB accordingly. Some SCM tools improve upon this by storing 'footprints' containing the source code version used and compile information within the generated executables. The source version of all in-house-developed applications and modules should be stored within the DSL, together with all of the other systems software required to generate and run executable versions, such as compilers and operating systems.

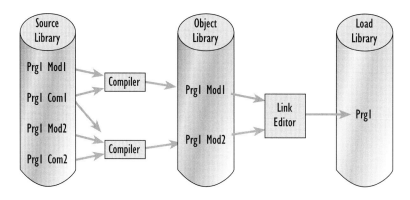

Figure 9.8 - The software build process

9.9.5   Electronic software distribution

Many organisations have large numbers of workstations and servers in the live environment that could require software Changes as part of a Release. Increasingly, this can require updates to software on more than one platform in a coordinated manner. The process of software distribution is not always smooth, whether manual or automated, because things can go wrong. Consequently, it is important to be able to record the progress of a given distribution and record individual failures (where, for instance, a few workstations did not receive a fix because of an error). It may even be required to insist on the back-out of a whole Release if it is only partially successful.

It is becoming increasingly difficult nowadays to achieve software distribution reliably and efficiently using manual processes, which is why there are a number of automated software-distribution tools on the market that can assist with this task. They range from simple file-transfer utilities to modules of large systems-management suites. Nevertheless, the introduction of such tools needs to be evaluated very carefully because they are not at all straightforward to use and they make increased demands on network bandwidth – which is often at a premium.

Being able to install an application automatically requires an understanding of how to do so manually and a general understanding of how software is installed and configured on the appropriate platform. Many applications come with their own installation routines, and sometimes it is a simple job to create a script to drive these in an automated way. However, this is not always sufficient and further Changes are sometimes required. Sometimes, special utilities are required to determine exactly what files are changed by installation routines by use of before-scans and after-scans – especially on workstations.

Features to look for (see Figure 9.9) in electronic software distribution tools include the following:

- *Assured delivery of software files.* Good systems include integrity checking of data sent and the ability to restart broken transmissions from the point of failure.

- *A variety of delivery options to make the most of an organisation's network capacity.* Some provide a courier mechanism via CD-ROM, for sending whole packages to remote installations in a controlled way by post. Another approach is that of 'fan-out' which employs intermediate servers at remote locations to help with the distribution.

- *The ability to store a new version of an application in a dormant state.* This is required for very rapid activation or deactivation when triggered.

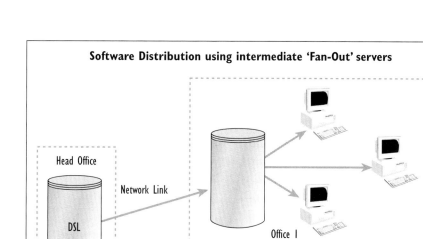

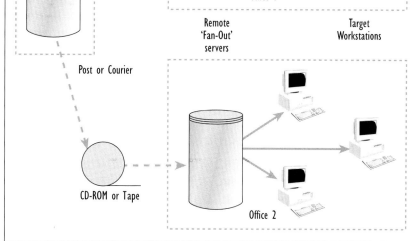

Figure 9.9 - Features of electronic software distribution

9.9.6   Software and hardware auditing tools

To be able to perform a successful Release it is important to have confidence in the target platform. This can be assisted through the use of automated tools to perform hardware and software audits. Such tools can determine exactly what software is installed and identify most critical aspects of hardware configuration.

Using tools like this, it should be possible to check for sufficient available disk space or some other prerequisite in the live environment a little while ahead of the distribution of the Release and so have time to rectify the situation in advance. As a consequence, there should be fewer failures during Release rollouts.

9.9.7   Desktop management tools

It is possible to restrict the changes that individual Users can make to client workstations and so make the target destination for new Releases much more reliable. Sometimes this can be achieved through correctly configuring operating system parameters; occasionally, additional software has to be used to increase control.

Whether electronic software distribution tools are used or not, it is a good practice to save standard workstation builds on a server and use some automation to perform the installation. There are a number of scripting languages that can help with this, and there are also dedicated software installation products that can be used.

It is the responsibility of Release Management to implement procedures to ensure that any installation files saved on servers are kept up-to-date when new Releases are lodged in the DSL.

9.9.8　Server management tools

Remote control and remote diagnostic facilities for live servers can aid fault determination and resolution during and after Release rollouts. Typical facilities provided include:

- remote control of operations on the server, for example to assist with making Changes to a server as part of a Release rollout
- remote monitoring of the event logs and other Problem logs on servers
- monitoring of processor, memory and disk utilisation
- management of the disk space on servers – for example to monitor usage, to reorganise files for improved performance, and to allocate more disk space to applications.

9.10　Impact of New Technology

9.10.1　The future of support tools

There is a trend towards a convergence of support tools in this arena, although there are currently many tools that overlap in their scope.

9.10.2　'Thin client'

Where companies choose deliberately to limit the amount of software installed on client workstations, they are able to reduce their support costs for both software distribution but also Problem Management because there is less to go wrong at a local level. There are several implementations of the so-called 'thin client' available, but they all follow the same principle of loading software dynamically over a network rather than storing it on each client workstation. This approach reduces the number of locations for the software to a few servers within an organisation, thus greatly reducing the overhead of distributing Changes to applications.

Some implementations of the 'thin client' require no modifiable software to be installed locally at all, and rely upon a control program in the firmware of the workstation to connect to the network and download the applications. This approach has the least administration overhead. Other methods depend on a locally installed operating system and the use of emulation software to run a remote session on the server. This approach, therefore, requires the management of the locally installed systems software.

9.10.3　Multi-tier systems

A growing number of systems consist of software that runs on more than one hardware platform. A common model is to make use of middle-tier application servers that issue requests for data on back-end database systems.

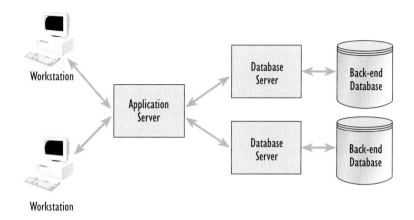

Figure 9.10 - Example of a multi-tier configuration

In Figure 9.10, several workstations are connected to a middle-tier application server, which accesses data on two different back-end database systems. In this example, it is quite possible that application software needs to be deployed on all three tiers: workstation, application server and database server.

Release Management should ensure that Changes to the application as a whole are coordinated across all of these platforms, along with any requisite hardware changes.

9.10.4 Internet applications

A variation on the multi-tier model is often used to provide Internet access to an organisation's systems alongside existing internal Users with normal workstations running Graphical User Interface (GUI) versions of the same or similar applications. A common model is to deploy a web server connected to the Internet for Users with web browsers. This would normally be connected via a firewall to prevent unauthorised access to the rest of the organisation's internal network.

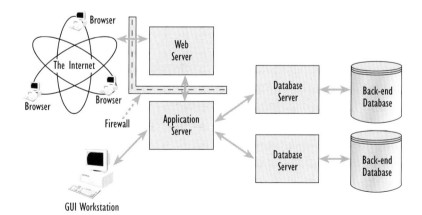

Figure 9.11 - Example configuration for web access

Figure 9.11 adds some further areas that need to be controlled, in addition to those in the multi-tier model:

- *The Internet network connection.* The settings in the routers at each end and the capacity of the line to the Internet need to be regulated. A new Release of an application might require additional bandwidth to be arranged to support additional numbers of concurrent Users.

- *The firewall.* This is often a dedicated server, which needs to be configured and supported. It is possible that hardware will need to be upgraded to support additional capacity or resilience requirements.

- *The web server.* This normally contains the web pages to be presented to the browser Users via the Internet. As well as hardware or software Changes to support additional capacity or resilience, it is very likely that new applications will need to deploy new or changed web pages to this server.

It can be seen, therefore, that Release Management has an increased role to play to ensure that all components of an IT service are changed in a coordinated manner with an Internet application. One challenge is that different parts of the IT department (or even some Users themselves) may need to be involved in this type of application, such as the networks team for the connections and firewall; the Web Master for the web server; the server team for the application server; and mid-range or mainframe teams for the back-end database systems. It is the role of Release Management to help bring all of these activities together smoothly.

9.10.5   Software updates via the Internet

It is becoming increasingly common for commercial software vendors to provide fixes and upgrades to their software available for downloading on the Internet. There are also huge numbers of complete applications that can simply be downloaded and installed.

It should be noted that, although the prospect of self-maintaining applications sounds attractive, there are dangers:

- any centrally held records of what software is installed on a given workstation, contained within the CMDB, rapidly become invalid unless they are under the control of a Change Management system and verified via a Configuration Management audit

- it is likely that such software updates are not thoroughly tested, and it is almost certain that regression testing of any other applications on the same workstation has not been performed; consequently, there is a risk that faults will be introduced

- it invalidates any controlled testing equipment, as it no longer reflects the live environment

- hardware or system software dependencies may not be correctly detected

- viruses can be introduced if correct procedures are not followed

- unauthorised Changes in the live environment can invalidate any future software or hardware Changes, unless they are preceded by very thorough software and hardware audits to spot any changes and check for the existence of known prerequisites.

In summary this practice should only normally be used by support staff on controlled test equipment, as part of the construction of a subsequent official Release. It should be strongly discouraged for use on live workstations.

9.11 Guidance for successful Release Management

What follows is a set of practical suggestions to make Release Management easier to implement and control. The suggestions are divided into the ITIL process that is affected. This demonstrates the close dependency of one process on another.

The best piece of advice, however, is to use the principles of Release Management in the implementation of Release Management itself, i.e. to make all Release Management procedures subject to controlled Change and kept under Configuration Management; and to bundle Changes to the procedures into planned 'Releases' with accompanying training and support documentation.

9.11.1 Configuration Management

1. Automate software and hardware auditing, and compare the reality found with the information in the Configuration Management Database.

2. Enforce strict record-keeping and controls on software-protection devices ('dongles') because they are valuable assets and often irreplaceable. Keep spares in case of emergencies.

3. Minimise the number of variants (both hardware and software) that exist in the live environment. This makes support much easier and more reliable. Keep an officially approved hardware and software list.

4. Provide mechanisms for Users to determine versions of software installed and hardware information. In other words, set up a 'Help About' function for a workstation as a whole, not just individual applications.

5. Check critical files for their integrity at start-up, for example using checksums.

6. Avoid continuing to pay maintenance on hardware or software that has been made redundant by a subsequent rollout. In addition, it may be possible to use the audit services of Configuration Management to check that no illegal copies of software are installed. This can be performed both as part of a distribution and via ad-hoc audits. This requires a fair degree of automation to do effectively.

7. Enforce strict desktop control via policies within the operating system to reduce the chance of the end Users changing the target platforms. Note that software developers typically need more open access, or even two workstations, to do their work.

8. Reduce the number of officially supported variations of target platform within an organisation.

9.11.2 Change Management

1. Limit through software controls the Changes that Users can make to the configuration of their PCs.

2. Hold a sequence of cutover planning meetings with all parties involved in the development, implementation and support of proposed Changes.

9.11.3 Release Management

1. Ensure that the software delivered to the live environment can be maintained from the source code saved through controlled build management procedures, with automated sequences of actions and strict version control of software source files .

239

2. Pilot new Changes with a 'model office' in the live environment – undertaken by a small number of real Users for a week or two after their training.

3. Automatically detect the need for software updates at start-up, and initiate them as required. This should, therefore, eliminate the risk of running out-of-date versions of software.

4. Automate the building, distribution and implementation of most or all of the software installed on workstations. Ideally, this should be driven from a centrally held 'model' to give the exact specification of the software to install.

5. Have permanent build-machines for specific platforms that can be allocated to projects and groups of similar applications.

6. Have representative and appropriate test environments that replicate the live hardware and software environments as closely as possible.

9.11.4 Application design issues

The design of the applications themselves can affect the task of Release Management. The following suggestions should be considered when reviewing an application's design:

1. The positioning of the application software, locally or centrally (see the next section), needs to be controlled.

2. If it is important that software updates are installed on time, then it might be acceptable to arrange 'time-outs' to be built into the application that prevent its use beyond a certain date. This is particularly useful for software that is released into an uncontrolled environment (e.g. outside the organisation).

3. Where parts of the application are split between different computers (e.g. a client–server arrangement, or an *n*-tier approach), it is important that all software components be consistent. It may be possible to build runtime checks into the application to verify that interfaces are compatible e.g. raise an error if an out-of-date version of a component on another platform is detected.

4. Consider all options for the positioning of data, for example distributed data against distributed applications. It may be required, for instance, to distribute and/or replicate centrally held data and possibly receive Changes back. A simpler scenario would be the distribution of static control data – e.g. look-up tables or a postcode database.

5. When making an application suitable for international use (covering different languages, locations and time zones) is required, it may be possible to design an application so that most of the files to be distributed are common and only a few are different for each country, the ultimate arrangement being a small number of configuration settings.

9.11.5 The positioning of software: what to put where

Consider minimising the amount of software installed on client workstations by deploying the executable software on servers instead. This will reduce the effort required to distribute software changes; however, it may increase the network traffic as a result. An extreme example of minimising the amount of software installed on client workstations is the 'thin client' model described in Paragraph 9.10.2.

Many applications require *some* files to be installed on every client PC, typically in shared directories. These runtime support files need to be managed very carefully, as they may well need to be updated along with new versions of the applications that use them. This can be particularly hard to manage where they are shared by several applications.

There is a line of thought that states that, given the rapidly decreasing prices of hard disks and their increasing capacity, you might as well install everything locally on each workstation (assuming, of course, that you have tools for remote distribution and workstation management). However, some organisations are successfully managing to operate such that any member of staff can use any PC. This has many benefits; for example, it makes the provision of 'hot-swap' equipment for faulty workstations very simple (as they are all identical). This approach can be achieved through a combination of techniques, for example:

- no data being stored locally on workstations, only on central fileservers
- dynamically loading as much software as possible over the LAN
- the use of clever 'caching' to reduce the demand on the LAN.

Even where sophisticated software distribution utilities are deployed, it may be simpler to have to keep a relatively small number of code servers up-to-date, compared with having to refresh code on thousands of PCs in a synchronised manner. There is no blanket answer for this problem, but it is recommended that organisations consider keeping the more volatile application code on their central servers. Although you may not be able change a purchased application, many do provide for being installed in this way and software developers should be strongly encouraged to consider these issues for any new applications.

The 'bottom line' is that an organisation should consider its approach and state that clearly as part of its Release policy.

| ANNEX 9A | Checklist to use when reviewing rollout plans |

- Are roles and responsibilities clear?
- Are the rollout procedures sound?
- Is there adequate budget and resource committed to complete the Release?
- Have all the necessary RFCs been raised and authorised, and is it planned to update the CMDB?
- Have all training issues been considered: end Users, IT support staff, Release Management staff?
- Has technical support for the rollout been properly planned and agreed?
- Are there any software licensing issues to consider during the rollout (e.g. software copyright protection schemes such as dongles, or authorisation passwords)?
- Have all the Capacity Management issues been considered and planned (e.g. response times and LAN traffic)?
- Do the plans conform to the organisation's Release policy? For example, a company might state that it intends to allow any person to access any application from any workstation; or they may allow or disallow individuals from installing their own software.
- Are there any software/hardware dependencies? For example, some software may only work on certain hardware combinations; or some software may only work with certain other software prerequisites.
- Does the rollout plan fit in with the established Service Management and support procedures?
- Are there any installation issues not yet resolved?
- Has operational acceptance testing been included in the plans?
- Is there a procedure to verify successful implementation of a Release?
- Are there any outstanding, hardware, cabling, network or environmental issues (e.g. power supplies)?
- Have clear acceptance criteria for the system going live been agreed?
- Is there a clear procedure for approving the stage sign-offs and the final sign-off of the Release?
- Does the rollout plan conflict with any other planned Changes?
- Has the emergency fix policy been determined?
- Has a thorough back-out plan been produced and tested?
- Has the schedule for a specific Release been published?
- Have the Service Desk, Technical Support, Service Level Manager and the Customers and Users been informed?
- Has the SLA and any OLAs or contracts been reviewed and revised?
- Has the Business Continuity Plan been updated to reflect the Changes?

ANNEX 9B Sample Release Management objectives for distributed systems

- Ideally, Users should have complete organisational flexibility: functions depend on people not their location. This implies that all workstations should have access to all facilities; however, the 'menu' for each User should belong to the User and be generated at log-on time.

- To enable the exchange of failing workstations, they should all be configured identically with no data held locally. This implies the same limited software on all workstations, with access to most software on servers.

- It should be possible to distribute small software changes to the entire network overnight, for instance to implement an emergency fix. This probably also implies that applications software resides only on servers.

- It should be possible to distribute synchronised updates of all components of an application over the network (i.e. PC changes and mainframe changes coordinated). This is easiest with a common distribution and control system.

- Users should have a single sign-on to all systems and facilities, and all their privileges and capabilities should be based on that sign-on.

- The control of User capabilities should be devolved to local Users, without them having to be aware of the underlying software mechanisms.

- The control and distribution of software should be an automated, low-overhead task once a 'Release' has initially been set up.

- There should be a guaranteed delivery/notice-of-receipt mechanism, with fail-safe locks on failing workstations, so that old code cannot continue to be used.

- Fast back-out from Changes across a network should be possible, together with the ability to 'freeze' failing applications.

10 SERVICE MANAGEMENT SOFTWARE TOOLS

The first question you should ask yourself on this topic is 'Do I really need software tools?' If you do, assess the need formally with a well-researched selection process.

If you look at the glossy brochures and listen to the sales talk, Service Management tools are indispensable. However, good people, good process descriptions, and good procedures and working instructions are the basis for successful Service Management. The need for, and the sophistication of, the tools required will depend on the business need for IT services and, to some extent, the size of the organisation.

In a very small organisation a simple in-house developed database system may be sufficient for logging and controlling Incidents. However, in very large organisation, a very sophisticated distributed integrated Service Management toolset may be required, linking all the processes with event-management systems. While tools can be an important asset in today's IT-dependent organisations, they are a means, not an end in themselves. When you are implementing Service Management processes, looking at the way your processes work and your need for management information should always be the starting point. This will provide information needed to define the specifications for a tool best suited to assist you.

Why the need? Here are some reasons:

- more sophisticated Customer demands
- a shortage of IT skills
- budget constraints
- business dependence on quality IT services
- integration of multi-vendor environments
- increasing complexity of IT infrastructures
- the emergence of international standards
- increased range and frequency of IT Changes.

Automated tools allow:

- the centralisation of key functions
- the automation of core Service Management functions
- the analysis of raw data
- the identification of trends
- preventive measures to be implemented.

10.1 Types of tools

Software tools range from simple to complex and from inexpensive to very expensive. They generally fall into one of the two following categories:

- CMDB & Help Desk; traditional Help Desk tools without separate databases and modules for the Service Management processes
- integrated Service Management tools comprising modern client-server-based tools, with or without a knowledge database.

10.2   Summary of tool-evaluation criteria

The following criteria should generally be used to assess software tools under consideration:

- an 80% fit to operational requirements
- a meeting of *ALL* mandatory requirements
- little (if any) product customisation
- ITIL compliance
- a sound data structure and handling
- business-driven not technology-driven
- administration and maintenance costs within budget.

Software tools should handle processes in conformity with the practices discussed in the IT Infrastructure Library. A set of guidance (the Appraisal and Evaluation Library) is available for the guidance of organisations wishing to select Service Support and Service Delivery tools. The prime areas to consider are:

- functional requirements support, and the level of integration with, for example, Service Delivery processes and tools
- data structure, data handling and integration, including the capability to support the required functionality
- integration of multi-vendor infrastructure components, and the need to absorb new components in the future – these will place particular demands on the data-handling and modelling capabilities of the tool
- conformity to international open standards
- flexibility in implementation, usage and data sharing
- usability: the overall ease of use permitted by the User interface
- service levels: performance and availability
- distributed clients with a centralised shared database (e.g. client-server)
- back-up, control and security provisions
- the quality of information provided by the supplier, and its validation by contact with other Users.

10.2.1   Service Management tools

Few enterprises have no Service Management tools, and many are considering replacing or upgrading those that are in use. The range and sophistication of tools for Service Management automation has grown rapidly in recent years.

Tools for the automation of core processes such as Incident logging and tracking have been supplemented by computer-integrated telephony, software capable of handling complex and multiple Service Level Agreements (with separate targets and business clocks) and remote support technology. Other tools include:

- interactive voice response (IVR) systems
- the Internet, internal electronic mail, voicemail
- self-help knowledge
- case-based reasoning/search systems

- network management tools (including remote support capabilities)
- system monitoring
- Configuration Management and Change Management systems
- release and distribution systems
- security monitoring and control, including password control, detection of violations, and virus protection
- capacity planning
- IT Service Continuity Management (including automatic back-ups).

Although some of the tools are not yet commonly used, there are few areas of Service Management that cannot be helped by automation. Some areas of Service Management are too resource intensive to be performed effectively without automation. Each tool for the automation of Service Management has advantages and disadvantages, but automation is still recognised as vital.

It is necessary to ensure that the combination of technology, processes and people are integrated and meet the needs of the Customers. Automation should be used to enhance Service Management, not replace it.

Automation is increasingly being treated as part of workflow management, linking each task in the life-cycle, from a new service being planned through to disposal. The technology should be used to complement and enhance service delivery, not replace it.

Automation that provides support for distributed computing has revolutionised the ability of an enterprise to diagnose Problems remotely, and in many cases also to fix them remotely (and therefore faster). Remote support technology has also made it possible for an enterprise to make changes by downloading the new versions of software and to monitor the capacity of the infrastructure, identifying capacity problems before they become serious.

Automation has enabled easier contingency planning, with work being switched in the event of a local overload or a serious problem that has taken the service out from a specific area.

Some final considerations:

- *supplier and product credibility and viability* – installed base and degree of support; consider issues such as the financial viability of the vendor (are they likely to be around in a few years when you need them?); also consider large time-zone differences between the supplier and your organisation and language differences
- *costs, including ongoing cost to upgrade and support* – consider which is better:
  - buying a standard package at reasonable initial cost, where the trade-off is that customisation may be very expensive and complex
  - or a more flexible package at higher initial costs where customisation maybe relatively easy and cheap
- *adaptability* – will the tool be able to meet organisation specific requirements and constraints in the years to come.

10.3   Product training

To ensure effective use of software tools, product training is required. Therefore budget provision should be made at the planning stage of the implementation project. Furthermore, the training supplier you employ should have a suitable portfolio of training programmes, covering the requirements of practitioners, supervisors and managers.

11 PLANNING FOR THE IMPLEMENTATION OF SERVICE MANAGEMENT

More and more organisations are recognising the importance of Service Management to their business. However, it is common for working practices to be based on historical or political considerations rather than the current needs of the business or best practice. It is therefore essential, before implementing any or all of the components of Service Management, to gain management commitment, to understand the working culture of your organisation, and to assess any existing processes and to compare these to the needs of the business and to best practice.

11.1 A Service Management project

To analyse the needs of the organisation and implement the desired solution requires a temporary organisation to be set up to undertake these activities. Thus this can readily be considered to be a project, or a series of projects, to implement the required Service Management processes.

One of the benefits of adopting a project approach to this activity is that you can undertake the necessary investigations and have designated decision points where you can opt to continue with the project, change direction, or stop.

The project needs to consider your current position and where you would like to be, and to plot the path between these states. For each option identified, you can begin to articulate:

- the business benefits
- the risks, obstacles and potential problems
- the costs of the move plus longer-term running costs
- the costs of continuing with the current structure.

You can then begin to see how the business needs can be supported and see the associated costs. The benefits can then be balanced against costs and risks. Undertaking the investigative work could be considered to be one project that can then be followed by an implementation project.

11.2 Feasibility study

It is essential to investigate and understand the current service levels and costs by baselining all appropriate aspects of the current service before making any major changes. This enables you to measure the impact of the improved service management processes on the baseline service levels and costs. (When baselining involves comparison with other enterprises, it is usually referred to as 'benchmarking'.)

Some advice is necessary before you start; the IT Infrastructure Library is not a magic wand. Do not expect miracles to happen when you implement the process framework. In the past, many organisations have tried to use process implementations as the basis for company reorganisations, or to assist with company mergers. Too many disparate goals for the project will lead to failure and disappointment. So, the targets and objectives associated with a Service Management project should relate to the objectives of the organisation itself. The target should be to enable the delivery of quality IT services aligned to business need.

11.3 Assessing the current situation

11.3.1 Introduction

Figure 3.1 represents a model that can be used by an organisation as the framework for process improvement. The model is also a framework for benchmarking. It can be used generically for any Change-related situation strategic, tactical or operational. The current situation is compared with best practices; the result is the input for the transition plans, together with the goals related to the Change process.

The transition plans describe the way that procedural Changes will take place and result in the actual Changes. Thanks to continuous measurement, *through the measurement of defined processes*, assessment of the Changes compared with the goals is possible, and may result in the changing of actions, facilitating the process of continuous improvement.

11.3.2 A 'health check'

A 'health check' based on the current procedures can be used as an objective way of assessing the effectiveness of Service Management processes in an organisation. This assessment should aim to identify those aspects that are functioning well, thus determining which best practices are in current use and should be retained, and also to pinpoint problem areas and constraints. Using the recommendations from a health check, you will be better equipped to define your implementation or improvement priorities.

To summarise, a health check should:

- objectively assess the effectiveness of your Service Management processes
- identify constraints and problem areas
- provide you with advice on how to manage your processes more effectively
- provide you with advice on how to improve your processes.

Non-IT-related issues that can influence your performance in delivering services such as people management and resource management can be assessed by using (self-) assessment provided by Total Quality Management methods. Be aware that in many cases it is these factors that have the major effect upon the actual performance from the Service Management processes. For further reading, see Appendix D, Quality.

Some examples of general topics that should be addressed by questions in a health check include:

- the existence of a strategic business plan
- how the plan supports IT planning
- the extent to which IT supports the needs of the business
- the alignment of IT and business growth plans.

Some examples of process topics, which should be addressed by questions in a health check, include:

- activities for each process
- the organisation of tasks and responsibilities
- communication lines between processes
- the overall control of Service Management
- an IT Infrastructure description

- control over Changes to the IT infrastructure
- the level of Customer satisfaction with IT services.

Some improvements will require major change to the current processes, within the organisation, and it may be a considerable time before they can be implemented. Wherever possible, some 'quick wins' should be implemented and communicated so that everyone involved can see that improvements are being achieved prior to the final implementation. Using the health check can assist in the identification of the quick-win areas.

Health checks and self-assessments can also help to determine the maturity level of your organisation. This is important if your target is better IT and business alignment. Maturity of process is an important issue, but has to be modified by the knowledge of what the business requires and will pay for in terms of maturity.

11.4 General guidelines on project planning

The CCTA project management method PRINCE2 (Projects IN Controlled Environments, version 2) is widely adopted internationally and is used to describe an approach to projects within the ITIL context. The guidelines below are consistent with a PRINCE2 approach.

11.4.1 Project characteristics

A project can be defined as:

> *a temporary organisation that is needed to achieve a predefined result at a predefined time using predefined resources.*

A 'temporary organisation' means that a project has a beginning and a clear ending and is conducted alongside day-to-day activities. By doing this, the project activity can be isolated from ongoing work.

PRINCE2 concentrates on creating an appropriate management environment to achieve the stated aim of the project. To achieve this, a PRINCE2 project requires the following to exist:

- a finite and defined lifespan for the project
- a set of defined and measurable business products (to achieve quality requirements)
- a set of activities to achieve the business products (i.e. the 'doing' of the project)
- a defined amount of resources
- a project organisation structure, with defined responsibilities, to manage the project.

Before starting a project, an organisation should have a vision about what the results are intended to be. By defining the means necessary to achieve the project result, it is possible to isolate these assets (people, budget, etc) from day-to-day activities. This increases the success rate of the project.

Before a project actually starts, management should have an overall 'feel' for the project and be able to document:

- project definition, explaining what the project needs to achieve – this should give background information, project objectives and scope, and it should outline the desired outcome and state constraints on the project
- the business case, describing how the project outcome will support business needs and justify its existence – including reasons for selection of the approach

- known quality expectations of the business solution
- acceptance criteria for the final outcome
- known risks
- a high-level plan identifying necessary roles and, if possible, assigning them to individuals, as well as identifying major 'go/no-go' decision points.

11.4.2 Business case for the project

The business case describes the added value of the project for the organisation: why should this project be carried out? Of course, to establish the answer, the project costs and revenues – perhaps this is more accurately described as savings – should be compared. The difficulty in doing this, however, is that while the *costs* are relatively easy to quantify (people, budget, etc.), this is not the case with *revenues*. Some ideas that you might find useful are described in Appendix E with its example cost–benefit analysis.

Particularly with process-oriented projects, assessing and describing the revenues/savings is a hard task. This has to do with the fact that process implementation results in higher quality service provision, higher service levels and a more flexible organisation; these are not always quantifiable financial results. Sometimes you find that you are making investments (or incurring costs, depending on your point of view) without knowing clearly the benefit; it is no use telling the budget holder that you sometimes have to take chances to if you're going to succeed. The business case should enable the reader to understand the value of investing in Service Management process improvement.

11.4.3 Critical success factors and possible problems

Successful Service Management should:

- provide a good understanding of the Customer's requirements, concerns and business activities, and deliver business-driven led rather than technology-driven services
- enhance Customer satisfaction
- improve value for money, resource utilisation and service quality
- deliver an infrastructure for the controlled operation of ongoing services by formalised and disciplined processes
- equip staff with goals and an understanding of Customers' needs.

Problems with Service Management processes that may be encountered include:

- excessively bureaucratic processes, with a high percentage of the total support headcount dedicated to Service Management
- inconsistent staff performance for the same process (often accompanied by noticeable lack of commitment to the process from the responsible staff)
- lack of understanding on what each process should deliver
- no real benefits, service-cost reductions, or quality improvements arising from the implementation of Service Management processes
- unrealistic expectations, so that service targets are rarely hit
- no discernible improvement.

Some of the major issues concerned with defining and running a successful Service Management function and the project to implement it are discussed in Appendix C.

11.4.4 Project costs

When you build the business case for a project, it is essential that you are clear about what the project costs are and what will be the ongoing running costs of the Service Management processes. Project costs are one-off costs, while the running costs form a commitment for the organisation that may involve long-term contracts with suppliers.

The costs of implementing IT Infrastructure Library processes clearly vary according to the scale of operations. The costs associated with the implementation and running of the processes are roughly categorised as follows:

- project management costs
- project delivery costs (consultancy fees, project team for implementation, process owner)
- equipment and software
- training costs (including awareness, training in specific tools, and training in business awareness)
- documentation costs
- ongoing staff and accommodation costs (for running the processes, including subsequent training needs).

The costs of failing to provide effective processes can be considerable. Some examples are provided in Appendix E.

11.4.5 Organisation

A project needs to be managed, as well as to produce something, in order to achieve the stated end result. Managing a project needs to take account of three viewpoints:

- business – will the outcome support a real business need?
- User – when using the product, will it achieve the objective the User wants?
- supplier/technical – can the product be created (particularly within any given constraints)? Can the product be supported effectively when in operation?

A project needs to balance these three views if it is to achieve a viable result that is 'fit for its business purpose' and be achievable within the other constraints of time and cost.

Typically senior managers provide direction in these areas but wish to leave the day-to-day activity of managing the project to a project manager. PRINCE2 identifies a project board to cover these three interests and provide direction and advice to the project manager without being involved in day-to-day activities.

The project board is responsible for ensuring that the project results in the desired outcome and so should ensure that quality assurance is applied to the project in an appropriate manner. This activity needs to be separated from the project manager to ensure the board gets an objective answer to the question 'Are things really going as well as we are being told?'

In a Service Management process-implementation/improvement project, the three viewpoints are likely to be represented thus:

- the business executive will probably be a director or board member
- the User role could be a (senior) Customer
- the supplier would be the IT manager.

11.4.6 Products

Many contemporary project management methods have a product approach. The advantage is that products – unlike activities – can be described even before the project starts. In this way, a certain outcome of the project can be guaranteed by setting norms for the products to be delivered.

The principle of product planning presupposes good product description and management. For further information, look at PRINCE2 or refer to your own project management approach.

11.4.7 Planning

After having defined the results in terms of products, the project manager should work out what other products need to be produced on the way to achieving the final outcome. A clear view of the activities can be built up for those products needed in the short-term (typically three to six months) with a high-level view of what is required in the longer term.

The project manager outlines the total project and produces a detailed plan for short-term activity. At this point, resources can be assigned to the activities to build products in the short term and skills requirements for the longer term can also be assessed.

While it is widely accepted that effective project planning and management are essential to project success, many IT projects continue to be poorly planned and badly managed. Often, people won't back out once (large) investments have been made. "*We've already invested heavily in this project, we can't stop now!*" has been used more than once in most organisations. Sometimes the runaway cost is the very reason for dissatisfaction and project cancellation should have taken place much earlier. To resist the temptation of an endless pursuit of a positive outcome of the project, an experienced project manager should assign a number of 'go/no-go' decision moments to the project.

This means that before the project is started, it is accepted that it may never be finished successfully. In fact, with each 'go/no-go' decision moment the business case of the project should be re-evaluated. In PRINCE2 these decision points come at the end of 'stages', where project progress to date is assessed and the ongoing viability of the future of the business case (and so the project) is actively revisited before the next stage is started.

11.4.8 Communication plan

Managing Change can only succeed with the correct use of communication. A Service Management project will involve a lot of people but, typically, the outcome will affect the working lives of many more. Implementing or improving Service Management within an organisation requires a change of mindset by IT management and IT employees as well as IT Customers and Users. Communication around this transformation is essential to its success.

In order to ensure that all parties are aware of what is going on and can play a relevant part in the project, it is advisable to clarify how the project will communicate with all interested parties. A well-planned and executed communication plan will have a direct positive contribution to the success of the project.

A good communication plan should be built on a proper conception of what communication is. Communication is more than a one-way information stream. It requires continuous attention to the signals (positive and negative) of the various parties involved. Managing communications effectively involves the following nine steps:

1. describe the communications process in the Change process from the start
2. analyse the communication structure and culture
3. identify the important target groups
4. assess the communication goals for each target group
5. formulate a communication strategy for each target group
6. choose the right communication media for each target group
7. write a communication plan
8. communicate
9. measure and redirect if necessary.

A communication plan describes how target groups, contents and media are connected in a timeframe. Much like a project plan, a communication plan shows how actions, people, means and budgets are to be allocated for the communication process.

11.5 Project review and management reporting

When a project is set up it is important to consider the reporting needs. Project management should be used to ensure appropriate decisions can be made. By exercising control over a project it should be possible to show that the project:

- is producing the required results, namely the results that meet predefined quality criteria
- is being carried out to schedule and in accordance with its previously agreed resource and cost plans
- remains viable against its business case (balancing benefits against costs/risks).

To support the decision-making processes, organisations should expect a number of reports throughout the life of a project. At the very least, a project should produce:

- regular progress reports
- post-completion project evaluation (of the way the project was run)
- post-completion project review to assess if the projected benefits have materialised.

As part of the need to evaluate the project it is essential to maintain records that enable the project to be audited. Auditing may cover compliance and efficiency as well as looking at improvements that have been achieved or that could still be attempted.

On completion of a project, management will require further, regular, reports to show how well the Service Management processes are supporting the business needs.

11.5.1 Progress reporting

Progress against plans should be assessed on a regular basis, so that problems can be identified early and can be dealt with in a timely manner. The project manager should ensure that progress reports are produced for the project board at regular, agreed, intervals. The reports should include statements regarding:

- achievements in the current period
- achievements expected in the next period
- actual or potential problems and suggestions for their prevention or resolution.

Progress reports should provide a clear picture of the status of the project against plan and the business case so that adequately informed decisions can be made as to whether or not to continue expending resources on the project. It is important to look at the risks, at any changes in these within the current period and, if appropriate, identify their impact on subsequent project activities.

If a problem arises between progress reports that the project manager is not authorised to sort out, then an interim report should be compiled for the project board without waiting for the next progress report to be due. Within this report, the project manager states the nature and scope of the problem that has arisen, identifies options for its resolution, and recommends a course of action.

11.5.2 Evaluation of the project

As the project draws to a close, it is important to analyse how the project was managed and to identify lessons that were learned along the way. This information can then be used to benefit the project team as well as the organisation as a whole. An End Project Report typically covers:

- achievement of the project's objectives
- performance against plan (estimated time and costs versus actuals)
- effect on the original plan and business case over the time of the project
- statistics on issues raised and changes made
- total impact of changes approved
- statistics on the quality of the work carried out (in relation to stated expectations)
- lessons learned
- a post-project review plan.

11.5.3 Post-project review

The business case will have been built from the premise that the outcome of the project will deliver benefits to the business over a period of time. Thus, delivery of benefits needs to be assessed at a point after the project products have been put into use. The post-project review is used to assess whether the expected benefits have been realised, as well as to investigate whether problems have arisen from use of the products.

Each of the benefits mentioned in the business case should be assessed to see how well, if at all, it has been achieved. Other issues to consider are whether there were additional benefits – or unexpected problems. Both of these can be used to improve future business cases.

If necessary, follow-up actions may be identified to improve the situation that then exists.

11.5.4 Auditing for compliance using quality parameters

Process quality parameters can be seen as the 'operational thermometer' of the IT organisation. Using them, you can determine whether the IT organisation is effective and efficient. Quality parameters need to be quantified for your own circumstances. However, this task will be easier once you have determined the required Service Levels and Internal Service Requirements. There are two types of quality parameters: process-specific and generic.

Generic quality parameters for IT Service Management:

Generic quality parameters that need to be considered include:

- Customer satisfaction
- staff satisfaction
- efficiency
- effectiveness.

Appropriate information should be collected to rate the organisation's performance relative to these parameters. The nature of the information required will vary depending on how you decide to judge each aspect, but what information is required should be clearly thought through from the start of the project so that measurement is possible during the post-project review.

Process-specific parameters

Process-specific metrics for each process are discussed in each of the process-specific chapters of this book.

11.5.5 Auditing for improvement using key performance indicators

Introduction to the 'Balanced Scorecard'

The 'Balanced Scorecard' is an aid to organisational performance management. It helps to focus, not only on the financial targets but also on the internal processes, Customers and learning and growth issues. The balance should be found between these four perspectives.[1]

The four perspectives are focused around the following questions:

1. *Customers.* What do our Customers desire?
2. *internal processes.* How do we generate the added value for our Customers?
3. *learning and growth.* How do we guarantee we will keep generating added value in the future?
4. *financial.* How did we do financially?

As you can see, the first three questions focus on the future, the last question reviews what has gone before. It is worthwhile discussing the Balanced Scorecard further at this point:

- The Balanced Scorecard is not complex, but to implement the scorecard successfully *is* complex. In practice, it can take an organisation up to three years to see the benefits of a Balanced Scorecard approach.

- The Balanced Scorecard is not an exclusive IT feature. On the contrary, many organisations use scorecards in other departments – even at board level.

- When implementing the Balanced Scorecard, it pays to start very conservatively. Start with three or four goals for each perspective. To do this, an organisation has to make choices; for many, this is extremely difficult and time-consuming to do.

- The most difficult part of using the Balanced Scorecard is not the implementation; it is the consolidation. Usually, consultants are employed to assist in the introduction of the Balanced Scorecard. The challenge is to keep measuring once they have gone. The

[1] Kaplan and Norton introduced the Balanced Scorecard in the early 1980s. Contemporary measurements from the time, particularly in US companies, focused on financial targets. Because financial figures are solely concentrated on past events, Kaplan and Norton sought a means to measure and steer using future activities as well. See the appropriate entry in the Bibliography to this book (Chapter 12).

danger is in the temptation to fall back on prior measuring techniques or not measuring at all.

The Balanced Scorecard is complementary to ITIL. It is a way of measuring the effectiveness of the performance of the organisation. Some of the links include the following:

- *the client perspective*: this is relevant to most disciplines and is particularly relevant to Service Level Management, where it is documented in Service Level Agreements

- *internal processes:* these of course cover the ITIL processes

- *finance:* Financial Management covers the way that costs are allocated to the organisation

- *learning and growth:* this refers to staffing, training and investments in software.

11.5.6   Management reporting

After implementation of an initial Service Management system, or some improvement to it, a regular system for management reporting has to be set up. The following types of management reports should be considered:

- IT management reports that are used for the planning and control of services

- reports matching achieved internal service levels, with service levels as described in Service Level Agreements

- internal process-management reports, used by the process manager to determine the process' efficiency and effectiveness and for auditing for compliance

- Service Management reports, which the Service Manager uses for higher-level process control.

12 BIBLIOGRAPHY

Note: that the entries in this Bibliography are given throughout in alphabetical order of title within each section.

12.1 References

Balanced Scorecard (The): Translating strategy into action

Robert S. Kaplan, David P. Norton / Hardcover / published 1996
Harvard Business School Press
ISBN: 0-87584-651-3

Capability Maturity Model (The): Guidelines for Improving the Software Process

Carnegie Mellon University, Software Engineering Institute, Addison-Wesley
ISBN 0-201-54664-7

Code of Practice for IT Service Management (A), DISC 0005

Extracts are reproduced with the permission of BSI under licence number PD\ 1999 0877. Complete copies of the standard can be obtained by post from BSI Customer Services, 389 Chiswick High Road, London W4 4AL.
www.bsi.ork.uk/disc/products, Tel: 020-8996 9001

Configuration Management: The Changing Image

Marion V. Kelly
McGraw-Hill/published: 1996.
ISBN: 0-07-707977-9

Cultures of work organisations (The)

Trice/Beyer (1993). Prentice Hall, N.J. U.S.A.
ISBN 0-13-191438-3

Industrial automation systems and integration — Product data representation and exchange — Part 44: Integrated generic resources: Product structure configuration - ISO 10303-44:1994

Edition: 1 (monolingual)
Number of pages: 51
Price code: U
Technical committee / subcommittee: TC 184 / SC 4
ICS: 25.040.40
Descriptors: automation, automation engineering, computer applications, data, data exchange, data representation, and industrial products

Industrial automation systems and integration — Product data representation and exchange — Part 203: Application protocol: Configuration controlled design - ISO 10303-203:1994

Edition: 1 (monolingual)
Number of pages: 581
Price code: XM
Technical committee / subcommittee: TC 184 / SC 4
ICS: 25.040.40
Descriptors: automation, automation engineering, computer aided design, computer applications, data, data exchange, data representation, design, industrial products, and protocols

259

Information technology — Software life cycle processes - ISO/IEC 12207:1995

Edition: 1 (monolingual)
Number of pages: 57
Price code: U
Technical committee / subcommittee: JTC 1 / SC 7
ICS: 35.080
Descriptors: computer software, computers, data processing, data processing equipment, and life-cycle

Information technology - Software life cycle processes - Configuration Management for Software - ISO/IEC DIS 15846

Edition: 1 (monolingual)
Technical committee / subcommittee: JTC 1 / SC 7
ICS: 35.080
Descriptors: computer software, computers, data processing, data processing equipment, and life-cycle

Information technology — Specification and standardisation of data elements — Part 5: Naming and identification principles for data elements - ISO/IEC 11179-5:1995

Edition: 1 (monolingual)
Number of pages: 14
Price code: G
Technical committee / subcommittee: JTC 1 / SC 14
ICS: 35.040
Descriptors: data elements, data processing, data representation, identification methods, information interchange, naming, and specifications

ISO 10007:1995

Quality management — Guidelines for Configuration Management
Edition: 1 (monolingual), Technical committee / subcommittee: TC 176 / SC 2, ICS: 03.120.10
Descriptors: general conditions, interfaces, quality assurance, quality assurance systems, quality management

ISO/IEC 12207:1995

Information technology — Software life cycle processes
Edition: 1 (monolingual), Technical committee / subcommittee: JTC 1 / SC 7, ICS: 35.080
Descriptors: computer software, computers, data processing, data processing equipment, and life-cycle

IT Infrastructure Library, (®ITIL), Service Support Set, Configuration Management, Change Management, Software Control and Distribution

CCTA, tel 01603 704567, *www.itil.co.uk*; The Stationery Office, Tel 020-7873 9090; or itSMF, tel: 01603 767181, *www.itsmf.com*.

Leading change

John P. Kotter/ hardcover/1996
Harvard Business School Press
ISBN: 0-875847-47-1

Managing Successful Projects with PRINCE 2, ISBN 0-11-330855-8

CCTA, tel 01603 704567; or The Stationery Office, tel 020-7873 9090
ISBN 0-11-330855-8

Methods and tools for Software Configuration Management

D. Whitgift, Wiley, 1991
ISBN 0-47-192940-9

New organisational wealth: managing and measuring knowledge-based assets (The)

Sveiby (1997). Berret-Koehler; San Francisco, U.S.A.
ISBN 157675014-0

Organisational transformations

Espejo/Schumann/Schwaninger/Bilello (1996). John Wiley&Sons; Chichester, England
ISBN 0-471-96182-5

Practical Software Configuration Management

Tim Mikkelsen & Suzanne Pherigo, 1997, Prentice Hall
ISBN 0-13-240854-6

PRINCE2 (reference manual)

ISBN 0-11-330685-7 - £55.00

Process Innovation

Davenport (1993). HBS, Boston, Massachusetts U.S.A.
ISBN 0-87584-366-2

Quality management -Guidelines for Configuration Management - ISO 10007:1995

Edition: 1 (monolingual)
Number of pages: 14
Price code: G
Technical committee / subcommittee: TC 176 / SC 2
ICS: 03.120.10
Descriptors: general conditions, interfaces, quality assurance, quality assurance systems, quality management

Service Quality

Brown/Gummesson/Edvardsson/Gustavsson (1991). Lexington Books; N.Y., U.S.A.
ISBN 0-669-21152-4

Structures in fives: designing effective organisations

Minzberg (1993). Prentice Hall, N.J. U.S.A.
ISBN 0-13-855479-X

12.2 Other Sources

BCS Configuration Management Specialist Group,

Email to cmsg@bcs.org.uk

European Foundation for Quality Management

Website at www.efqm.org. '…the battle for Quality is one of the prerequisites for the success of your companies and for our collective success.' (Jacques Delors)

W. Edwards Deming Institute (The)

Website at://www.deming.org. 'We should work on our process, not the outcome of our processes.' (W. Edwards Deming)

ISO 9000 Information Forum

Website at://www.iso-9000.co.uk

British Standards Institution

Website at://www.bsi.org.uk

APPENDIX A: TERMINOLOGY

A.1 List of acronyms

ACD	Automatic Call Distribution
BSI	British Standards Institution
CAB	Change Advisory Board
CAB/EC	Change Advisory Board/Emergency Committee
CASE	Computer-Aided Systems Engineering
CCTA	Central Computer and Telecommunications Agency
CI	Configuration Item
CMDB	Configuration Management Database
COP	Code of Practice
CTI	Computer Telephony Integration
DHS	Definitive Hardware Store
DSL	Definitive Software Library
EDI	Electronic Data Interchange
EFQM	European Foundation for Quality Management
FSC	Forward Schedule of Change
GUI	Graphical User Interface
ICAM	Integrated Computer-Aided Manufacturing
ICT	Information and Communications Technology
IDEF	ICAM Definition
IP	Internet Protocol
IR	Incident Report
ISO	International Standards Organisation
IT	Information Technology
IVR	Interactive Voice Response
KER	Known Error Record
KPI	Key Performance Indicator
KSF	Key Success Factors
LAN	Local Area Network

MBNQA	Malcolm Baldridge National Quality Award
MTBF	Mean Time Between Failures
OLA	Operational Level Agreement
PC	Personal Computer
PIR	Post-implementation Review
PR	Problem Record
PRINCE	Projects IN Controlled Environments
PSA	Projected Service Availability
RFC	Request for Change
SCI	Software Configuration Item
SCM	Software Configuration Management
SIP	Service Improvement Program
SLA	Service Level Agreement
SLM	Service Level Management
TOR	Terms of Reference
TP	Transaction Processing
VOIP	Voice Over Internet Protocol
WAN	Wide Area Network
WIP	Work in Progress
WFD	Work flow diagram

A.2 Glossary of terms

Availability
: Ability of a component or service to perform its required function at a stated instant or over a stated period of time. It is usually expressed as the availability ratio, i.e. the proportion of time that the service is actually available for use by the Customers within the agreed service hours.

Build
: The final stage in producing a usable configuration. The process involves taking one of more input Configuration Items and processing them (building them) to create one or more output Configuration Items e.g. software compile and load.

Category
: Classification of a group of Configuration Items, Change documents or Problems.

Change
: The addition, modification or removal of approved, supported or baselined hardware, network, software, application, environment, system, desktop build or associated documentation.

Change Advisory Board
: A group of people who can give expert advice to Change Management on the implementation of Changes. This Board is likely to be made up of representatives from all areas within IT and representatives from business units.

Change authority
: A group that is given the authority to approve Change, e.g. by a project board. Sometimes referred to as the Configuration Board.

Change control
: The procedure to ensure that all Changes are controlled, including the submission, analysis, decision making, approval, implementation and post implementation of the Change.

Change document
: Request for Change, Change control form, Change order, Change record.

Change history
: Auditable information that records, for example, what was done, when it was done, by whom and why.

Change log
: A log of Requests for Change raised during a project, showing information on each Change, its evaluation, what decisions have been made and its current status, e.g. raised, reviewed, approved, implemented, or closed.

Change Management
: Process of controlling Changes to the infrastructure or any aspect of services, in a controlled manner, enabling approved Changes with minimum disruption.

Change record
: A record containing details of which CIs are affected by an authorised Change (planned or implemented), and how.

Classification	Process of formally grouping Configuration Items by type, e.g. software, hardware, documentation, environment, application.
	Process of formally identifying Changes by type e.g. project scope Change request, validation Change request, infrastructure Change request.
	Process of formally identifying Incidents, Problems and Known Errors by origin, symptoms and cause.
Closure	When the Customer is satisfied that an incident has been resolved.
Computer Aided Systems Engineering	A software tool for programmers. It provides help in the planning, analysis, design and documentation of computer software.
Configuration baseline	Configuration of a product or system established at a specific point in time, which captures both the structure and details of that product or system, and enables that product or system to be rebuilt at a later date.
	A snapshot or a position which is recorded. Although the position may be updated later, the baseline remains unchanged and available as a reference of the original state and as a comparison against the current position (PRINCE2).
Configuration control	Activities comprising the control of Changes to Configuration Items after formally establishing its configuration documents. It includes the evaluation, coordination, approval or rejection of Changes. The implementation of Changes includes changes, deviations and waivers that impact on the configuration.
Configuration documentation	Documents that define requirements, system design, build, production, and verification for a Configuration Item.
Configuration identification	Activities that determine the product structure, the selection of Configuration Items, and the documentation of the Configuration Item's physical and functional characteristics, including interfaces and subsequent Changes. It includes the allocation of identification characters or numbers to the Configuration Items and their documents. It also includes the unique numbering of configuration control forms associated with Changes and Problems.
Configuration item (CI)	Component of an infrastructure – or an item, such as a Request for Change, associated with an infrastructure – that is (or is to be) under the control of Configuration Management. CIs may vary widely in complexity, size and type, from an entire system (including all hardware, software and documentation) to a single module or a minor hardware component.

Configuration Management	The process of identifying and defining Configuration Items in a system, recording and reporting the status of Configuration Items and Requests for Change, and verifying the completeness and correctness of Configuration Items.
Configuration Management tool	A software product providing automatic support for Change, Configuration or version control.
Configuration Management Database (CMDB)	A database that contains all relevant details of each CI and details of the important relationships between CIs.
Configuration Management plan	Document setting out the organisation and procedures for the Configuration Management of a specific product, project, system, support group or service.
Configuration structure	A hierarchy of all the CIs that comprise a configuration.
Customer	Recipient of a service; usually the Customer management has responsibility for the cost of the service, either directly through charging or indirectly in terms of demonstrable business need.
Definitive Software Library (DSL)	The library in which the definitive authorised versions of all software CIs are stored and protected. It is a physical library or storage repository where master copies of software versions are placed. This one logical storage area may in reality consist of one or more physical software libraries or filestores. They should be separate from development and test filestore areas. The DSL may also include a physical store to hold master copies of bought-in software, e.g. a fireproof safe. Only authorised software should be accepted into the DSL, strictly controlled by Change and Release Management. The DSL exists not directly because of the needs of the Configuration Management process, but as a common base for the Release Management and Configuration Management processes.
Delta Release	A Delta, or partial, Release is one that includes only those CIs within the Release unit that have actually changed or are new since the last full or Delta Release. For example, if the Release unit is the program, a Delta Release contains only those modules that have changed, or are new, since the last full release of the program or the last Delta Release of certain modules. See also 'Full Release'.
End-User	See 'User'.

Environment	A collections of hardware, software, network communications and procedures that work together to provide a discrete type of computer service. There may be one or more environments on a physical platform e.g. test, production. An environment has unique features and characteristics that dictate how they are administered in similar, yet diverse, manners.
Expert User	See 'Super User'.
Forward Schedule of Changes	A schedule that contains details of all the Changes approved for implementation and their proposed implementation dates. It should be agreed with the Customers and the business, Service Level Management, the Service Desk and Availability Management. Once agreed, the Service Desk should communicate to the User community at large any planned additional downtime arising from implementing the Changes, using the most effective methods available.
Full Release	All components of the Release unit that are built, tested, distributed and implemented together. See also 'Delta Release'.
Impact	Measure of the business criticality of an Incident. Often equal to the extent to which an Incident leads to distortion of agreed or expected service levels.
Incident	Any event that is not part of the standard operation of a service and that causes, or may cause, an interruption to, or a reduction in, the quality of that service.
Interface	Physical or functional interaction at the boundary between Configuration Items.
Known Error	An Incident or Problem for which the root cause is known and for which a temporary Work-around or a permanent alternative has been identified. If a business case exists, an RFC will be raised, but, in any event, it remains a known error unless it is permanently fixed by a Change.
Life-cycle	A series of states connected by allowable transitions. The life cycle represents an approval process for Configuration Items, Problem Reports and Change documents.
PD0005	Alternative title for the BSI publication *A Code of Practice for IT Service Management*.
PRINCE2	The standard UK government method for project management.
Priority	Sequence in which an Incident or Problem needs to be resolved, based on impact and urgency.
Problem	Unknown underlying cause of one or more Incidents.

Process	A connected series of actions, activities, Changes etc. performed by agents with the intent of satisfying a purpose or achieving a goal.
Process Control	The process of planning and regulating, with the objective of performing a process in an effective and efficient way.
Release	A collection of new and/or changed CIs which are tested and introduced into the live environment together.
Request for Change (RFC)	Form, or screen, used to record details of a request for a Change to any CI within an infrastructure or to procedures and items associated with the infrastructure.
Resolution	Action that will resolve an Incident. This may be a Work-around.
Role	A set of responsibilities, activities and authorisations.
Service Level Agreement	A written agreement between a service provider and Customer(s) that documents agreed service levels for a service.
Service Request	Every Incident not being a failure in the IT Infrastructure.
Software Configuration Item (SCI)	As 'Configuration Item', excluding hardware and services.
Software Environment	Software used to support the application, such as operating system, database management system, development tools, compilers, and application software.
Software Library	A controlled collection of SCIs designated to keep those with like status and type together and segregated from unlike, to aid in development, operation and maintenance.
Super User	In some organisations it is common to use 'expert' Users (commonly known as Super, or Expert, Users) to deal with first-line support problems and queries . This is typically in specific application areas, or geographical locations, where there is not the requirement for full-time support staff. This valuable resource needs, however, to be carefully coordinated and utilised.
System	An integrated composite that consists of one or more of the processes, hardware, software, facilities and people, that provides a capability to satisfy a stated need or objective.
Urgency	Measure of the business criticality of an Incident or Problem based on the impact and on the business needs of the Customer.
User	The person who uses the services on a day-to-day basis.

Version	An identified instance of a Configuration Item within a product breakdown structure or configuration structure for the purpose of tracking and auditing change history. Also used for software Configuration Items to define a specific identification released in development for drafting, review or modification, test or production.
Version Identifier	A version number; version date; or version date and time stamp.
Work-around	Method of avoiding an Incident or Problem, either from a temporary fix or from a technique that means the Customer is not reliant on a particular aspect of a service that is known to have a problem.

APPENDIX B: PROCESS THEORY AND PRACTICE

B.1   Process theory

This Appendix provides a general introduction to process theory and practice, which is the basis for the ITIL process models. We become aware of 'process' through process models that serve to define workflows and provide guidance on performing it. A process model enables understanding and helps to articulate the distinctive features of a process.

A process can be defined as

a connected series of actions, activities, changes etc, performed by agents with the intent of satisfying a purpose or achieving a goal.

Process control can similarly be defined as

the process of planning and regulating, with the objective of performing a the process in an effective and efficient way.

Processes, once defined, should be under control; once under control, they can be repeated and become manageable. Degrees of control over processes can be defined, and then metrics can be built in to manage the control process.

The output produced by a process has to conform to operational norms that are derived from business objectives. If products conform to the set norm, the process can be considered *effective* (because it can be repeated, measured and managed). If the activities are carried out with a minimum effort, the process can also be considered *efficient*. Process results metrics should be incorporated in regular management reports.

B.1.1   The product-oriented organisation

Process activities exist in many organisations. However, they are often carried out throughout an organisation, but without any process-oriented coordination. This results in problems, which have to be addressed during process implementation. Some examples include:

- ■ processes lacking a clear purpose and focus on business results
- ■ similar processes with inconsistent approaches
- ■ actions or processes performed many times instead of once
- ■ activities that are missing
- ■ no focus on existing business-oriented results.

B.1.2   Moving towards a process-oriented organisation

Since processes and their activities run through an organisation, they should be mapped and coordinated by process managers. Figure B.1 shows how process activities may be assigned to people in several different organisational units. The simple box diagram indicates the apparent consecutive flow of processes in a linear sequence. Reality is better reflected in the organisational view, where the flow is clearly non-linear and where it is possible to think of delays and interactions that might take place.

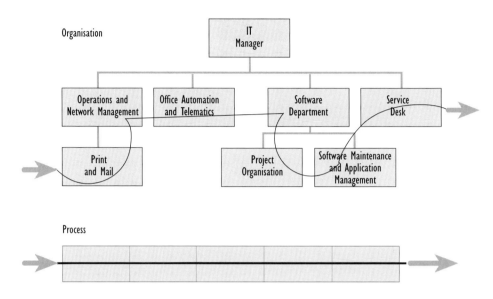

Figure B.1 - Process mapped to organisational unit

In a product-oriented organisation, the flow of activities and processes in Figure B.1 is not generally recognised *at all*; the focus is on the product, and management and control is often lacking. The evidence is in the lack of any useful metrics related to the production process, because the process activities are not clear or even not identified.

B.1.3   The process approach

The model shown in Figure B.2 is a generic process model. Data enters the process, is processed, data comes out, the outcome is measured and reviewed. This very basic description underpins any process description. A process is always organised around a goal. The main output of that process is the result of that goal.

Working with *defined* processes is a novelty for many organisations. By defining what your activities are, which inputs are necessary and which outputs will result from the process, you will be able to work in a more efficient and effective manner. Measuring and steering your activities increases this efficacy. Finally, by adding norms to the process, you can add quality measures to your output.

The approach underpins the 'plan–do–check–act' cycle of any quality-management system. Plan the purpose of your process in such a way that that the process action can be audited for successful achievement and, if necessary, improved.

The output produced by a process has to conform to operational norms that are derived from business objectives. If the products conform to the set norm, the process can be considered effective. If the activities are also carried out with a minimum effort, the process can also be considered efficient. Process-measurement results should be incorporated in regular management reports.

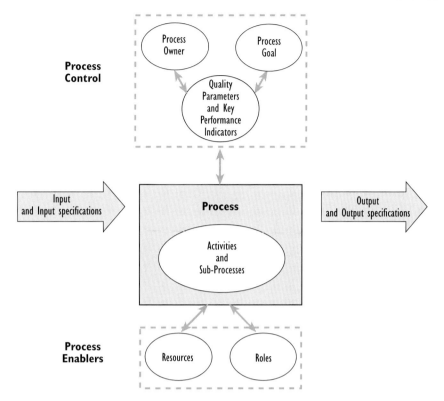

Figure B.2 - The generic process model

'Norms' define certain conditions that the result should meet. By defining norms, you introduce quality aspects to the process. Even before you start, you can think about what the outcome should look like. This enables you to:

- consider inputs and activities beforehand because you know what to do

- measure and steer effectively because you know what to measure

- assess whether the result fulfilled your expectations, because you know what to expect.

Defining objective norms is a tedious task and also often very complex since objectivity can often be subjective (to slightly misquote Woody Allen).

To discover whether or not your activities are contributing optimally to the business goal of the process, you should measure their effectiveness on a regular basis. Measuring allows you to compare what you have actually done to what you set out to do and to consider the improvement that may be needed.

B.2 Process modelling case study: Service Support example.

B.2.1 Introduction

An international manufacturing company had outsourced its IT services to an external supplier. The supplier planned to improve the Service Support processes by means of a detailed understanding of the current practices (including points of escalation and authorisation) and through development of the processes in line with recognised 'best practice' guidance.

Initial analysis indicated that there were approximately 20 Service Support subprocesses for dealing with service requests, change requests and the resolution of hardware and software problems. The initial state of these subprocesses, all of which had an element of interaction with the Customer, was documented by the supplier and his Customer using work flow diagrams (WFDs) and through brief functional descriptions. The WFD approach and existing terminology for roles, for types of requests and for calls had been used to aid Customer understanding.

The documentation of the Service Support subprocesses and the adoption of better working practices was initiated early in the contract. When both parties had agreed the baseline, a plan to consolidate the documentation into a more generic process set was created.

It was also intended that the supplier could better serve the international nature of its client's business through a central Service Desk, which it had established already for other international clients and which used an ITIL-compliant process for call capture and tracking to resolution. A joint management team was planning a project to transfer first-line support from the existing support structure to the Service Desk. It was imperative that this move would at least sustain, and perhaps improve, the perceived quality of Service Support.

The supplier was now faced with the difficulty of comparing and contrasting the description of practice within the central Service Desk with that represented in the WFDs of the current support structure. A suitable modelling approach had to be found which could provide the basis for consolidation of the existing documentation, support the move to the central Service Desk, and enable the process-improvement project to be implemented.

B.2.2   The approach

Although the existing diagrams of the target Service Desk appeared outwardly similar to the WFDs of the current support operations, the diagrams were difficult to compare because of the differences in terminology and notational semantics.

It was decided that both would be 'reverse-engineered' to recover the basic design elements and the underlying subprocess purpose, and to redocument them so that they would be directly comparable.

A simple process-modelling formalism was adopted that had been previously used to produce generic reference models for ITIL guidance (as this would later facilitate the longer-term process - improvement programme and recognition of better practice).

The formalism consists of four basic constructs as shown in Figure B.3. The notation facilitates the diagrammatic representation of the scope of a process from a particular perspective and enables the dynamics of the process to be shown in terms of the actions and interactions undertaken by the people who perform specific roles.

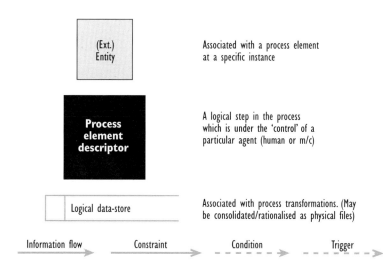

Figure B.3 - Process model notation

B.2.3   Process analysis

The existing support function was believed to consist of two subprocesses:

- handling of standard calls and requests
- break/fix call resolution and request completion.

These were compared and contrasted with the two Service Desk subprocesses, namely:

- request verification and incident definition
- Customer support and escalation.

The process-modelling exercise indicated that there were a number of explicit roles and logical datastores associated with the process that had not been expanded in the original WFDs, – for instance, the role of local service co-ordinators, and status changes to the configuration data. Furthermore, the exercise facilitated the review of the existing process, for example, in raising queries about the approval mechanism for requests and their assignment to various support areas.

The comparison identified improvements to be gained in the move from the local support structure to the central Service Desk as:

- an enhanced ability to verify User identity
- an increased level and content of first-line support
- an improved knowledge base for assigning unresolved incidents and requests.

Similarly, the gap analysis of break/fix call resolution and request completion versus Customer support and escalation showed some significant potential process improvements, including;

- time-stamping and automated support for incident progress monitoring at the Service Desk
- scheduled negotiation and agreement with the User and estimated fix time provided by the existing Service Desk.

Figure B.4 depicts the subprocess for Customer support and Service Desk escalation. It should be noted that the process is dependent upon a process support tool for the monitoring of Incident progress, and that contingency planning measures need also to be considered.

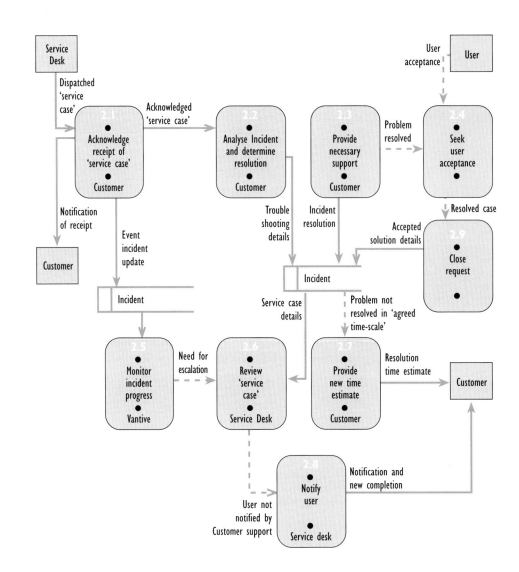

Figure B.4 - Customer support and Service Desk escalation

In studying the above model, a number of questions were raised concerning:

■ how the User would be provided with an estimated completion time
■ possible escalation routes, beyond simply notifying the User of any slippage
■ resolving who has responsibility for seeking User acceptance, and for closing the request, including details of Problem resolution
■ the development of a Problem Management role on the Customer site.

Once the Service Support functions had been modelled in the way shown in Figure B.3 and Figure B.4, it was also possible to compare them with a target generic ITIL goal model for the respective Service Support functions.

As a result of this comparison, a number of areas for improvement were identified in that part of the support function that remained within the Customer site, i.e. predominantly Change Management, Configuration Management, Problem Management and second-line support.

B.2.4 Conclusion

The process-modelling exercise was initiated using WFDs and functional descriptions. This methodology was initially more familiar and useful to the Customer groups involved than the more formalised generic process models either in use by the service supplier or available from the best-practice sources such as ITIL. The approach therefore enabled both parties to baseline the points of authorisation, escalation and the general workflow through the Service Support functions.

The consolidation and redocumentation of the Service Support processes bridged the gap between the company's localised processes and procedures and the generic target ones. It enabled the process improvement team and Service Desk deployment teams to address interface gaps between the centralised desk and the local support structure, and also to create a planned improvement path between the current process set and ITIL best practice.

The main areas for focus following the redocumentation and comparison were:

- the role of Problem Management in ensuring recovery coordination from significant Incidents
- the rerouteing of wrongly assigned Incidents or Requests for Change
- the provision of management information on Incidents, Problems and Requests for Change
- the links to procurement and Configuration Management.

APPENDIX C: IMPLEMENTING SERVICE MANAGEMENT PROCESSES – ISSUES TO CONSIDER

When implementing, or improving, any aspects of Service Management processes, there are a wide range of issues to take into consideration. This Appendix looks at some of the issues that need to be taken into account when deciding to implement, or change, Service Management processes. The topics covered also look at planning the project for such an implementation.

C.1 Process implementation

A practical implementation of Service Management should include:

- earning and communicating 'quick wins' to demonstrate the benefits of Service Management
- starting with something simple and adopting a phased approach
- involving Customers, especially those that have been critical of the service
- explaining the differences that will be seen by Customers and Users
- including third-party service suppliers
- managing the changes, and explaining what is being done (and why) to everyone involved or affected – support staff are often cautious about changes, and it is particularly important that they understand the benefits in order to overcome their resistance
- educating staff and managers to become *service* managers.

Vital elements to consider are:

- the extent of the organisation
- the resources of your disposal, including staff numbers
- the level of maturity of staff, of the processes and of the organisation
- the impact of IT on the business
- the culture of the organisation
- continuous communication with the User population.

C.2 Applicability / scalability

The size of an organisation is an important factor when implementing ITIL processes. In a small organisation, many of the roles defined may well be the responsibility of one person.

Based on best practices, the organisation should develop the combinations that work best for it:

- There is a tension between Incident Management and Problem Management, because of their different goals. Incident Management is responsible for minimising the effect of Incidents for Users. Problem Management's task is to find the underlying Problem and is less interested in the continuity of the Users' activities. When combining these two roles, this tension should be acknowledged.

- There is a similar tension between Problem Management and Change Management. When combining these roles, there is the danger of Changes being implemented too quickly by Problem Management. One would do well to separate these functions to ensure that the proper checks and balances exist.

- Configuration Management and Release Management are roles that are quite commonly shared. Both roles have an administrative component and are concerned with maintaining an up-to-date database.

- Configuration Management and Change Management can also be easily shared, because both roles are centred on CMDB information, and no direct conflict of interest exists between the roles.

C.2.1   Large and small IT units

In small IT units, one group (or individual) has responsibility for a wide variety of processes. Typically, such a person or group is much more effective in performing one role better than the others. The range of personalities and skills in the group determines which of the processes is done most effectively.

Conversely, a large organisation is able to allocate individual processes to specialist groups composed of people with specialist skills who also have a personality that is a good match for the process. However, over specialisation has its disadvantages, as specialisation may be perceived as tedious and demotivating if an individual is simply left in place without looking after their needs and aspirations.

C.3   Process implementation projects: a checklist

Most organisations planning to implement ITIL will already have their own 'best practices' in place. ITIL is a best-practice framework, so a totally greenfield situation will hardly ever be found. Some other methods advocate discarding your own best practices; the ITIL view is that those elements that are working for you should not be discarded unless they will not be able to fit within your vision for the future.

> IT Infrastructure Library process assessment services are commercially available, and can help you to determine the way in which processes, activities and communication lines are already in place in your organisation. Furthermore, they can help you to determine the maturity level of your process framework. Simple self-assessment could also be provided.

The following checklist is of a general nature, since these topics are discussed in detail in the process-specific chapters. The checklist can function as a guideline for Service Managers controlling the overall implementation of processes.

C.3.1   Procedures

- establish the procedure framework
- implement reactive procedures
- implement proactive procedures
- implement supporting tools
- establish a managed documentation system
- establish control over procedures used.

C.3.2 Dependencies

- establish a dependency and relationship framework
- describe inter dependencies with all other processes within the model, both operational and tactical
- establish process interfaces with the IT directorate – these interfaces will be crucial at the outset of process implementations, although the role of the IT directorate relative to tactical matters should diminish over time as tactical processes are put in place
- include vendor relationships
- establish a Customer liaison function on an operational level to organise publicity campaigns.

C.3.3 People

- implement the staff training plan and make this an ongoing activity-focus on both social and technical skills
- assign roles within the ITIL model to people, and make this part of their function description
- delegate tasks and authorisations as low as possible in the organisation.

C.3.4 Timing

- control the project timescale because other stages or projects may depend on it
- consider the timing of 'going live', including the timing and communication of the 'go live' event, as well as any special considerations for the 'go live' day and the period of days or weeks immediately after the 'going live'.

C.4 Impact on an organisation

An often-asked question in this regard is: "Do I have to change my organisational structure?" The question often crops up because the ITIL process approach means that processes have to be managed over more than one department within traditional hierarchical company structures. Some organisations have tried the 'matrix' organisational approach, but whatever structure you choose, there will always be benefits and disadvantages connected with each. Consider the following examples:

C.4.1 Hierarchical structure

+ the traditional role model

+ clear lines of communication

+ clear function and task descriptions within each department

− may result in a bureaucracy if you describe procedures in too much detail

− difficult to place process roles in this model

− process approach will require a complex communication structure.

C.4.2 Matrix organisation

+ process oriented structure

+ flexible

+ clear communication model

− no (or less) clear responsibilities

− no (or less) clear leadership roles (informal leadership).

C.4.3 Self-learning teams (coaching management)

+ continuous quality improvement from within

+ equality within the different teams

− requires quality awareness

− no control over performance

− possible role confusion.

C.5 Benchmarking

In some circumstances, it may be possible to compare a service with that provided by other organisations. This comparison is only useful to the degree that the compared organisations are either the same or very similar. In the latter case, the differences should be understood and quantified before the comparison can provide useful information. Benchmarking is used to find out if a service is cost-effective, responsive to the Customer's needs and effective in comparison with outside. Some Customers use benchmarking to decide if they should change their service provider.

A number of organisations provide benchmarking services. These generally fall into four categories:

1. a baseline set at a certain point in time for the same system or department (service targets are a form of benchmark)
2. comparison to industry norms provided by an external organisations
3. direct comparisons with similar organisations
4. comparison with other systems or departments within the same company.

Differences in benchmarks between organisations are normal. All organisations and service provider infrastructures are unique, and most are continually changing. There are also intangible but influential factors that cannot be measured, such as growth, goodwill, image and culture.

Of the four types of benchmark listed above, the first is usual for Service Management. The second and third involve comparisons with other organisations. Comparison against industry norms provides a common frame of reference but may be misleading if the comparisons are used without an understanding of the differences that exist across a wide variety of organisations. The differences between organisations may be greater than the similarities, and comparison with a 'typical' result may not be useful as a consequence.

Direct comparison with *similar* organisations are most effective if there is a sufficiently large group of organisations with similar characteristics. It is important to understand the size and nature of the business area, including the geographical distribution and the extent to which the service is used for business, or time critical, activities.

The culture of the Customer population also has an influence. Many support services are influenced by the extent to which Customers will or will not accept restrictions on what they may do with the technology provided. For example, it is difficult to have good security standards with Customers who will not keep their passwords secure, or who load unlicensed or untested software. Finally, comparison with other groups in the same organisation normally allows a detailed examination of the features being compared, so that it can be established whether or not the comparison is of 'like with like'.

Most benchmarks include some financial measures, such as 'cost per unit', and an assessment of cost-effectiveness is a common reason for benchmarking against other organisations. This is particularly so for organisations that have only limited historical information and that are therefore unable to use service or financial trends to measure objectively whether the service is getting better or worse. Financial benchmarking is very difficult. Establishing genuine baselines is nearly impossible, and organisational factors involved in arriving at the cost of similar processes make it hard to make true comparisons.

C.6   A sample implementation strategy

In general, the impact of current weaknesses on IT service quality should determine priorities. For example, if User services are less affected by 'real' errors than those that arise from poor implementation of Changes, Change Management should have priority. While each organisation should therefore set its own priorities, the following phased approach may be used as a starting point:

C.6.1   Phase 1:

- determine the baseline
- start with an assessment to determine priorities.

C.6.2   Phase 2:

- survey the services/system(s) currently used by the organisation for providing day-to-day User support and for handling Incidents, Problems and Known Errors
- review the support tools used, and the interfaces to Change Management and Configuration Management, including inventory management, and the operational use of the current system within the IT provider; identify strengths to be retained, and weaknesses to be eliminated
- identify and review the agreements in place between service providers and Customers.

C.6.3   Phase 3:

- determine and document service level requirements
- plan and implement the Service Desk using tools designed for this function that support Incident control – these tools should either support, or be capable of integration with, tools for Problem Management, Configuration Management and Change Management

■ implement at least the inventory elements of Configuration Management that are required for Incident Management and Change Management.

C.6.4 Phase 4:

■ extend the Incident control system in order to allow other domains, such as Computer Operations and Network Control staff, to log Incidents directly

■ negotiate and set up SLAs.

C.6.5 Phase 5:

■ develop the management reporting system.

C.6.6 Phase 6:

■ implement the balance of 'reactive' Problem Management (Problem control, error control and management reporting) and Configuration Management

■ realise the proactive parts of Problem Management as staff are released from reactive duties by gradually improving service quality

■ establish the Release Management process.

This six-phased approach reduces the development overhead experienced at any given time for the four IT infrastructure management systems under consideration (Incident Management, Problem Management, Change Management and Configuration Management). It should, nevertheless, be noted that, although busy sites will appreciate this smoothing of the development bulge, the approach will increase the overall time scale for implementation.

C.7 Process improvement

Regrettably, even a high standard of Service Management may not be adequate for rapid and major Changes. This can be an issue, for example, when two organisations merge and two sets of Service Management processes, functional groups and support technology have to be rationalised. The most common reason for normal service tuning not being adequate are when one or more of the components of Service Management are missing or deficient, so that the service has degraded and Customers are dissatisfied with its quality or cost.

Under these circumstances, management is faced with a potential or real crisis and should react by initiating a project or series of projects to address the situation. These are required to make much faster improvements to the service, costs or the processes than are possible within the scope of normal ongoing Service Management.

Projects may be directly related to the activities of Service Level Management. For example they may be part of a Service Improvement Programme (SIP) or may be focused on improving Customer and/or staff satisfaction. However, apart from this reactive reason to start a process improvement project, many proactive ones should also be considered, such as:

■ providing the operational processes with a tactical planning horizon

■ aiming for a higher IT maturity level

■ improving alignment with, and support for, business objectives

- reducing costs or improving business profits
- implementing a planning and control system
- increasing quality awareness amongst staff
- 'making the feedback loop work'.

In all cases, management needs to have a clear view of the Service Catalogue and the internal service requirements, and also needs to have a so-called 'Helicopter View' of the IT organization.

More guidance can be obtained from the CCTA ITIL book on Planning and Control for IT Services (ISBN 0 11 330548 6), which covers information flows and the development of an appropriate planning-and-control system to meet the requirements of an organisation.

APPENDIX D: QUALITY

D.1 Quality Management

Quality Management for IT Services is a systematic way of ensuring that all the activities necessary to design, develop and implement IT services which satisfy the requirements of the organisation and of Users take place as planned and that the activities are carried out cost effectively.

The way that an organisation plans to manage its operations so that it delivers quality services, is specified by its quality management system. The quality management system defines the organisational structure, responsibilities, policies, procedures, processes, standards and resources required to deliver quality IT services. However, a quality management system will only function as intended if management and staff are committed to achieving its objectives.

D.1.1 Ongoing quality improvement: The Deming Cycle

'We have learned to live in a world of mistakes and defective products as if they were necessary to life. It is time to adopt a new philosophy...'
(W.Edwards Deming, 1900–93)

W. Edwards Deming is best known for his management philosophy establishing quality, productivity, and competitive position. As part of this philosophy, he formulated 14 points of attention for managers. Some of these points are more appropriate to Service Management than others, for example:

> Excerpts from Deming's fourteen points relevant to Service Management
>
> - break down barriers between departments (improves communications and management)
> - management should learn their responsibilities, and take on leadership (process improvement requires commitment from the top; good leaders motivate people to improve themselves and therefore the image of the organisation)
> - improve constantly (a central theme for Service Managers is continuous improvement; this is also a theme for quality management. A process-led approach is key to achieving this target)
> - institute a programme of education and self-improvement (learning and improving skills have been the focus of Service Management for many years)
> - training on the job (linked to continuous improvement)
> - transformation is everyone's job (the emphasis being on teamwork and understanding).

For quality improvement, Deming proposed the Deming Cycle (or Circle). The four key stages are plan, do, check and act, after which a phase of consolidation prevents the 'Circle' from 'rolling down the hill' as illustrated in Figure D.1. The consolidation phase enables the organisation to take stock of what has been taking place and to ensure that improvements are embedded. Often, a series of improvements have been made to processes that require documentation (both to allow processes to be repeatable and to facilitate recognition of the achievement of some form of quality standard).

As discussed in Appendix B – Process theory and practice, the cycle is underpinned by a process-led approach to management, where defined processes are in place, the activities are measured for compliance with expected values, and outputs are audited to validate and improve the process.

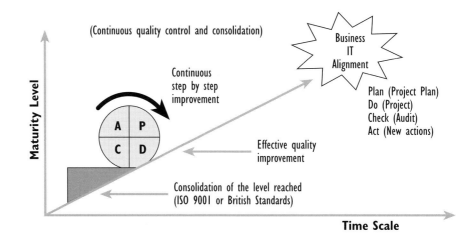

Figure D.1 - The Deming Cycle

D.1.2   Quality standards

International Standards Organisation ISO 9000

An important set of International Standards for Quality Assurance is the ISO 9000 range, a set of five universal standards for a Quality Assurance system that is accepted around the world. At the turn of the millennium, 90 or so countries have adopted ISO 9000 as the cornerstone of their national standards. When you purchase a product or service from a company that is registered to the appropriate ISO 9000 standard, you have important assurances that the quality of what you will receive will be as you expect. For reference purposes, *ISO Standards* can be ordered directly from the International Standards Institute (see Chapter 12, Bibliography, for details).

The most comprehensive of the standards is ISO 9001. It applies to industries involved in the design, development, manufacturing, installation and servicing of products or services. The standards apply uniformly to companies in any industry and of any size.

More detailed guidance of the IT Infrastructure Library (including comprehensive mapping of ISO clauses to IT Infrastructure Library processes) can be obtained from the ITIL book on Quality Management for IT Services – ISBN 0-11-330555-9. This book is concerned primarily with putting in place in IT services an ISO-9001-conformant Quality Management system based on Service Management processes; it also touches upon organisational and planning-and-control aspects.

The BSI Code of Practice for IT Service Management is a modern update of the original document PD0005, which was published in 1995. The new code has been written to serve as an introduction to Service Management, and in fact can be used as an introduction to the IT Infrastructure Library. However, the guide is not an official BSI *standard*; indeed a *standard* for Service Management does not yet exist. The IT Infrastructure Library is in many countries the *de facto* standard, and with the help of BSI and ISO it is hoped that a true international standard, based on the ITIL will soon be in place. The BSI Code of Practice covers the established Service Support and Service Delivery processes, as well as some additional topics such as implementing processes. The BSI Code can be ordered from the British Standards Institute (see Chapter 12, Bibliography, for details).

D.1.3   Total Quality Systems: EFQM

'...the battle for quality is one of the prerequisites for the success of your companies and for our collective success.'*
(Jacques Delors)

The EFQM excellence model

The European Foundation for Quality Management (EFQM) was founded in 1988 by the Presidents of 14 major European companies, with the endorsement of the European Commission. The present membership is in excess of 600 very well respected organisations, ranging from major multinationals and important national companies to research institutes in prominent European universities.

EFQM provides an excellent model for those wishing to achieve business excellence in a programme of continuous improvement.

EFQM mission statement

The mission statement for EFQM is:

> *To stimulate and assist organisations throughout Europe to participate in improvement activities leading ultimately to excellence in Customer satisfaction, employee satisfaction, impact on society and business results; and to support the managers of European organisations in accelerating the process of making Total Quality Management a decisive factor for achieving global competitive advantage.*

Depiction of the EFQM excellence model

The EFQM Excellence Model consists of 9 criteria and 32 subcriteria. It is illustrated in Figure D2.

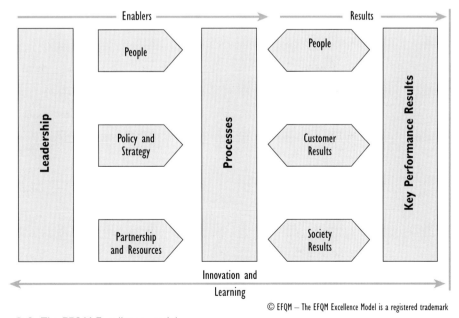

© EFQM – The EFQM Excellence Model is a registered trademark

Figure D.2 - The EFQM Excellence model

*Jacques Delors, President of the European Commission, at the signing of the letter of intent in Brussels to establish EFQM on 15 September 1988.

In the model there is explicit focus on the value to Users of the 'Plan–Do–Check–Act' cycle to business operations,* and the need to relate everything that is done, and the measurements taken, to the goals of business policy and strategy.

Self-assessment and maturity: the EFQM maturity scale

One of the tools provided by EFQM is the self-assessment questionnaire. The self-assessment process allows the organisation to discern clearly its strengths, and also any areas where improvements can be made. The questionnaire process culminates in planned improvement actions, which are then monitored for progress.

In this assessment, progress can be checked against a five-point maturity scale:

1. product orientation
2. process orientation (the maturity stage aimed for by the original ITIL)
3. system orientation (the maturity target for ITIL-compliant organisations in the new millennium)
4. chain orientation
5. total quality.

Quality awards

To demonstrate a successful adaptation of the EFQM model, some companies aim for the European Quality Award, a process that allows Europe to recognise its most successful organisations and promote them as role models of excellence for others to copy.

The US equivalent to this award is the Malcolm Baldridge Quality Award for Quality management. The Malcolm Baldrige National Quality Improvement Act of 1987, established an annual US National Quality Award. The purpose of the Award was (and still is) to promote awareness of quality excellence, to recognise quality achievements of US companies, and to publicise successful quality strategies.

For the Malcolm Baldridge Award, there are three categories:

- manufacturing companies or subunits
- service companies or subunits
- small businesses.

The criteria against which firms are judged are:

1. leadership
2. strategic planning
3. customer and market focus
4. information and analysis
5. human resource development and management
6. process management
7. business results.

---

* See the paragraph on W. Edwards Deming.

For the European Quality Award, there are four possible categories:

- companies
- operational units of companies
- public-sector organisations
- small and medium enterprises.

The criteria against which candidate organisations are measured are:

1. leadership
2. people
3. policy and strategy
4. partnerships and resources
5. processes
6. people results
7. customer results
8. society results
9. key performance results.

In the EFQM Excellence model the first four criteria are defined as enablers. Best practice in IT Infrastructure Library process implementations show that placing proper emphasis on these topics will increase the chances for success. The key points for the four enablers are as follows:

- *Leadership*
  - organise a kick off session involving all of your people
  - be a role model
  - encourage and support your staff.

- *People management*
  - create awareness
  - recruit new staff and/or hire temporary staff to prevent service levels being affected during implementation stages
  - develop people through training and experience
  - align human resource plans with policy and strategy
  - adopt a coaching style of management
  - align performance with salaries.

- *Policy and strategy*
  - communicate mission, vision and values
  - align communication plans with the implementation stages.

- *Partnerships and resources*
  - establish partnerships with sub-contractors and customers
  - use financial resources in support of policy and strategy
  - utilise existing assets.

Readers interested in either of the quality programmes mentioned above should refer to Chapter 12, Bibliography, for details of contacts.

APPENDIX E: EXAMPLE COST-BENEFIT ANALYSIS FOR SERVICE MANAGEMENT PROCESSES

This Appendix is intended as an example of how to quantify the costs and benefits of implementing the processes described in the IT Infrastructure Library. It is not intended to be comprehensive. Please be sure to substitute your own organisation's specific assumptions, purposes, costs, and benefits to get an example that is more suitable to your own circumstances.

In this example the following assumptions are made:

- all employees cost $50 an hour
- your organisation comprises 500 Users
- the total number of Incidents is 5,000 per year
- the average time to fix an Incident is 10 minutes
- a working year has 200 days.

Example costs and benefits are set out below.

Process	Purpose	Cost/benefit examples
Configuration Management	Controlling the IT infrastructure Ensuring that only authorised hardware and software is in use	Following the implementation implementation of Configuration Management, the Service Desk has a much greater insight into the relationship between Users, CIs and Incidents. The 3 people assigned to Incident matching can be reduced to 2, resulting in a benefit of 200x8x$50=$83,300 per year.
Incident Management	Continuity of the service levels Underpin Service Desk function	The implementation of Incident Management has resulted in a decrease in down time per User; this is defined as the amount of time a User is on the phone to the Service Desk or cannot work because of a failure. If the downtime per User has gone down by 1 minute per person per day, this would save the organisation 500×200×$50×1/60 = $83,300 per year.
Problem Management	Minimise disruption of the service level	Suppose that the implementation of Problem Management decreases the amount of recurring Incidents by 500 (10% of total) per year. This means a revenue of 500×$50×10/60 = $4,000 per year.
Change Management	Efficient handling of Changes	Two Changes are implemented simultaneously, resulting in a major problem. The Customer support system fails, resulting in the loss of 50 Customers with an average purchasing power of $500. This has just cost your company $25,000.

Release Management	Ensuring authorised software modules are used Provide means to build Change Releases Automating release of software	Suppose that a new software module is released containing a bug. The previous version should be reinstalled, but due to poor version management, the wrong version is used, resulting in a system shutdown that lasts for 3 hours and affects two-thirds of all employees. This would cost the organisation 500×$50×3× 2/3= $50,000.
Service Level Management	Agree on and control the service levels Understand business needs	Thanks to a clear set of agreements, the Service Desk is less troubled with calls that are not part of the services offered. In this way the 4 Service Desk employees work 5% more efficiently, resulting in a gain of 4×5%×$50×8×200 = $ 16,000 a year.
Availability Management	Ensure high availability of services	Due to a physical error on a hard disk, a server supporting 100 people crashes. It takes 3 hours to have a new disk delivered and installed before starting up the system again. Costs: 100×3×$50 = $15,000. On a critical system, Availability Management processes would have highlighted the need for a mirror disk, which could automatically take over.
Capacity Management	Ensure the optimal use of IT	There is an overcapacity of 20%. Assuming your IT infrastructure cost you $5 million, you could gain up to $1 million by implementing Capacity Management and frequently reassessing the necessary capacity .
IT Service Continuity Management	Ensure quick recovery after a disaster	A water pipe breaks, flooding the server room. It takes 2 days to be fully operational. The average User has missed 10 hours of work. Total costs (apart from the pumping): 500×10×$50 = $250,000. Please note that a good contingency plan doesn't come cheap; however, the recovery costs (as in this example) could be dramatic – that is, if your organisation is still in business!
Financial Management	Provide insight, control and charge the costs of IT services	Imagine that the costs of IT services are charged to the departments that take them. A 10% reduction in the requests for new services would directly result in a 10% reduction of IT expenditure. The insight into the real costs in IT services proves to be surprising in practice; most Users don't have a clue about the costs.

APPENDIX F: THE SERVICE-SUPPORT PROCESS MODEL

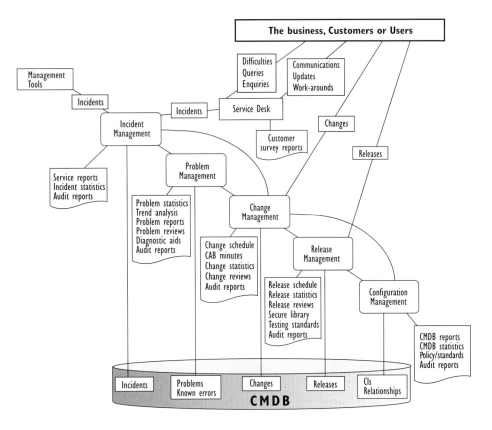

Index

Note: **Bold** page numbers indicate main topics; *italic* numbers refer to illustrations

accountability 61-62
ACD *see* Automatic Call Distribution
actioned infrastructure events 34
active listening 62-63
adaptability, management tools 247
allocation of Problems 102-104
applicability 279-280
applications
   design 240
   development 169-170, 201-202
   management 15
approval of Change 186
archives 67-68, 146, 149
assessment
   Change Management 185-186
   error 107-108
   project management 255
   Service Management software 250-251
   see also evaluation
asset management 121, 127
audits
   automated tools 148
   Change Management process 198-199
   Configuration Management 122, 123, 135, 148, 154
   key performance indicators 257-258
   Problem Management metrics 113
   quality parameters 256-257
   Release Management 235
   software and hardware tools 235
Automatic Call Distribution (ACD) 40
automatic systems
   audit tools 148
   Build process 233, *234*
   Release procedures 217-218, 224
   Service Management 246-247
   software tools 245
Availability management 13, 14, 294

back-out plans 169, 188, 190, 211, 218
Balanced Scorecard 257-258
baselines
   Configuration 123-124, 142
   identification 142
   Service Management 249, 282
basic Change Management procedures
         170-173, *171-173*
benchmarking 249, 250, 282-283
   see also baselines
best practice 1-2, *18*, 23, 165, 291
big bang approach 226, 227
brainstorming 120
breaches of service 50-51
British Standards Institute (BSI), Code of
   Practice for IT Service Management 8, *8*, 168, 181, 288
BSI *see* British Standards Institute
Build
   Change Management 187-188, 190-191
   management 210, 221, 232-234
   process 233, *234*
   Release Management 219, 223-224
business as usual 24, 36

C&CM plan *see* Change and Configuration
   Management plan
CAB *see* Change Advisory Board
CAB/EC *see* Change Advisory Board
   Emergency Committee
capacity management 14, 176, 294
cascading information 112
categorisation
   Change 183-184
   Incidents 71, 105, 110
   Problems 110, *116-117*
cause-and-effect diagrams *120*
Central Function for Change, Configuration
   and Release Management 158-161
central Service Desks 39-40

Change
 Configuration structures 124, 140
 definition 168
 Release Management 203
 review 191
 see also Change Management
Change Advisory Board (CAB)
 Change reviews 12, 191
 establishment of 175-176, 193-194
 meetings 184-185
Change Advisory Board Emergency
 Committee (CAB/EC) 176
Change and Configuration Management plan
 (C&CM plan) 159-161
Change Management **165-202**
 authorisation of 153
 central function for 158-161
 Configuration Management relations 12,
   151-152, *151, 152*, 154, 167
 cost-benefit analysis 293
 Release Management relationships 12, 167,
   219-220, *219*, 231, 239
charging 30
CIs *see* Configuration item
classification
 Incidents 42-43, 81-83, 90
 Problems 102-104
client-server applications, responsibility
 matrix 218, *219*
closure 42, 85-86, 108
CMDB *see* Configuration Management
 Database
coaching management 282
Code of Practice for IT Service Management
 (PD0005) 8, *8*, 288
 Change Management 168, 181, 198
coding systems 42, 90, 91, *116-117*
commitment 19-20, 46
common structured interrogation techniques
   63
communication
 customers needs 23
 Incident Management 86-87
 plans 254-255

Release Management 228
Service Desks 46
compliance 181, 198-199, 256-257
computerisation of services desks 43-44
Configuration
 baselines 123-124, 142
 breakdown *123*, 138, *139*
 control 121, 123, 144-147
 identification 122-123, 137-143
 librarians 163
 multi-tier systems 236-237, *237*
 Release Management 223-224
 Service Desks 41
Configuration items (CIs)
 attributes of 164
 breakdown 122-123
 CMDB population 134
 critical 156
 error identification 106
 Incident Management 76
 labelling 143
 life-cycles 141
 naming conventions 143
 Problem identification 102
 relationships 141
 selection of 138-140
 software tools 199
Configuration Management **121-164**
 cost-benefit analysis 293
 inter-relationships 11-12, *12*, 151-153, *167*
 Release Management relationships 231, 239
 tools 153-155, 157, 199
Configuration Management Database
 (CMDB)
 Configuration items (CIs) 164
 description **124**
 DSL relationship *209*
 housekeeping 149
 Incident Management planning 79
 inconsistencies 82
 interfacing *151*
 management relationships *12*, 151-152,
   151, 152
 populating 133-134

Problem impacts	103
Release Management	203, 210, 218
updating	147
confirmation	31-34
conformance	23
consistency	23
contingency measures	211, 247
control	
Configuration items (CIs)	144-147
Configuration Management	121, 123
level of	156
cost-benefit analysis	252, **293-294**
costs	
Change Management	180
charging for support services	30
Configuration Management	135-136
customer care	24-25
effectiveness	283
Problem Management	101
project planning	253
Release Management	222
Service Management	247, **293-294**
credibility	247
critical	
Configuration items	156
outage plan	179
success factors	68, 79, 252
cross-reference information	233
culture	20-22
customers	
databases	64
definition	7
interaction	31-32, 52
needs of	22-24, 51, 55
relations	2, 15, 61-62
satisfaction	20-21, 22, 24, 29, 45, 53
support	275, *276*
users	7, 57-58
daily reviews	66
Definitive Hardware Store (DHS)	210
Definitive Software Library (DSL)	
CIs	125
CMDB relationship	*209*

management inter-relationships	*151*, *152*, *152*
populating	133-134
Release Management	208-209
software	143, 215-216
Delta Release	207-208
The Deming Cycle	287-288, *288*
dependencies	281
design	
global support	41-42
Release Management	223-224, 240
desktop management tools	235-236
detection of Incidents	80-81
DHS *see* Definitive Hardware Store	
diagnosis	83-84, 104
distribution	
electronic software	234, *235*
Release Management	217-218, 221, 228-229, 243
document libraries	125, 141-142
documentation	96, 143, 182, 214
DSL *see* Definitive Software Library	
education	59-63
effectiveness	36-37, 191-192, 271
efficiency	191-192, 271
EFQM *see* European Foundation for Quality Management	
electronic customer registration	45, 50
electronic software distribution	234, *235*
email	45
empathy	61
empowerment	49
End Project Report	256
engineering reports	111
enterprise systems	155
environmental infrastructure processes	16
errors	
categorisation of	*116-117*
control	105-109, *106*
cycle	*107*
handling of	97-98
see also known errors; unknown errors	

escalation

    functional versus hierarchical   75-76

    Incident resolution   86-87

    management   50-51

    Service Desks   275, *276*

European Foundation for Quality

    Management (EFQM)   2, 20, 289-291, *289*

evaluation   252, 255, 256

    see also assessment

expert users   52

failed Releases   211, 225

feasibility studies   249

financial management   14, 186, 294

firewall   238

first-line support   74-75, 75, 87-88

    see also Service Desks

fix rates   55-56

flowcharts   177

Forward Schedule of Changes (FSC)

    176-178, 177

front-line support   55

FSC *see* Forward Schedule of Changes

full Release   207

functional escalation   75-76

generic

    process model   *273*

    quality parameters   257

global support   41-42

Graphical User Interface (GUI)   237

GUI *see* Graphical User Interface

hardware Releases   205, 217

health checks   250-251

helicopter view   285

help desks   29

hierarchical

    escalation   75-76

    structures   281

high-risk Configuration items   156

housekeeping, CMDB   149

ICT infrastructure management   15

identification

    CIs   121, 122-123, 142

    Configuration structures   137-143

    customer   64

    error   106

    Problem   101-102

    Release   207

    software and document libraries   141-142

image   56

impact

    Change Management   176, 184, 185-186

    Incident Management   83

    new technology   156, 200-202, 236-238

    Problem classification coding   103, 104

    Service Management implementation

    281-282

    technology and Change Management

    200-202

implementation

    Change Management   187-188, 194-197

    Configuration Management   127-136,

    131-133, 134-135

    phased Release Management   226-227,

    226, 227

    Problem Management   99-100

    Release Management   221-223

    Service Desks   68

    Service Management   **249-258, 279-285**

    strategies   283-284

    urgent Changes   190-191

impressions   56, 61

in-house software   144-145, 245

Incident Management   **71-94**

    CMDB   *151*

    cost-benefit analysis   293

    inter-relationships   13

    Problem Management contrast   97-98

    role of   87-88

Incident-matching process flow   *102*

Incidents

    categorisation of   71, 105, 110

    Change Management   169

    classification of   42-43, 81-83, 90

    closure   85-86

difficult types 48
handling 73-74, *94*
infrastructure events 34
investigation *93*
life-cycle *73*, 92
priority of 76
registration inputs *32*
relationships 76-78, *77*
reporting and review 65-68
resolution 84-85
independent Change 137
indicators
  Change Management 192
  Configuration Management 150-151
  key performance 88, 150-151, 229-230
  Release Management 229-230
information
  cascading 112
  customer 32, 48
  management 112
  support organisations 111-112
infrastructure
  Configuration 138-140, *139*
  Incident model 34, *35*
  management 169
  Release unit 206-207
installation *33*, 228-229
integrity 146-147
interactive voice response systems 45
International Standards Organisation
  ISO 9000 2, 3, 288
  ISO 9001 22
Internet
  Change Management 201
  Release Management 237-238
  software updates 238
  technology 35-36
interpersonal skills 59
interrogation techniques 63
investigation 83-84, 104, 105
Ishikawa diagrams *120*
ISO *see* International Standards Organisation
IT Infrastructure Library (ITIL) **1-8**
IT service continuity management 15, 294
IT Service Management Forum (itSMF) 3

ITIL *see* IT Infrastructure Library
itSMF *see* IT Service Management Forum

jigsaw concept 4-5, *4*, 6

Kepner and Tregoe analysis 118-119
key performance indicators (KPIs)
  Configuration Management 150-151
  Incident Management 88
  Release Management 229-230
key success factors 99-100
known errors
  control of 105-106
  definition 77
  error control system 106
  identification of 96-97
KPIs *see* key performance indicators

labelling of CIs 143
licences 125, 146, 224
life-cycles 170-173
listening 62-63
local Service Desks 39
logging 182

Malcolm Baldridge Award 290
management
  application 15
  Availability 14
  capacity 14
  Change 12, **165-202**
  coaching 282
  commitment of 19-20, 46
  Configuration 11-12, **121-164**
  customer relationship 15, 24
  escalation 50-51
  financial 14
  ICT infrastructure 15
  Incident 13, **71-94**
  information 112
  IT service continuity 15
  Problem 13
  projects 16, 253
  relationships **11-16,**

Release 12, **203-243**
  reporting 150, 197-199, 230-231, 258
  security 15
  server tools 236
  service breaches 50-51
  Service Desks 60, 65-66
  service level 13-14
  see also Code of Practice
managers
  Change 193, 194
  Configuration 162-163
  Incident 87
  Problem 114
  Release 220
  service desk 60
marketing, Service Desks 65
matrix organisation 282
maturity scales 290
metrics
  Change Management 176, 197-199
  Problem Management 112-114
  target effectiveness 36-37
module hierarchy diagram *233*
monitored infrastructure events 34
monitoring
  Configuration Management 135
  Incident Management 34-35, 46, 81, 86-87
  Problem/error resolution 108
  Release Management 229-230
  service desk workload 52
monthly management reviews 66
multi-tier systems 236-237, *237*
multiplatform environments 44

n-line support 75, *75*
naming conventions of CIs 143
networks 140, *140*, 238
normal service operation 71

OLAs *see* operational level agreements
ongoing quality improvement 287-288
operational level agreements (OLAs) 13

organisation
  product-oriented 271-272, *272*
  project management 253
  Service Management impacts 281-282
outsourcing 47-48, 178-179
overheads 135
ownership 61-62, 86-87

packaged Releases 186-187, 208
PD0005 *see* Code of Practice
personality 59
phased implementation 226-227, *226*, *227*
phone systems 45
physical Configuration audits 148
PIR *see* Post Implementation Review
planning
  central function for Change, Configuration
    and Release Management 159-160
  Change Management 194-197
  Configuration Management
    121, 122, 127-137, *131*
  Incident Management 78-80
  management commitment 20
  operational processes 182
  Problem Management 99-100
  project guidelines 251-255
  Release Management 206, 214-221
  Service Management **249-258**
policy Release 206, 215-216
Post Implementation Review (PIR)
    108, 175, 190-191
post-project reviews 256
preventative action 110-111
PRINCE2
  Change Management 200-201
  project management 16, 251, 253, 254
  Release Management 216, 232
priority
  allocation of 183
  coding systems 91
  Configuration Management 129
  Incident Management 83
  Problem classification 103
  ratings 183

proactive Problem Management   96, 97, 98, 109-111, 115

proactive service reports   67

Problem Management   **95-120**

   CMDB   *151*

   Configuration Management relationships   151-152, *151*

   cost-benefit analysis   293

   relationships   13

   Release Management relationships   231

Problems

   allocation   102-104

   analysis   118-119

   categorisation of   110, *116-117*

   Change Management   180-181

   classification of   102-104

   control   100-105, *101*

   definition   77, 118

   diagnosis   104

   handling of   97

   identification   101-102

   impact of   83

   investigation   104

   prevention   109-111

   recording   101-102

   records of   76-77

   Service Management   252

   support responsibilities   115

procedures

   process implementation   280

   Release Management   216

   Service Desks   63-65

process

   analysis   275-276

   approach   272-273, *273*

   control   271

   definition   *19*, 271

   implementation   279, 280-281

   improvement   *18*, 284-285

   models   177, 273-277, 274, *275, 296-297*

   theory   **271-277**

product approach   254

product-oriented organisation   271-272, *272*

professionalism   60, 61

program management   165, *166*

progress reports   74, 255-256

project management

   Change Management   165, *166*

   Release Management relationship   232

   reporting   255-258

   review   255-258

project planning   249, 251-255

Projected Service Availability (PSA)   177

PSA *see* Projected Service Availability

public domain framework   1

quality

   Change Management   188

   compliance parameters   256-257

   control of software   145

   management   2-3, 287-291

   Service Desks   27, 46

quarterly management reports   197

quick wins   58, 59, 79

reactive Problem

   control   100, *101*

   management   96

   support responsibilities   115

records

   archives   67-68

   error   106

   Incidents   80-81

   Problem   101-102

   urgent Changes   190-191

registration   34-35, 49, 144

rejected Releases   225

relationships   **11-16**

   Change Management   *167*

   Configuration Management   151-153, *151, 152*

   Incident Management   *77, 78-79*

   Release Management   231-232

Release

   Configuration baseline   124

   controls   145

   documents   69

   Service Desks   57-58

Release Management	**203-243**
central function for	158-161
Configuration Management	151-152,
	151, 152, 154
cost-benefit analysis	294
definitive library software	133-134
life-cycle	*141*
relationships	12, *167,* 231-232
Release strategy	108
Releases	
acceptance of	224-225
concurrent Changes	186
definition	205
identification	207
packaged	186-187
policy	215-216
software distribution	221
types of	207-208
unit	206-207
remote control	236
reporting	
Change Management	197-199
Incidents	65-68
management	150, 230-231, 258
Problem/error control	112-113
project management	255-258
requests	
common structured dialogue	63
fix rates	55
registration of	49
support workloads	54
urgent	50
workload monitoring	52
Requests for Change (RFCs)	14, 71
Change Management	173-175
definition	77
error assessment	107
priority allocation	183
resolution	76, 77, 108, 169
resources	36, 53, 185-186
responsibility	
Change Management	176, 192-194, 194
matrix	218, *219*

reviews	
Change Management	191, 195, 197
Configuration Management	135
Incidents	65-68
post-implementation of Changes	175
post-project	256
project management	255-258
RFCs *see* requests for Change	
rollout planning	216, 222, 225-227, *226,* 242
satisfaction surveys	53
scalability	279-280
schedules	
Change	186-187
installation confirmation	*33*
SCM *see* Software Configuration Management	
second-line support	49, 53-54, 74-75, *75,* 88
security	15, 201
self-assessment	250-251, 290
self-learning teams	282
self-service	45, 50
server management tools	236
service	
breaches	50-51
catalogue	56
culture	22, 25
delivery	11
provision	149, 178-179
quality	27, 46, 188
reports	67
requests	169
support	6, 273-277, *296-297*
Service Desks	**27-69**
CMDB inconsistencies	82
Incident Management	76, 79, 81, 86, *94*
information dissemination	112
management relationships	13
process modelling	274, 275, *276*
Release Management relationships	231
Service Improvement Programme (SIP)	284
Service Level Agreements (SLAs)	
customer care	23
Incidents	48, 82
monitoring	108

normal service operation 71
resolution time 75-76
service breaches 51
Service Desks 45
target effectiveness metrics 37
Service Level Management (SLM)
cost-benefit analysis 293
management relationships 13-14
process improvement 284
Service Management
benefits 17
Change Management review 191, 197
Code of Practice 8, *8*
cost-benefit analysis **293-294**
implementation **279-285**
ITIL **1-8**
management reports 258
planning **249-258**
software tools **245-247**, 250-251
training 25
service-profit chain model 27, *28*
silver bullet lifecycle 46, *47*
SIP *see* Service Improvement Programme
SLAs *see* Service Level Agreements
SLM *see* Service Level Management
small support units 53
software
auditing tools 235
Build process 233, *234*
Change Management 169-170, 199, 201-202
CMDB 153
Configuration Management 125, 154
distribution 221, 234, *235*
error control 107-108, *107*
hardware auditing tools 235
identification of 141-142
in-house 144-145
infrastructure *206*
licences 125
positioning of 240-241
product training 247
quality control 145
Release Management 205, 217, 221, 231

service desk 44-45
Service Management **245-247**
updates 238
Software Configuration Management (SCM)
tools 232
specifications 23, 56-57
staff
C&CM plan 160-161
Change Management 180, 196
Configuration Management 129-130, 132, 136, 162-163
Incident-handling 87-88
Problem Management 114-115
process implementation 281
Release Management 220-221
second-line awareness 53-54
Service Desks 36, 51-52, 55-56, 60, 61, 63
standard Change procedures 170-173, *173*, 177
standards 2
status
accounting 121, 123, 147-148
updates 48
super user 52
support
Incident Management 74-75, *75*
information provision 111-112
maintenance of 46
Problems of 28-29
tools 195-197, 180, 236
surveys of customer satisfaction 53
symptoms of Incidents 42
systems design
Change Management 194-195
Configuration Management 130-131

targets 36-37, 150-151
teamwork 60, 61
technical approval 186
technology 43-48, 156, 200-202, 236-238
telephone response times 50
terminology 61-62, **263-270**
testing
Changes 187-188, 190-191
Release Management 210

thin client   236
third-line support   74-75, *75*
timing
  Change Management   196-197
  Incident Management   78-80
  Problem Management   99-100
  process implementation   281
tools
  Change Management   180, 195-197
  Configuration Management   157
  desktop management   235-236
  evaluation criteria   246-247
  future of   236
  Incident Management   88-89
  Release Management   232-236
  Service Management   **245-247**
  types of   245
total quality systems   289-291, 20, 250
TP *see* transaction processing
tracking   86-87
training
  C&CM plan   160-161
  monitoring of   54
  Release Management   221, 224, 228
  Service Management   25, 59-63
  software product   247
transaction processing (TP)   206
trend analysis   110

unknown errors   76-77
update activities, Incident life cycles   74
urgency   83, 103
urgent
  Changes   188-191, *189*
  requests   50
users   7, 57-58
  see also customers

value for money   23
vendor partnerships   47-48
vendor-maintained products   107
verification   122, 123, 148
versions, variants contrast   157
viability   247
virtual Service Desks   39-40, *40*
voicemail   45

WAN *see* wide-area networks
web servers, Release Management   238
weekly management reviews, Service Desks 67
WFD *see* workflow diagrams
Wide Area Networks (WAN)   45, 140
work-around   76, 77, 77, 84
workflow
  diagrams (WFDs)   274
  Incident life cycle   73-74
workload   52, 54, 66

Printed in the United Kingdom by The Stationery Office
TJ4740 C40 06/01